365
ESSENTIAL
QUESTIONS
FROM THE
BIBLE

365
ESSENTIAL
QUESTIONS
FROM THE
BIBLE

A DAILY DEVOTIONAL

BARBOUR BOOKS
An Imprint of Barbour Publishing, Inc.

Published by Barbour Books, an imprint of Barbour Publishing, Inc., P.O. Box 719, Uhrichsville, Ohio 44683, www.barbourbooks.com

Our mission is to publish and distribute inspirational products offering exceptional value and biblical encouragement to the masses.

 Member of the
Evangelical Christian
Publishers Association

Printed in the United States of America.

INTRODUCTION

Welcome to *365 Essential Questions from the Bible*—questions that Almighty God has asked mortal men. In fact, this book actually contains more than 365 questions, since we frequently left groups of questions together if they were all asking the same basic thing.

When you think of God asking questions, probably the example that springs to mind is His very *first* question. After Adam and Eve disobeyed Him and sinned, they heard the Lord walking through the garden of Eden, and they hid. So God called to Adam, "Where are you?" (Genesis 3:9 NIV). As you probably realize, God already *knew* where Adam and his wife were. The purpose of His question was to give them an opportunity to come forward and confess what they'd done. In His Father's heart of love, God wanted to deal with the sin and restore the relationship.

This is why He says, "Come now, and let us reason together. . . . Though your sins are like scarlet, they shall be as white as snow" (Isaiah 1:18 NKJV). And a good portion of God's reasoning consists of probing, rhetorical questions. This was the purpose behind many of the questions He asked through prophets such as Isaiah, Jeremiah, and Ezekiel.

God also questioned His people when they didn't have their facts straight and were basing their attitudes and actions on mistaken assumptions. He then asked questions, as He did with Job when the suffering patriarch doubted His wisdom and fairness. God told him, "Brace yourself like a man, because I have some questions for you, and you must answer them" (Job 38:3 NLT). This was followed by four entire chapters of questions.

The Lord wanted to reason things through with Job, not because He didn't know the answers, but to get Job—and us—to *think*. Of course, Job didn't know the answers to many of the questions, but he did understand the *underlying* thought: "I am the Lord God, the Almighty. Can you trust Me even though you can't understand what I'm doing?"

Finally, God asked questions in the Bible to draw His people's attention to new things He was doing, to prepare their hearts, and to cause them to consider things they'd never considered before. God is not only our loving Father, but He is also a master Teacher. He wants us to think things through thoroughly. He wants us to learn the truth and have our facts straight. Are you willing to be taught by the Lord?

HIDING FROM GOD?

*Then the LORD God called to Adam
and said to him, "Where are you?"*
GENESIS 3:9 NKJV

———————

There's something inside of fallen human beings that makes us think our best course of action when we stumble or fall is to hide from our heavenly Father—make that, *try* to hide from Him.

Adam knew he had messed up—badly—and he set the tone for what so many people have been doing ever since. Instead of approaching his Creator and restoring fellowship with Him, Adam hid. For the first time ever, he felt so much shame that he couldn't face God.

King David had his moments of sin and imperfection when he probably wanted to hide from God as well. But he knew there was nowhere he could go to avoid the Lord's watchful eyes: "Where can I go from Your Spirit? Or where can I flee from Your presence?" (Psalm 139:7 NKJV).

When we mess up—and we all do, sometimes royally—our first response should be to run *to* God, not *away* from Him. When we do that, He promises to forgive us, cleanse us, and restore us to fellowship with Himself. "If we confess our sins," the apostle John wrote, "he is faithful and just and will forgive us our sins and purify us from all unrighteousness" (1 John 1:9 NIV).

There's only one way we'll find that kind of restoration and cleansing, and that's when we present ourselves to God as sinners in need of His amazing forgiveness.

HE HEARS OUR CRIES FOR HELP

What is the matter, Hagar?
GENESIS 21:17 NIV

Genesis 21:8–17 is the story of a woman and her son who had been abandoned and forced to fend for themselves. Abraham, at the insistence of his wife, reluctantly sent his Egyptian servant, the mother of Ishmael, away with little more than a canteen full of water and some bread.

It wasn't long before Hagar came to the end of her rope. Alone and without food or water, she lost hope. Convinced that Ishmael was going to die, she began to weep (21:15–16). But when God heard her cries and Ishmael's voice, He sent an angel to comfort Hagar then to cause her to see a nearby source of water.

Abraham was worried sick about his son Ishmael, but he was severely limited in what he could do. God, however, was under no such limitation. As He still does for us to this day, He reached into a hopeless situation and offered comfort and provision.

God didn't forget Hagar and Ishmael. And He'll never forget us, His chosen people, when we're in a place where we're in short supply of hope and comfort. The apostle Paul summarized this promise when he wrote, "My God will meet all your needs according to the riches of his glory in Christ Jesus" (Philippians 4:19 NIV).

Feeling short on hope today? Don't be afraid to cry out to the God who promises to meet all your needs.

LOVE FOR ONE ANOTHER

What will he sleep in?
EXODUS 22:27 NKJV

Much of the Law Moses passed down to the people dealt with treating others with justice and compassion. The Lord identified Himself as a God who was compassionate and concerned about the plight of the poor and disadvantaged.

Today's question is part of a passage in which God tells His people, "If you ever take your neighbor's garment as a pledge, you shall return it to him before the sun goes down. For that is his only covering. . . . What will he sleep in? And it will be that when he cries to Me, I will hear, for I am gracious" (Exodus 22:26–27 NKJV).

The "pledge" in this passage is very much like modern-day collateral on a loan, and God wanted His people to understand that He would not be pleased with those who took advantage of the needy by keeping their cloak—usually the only one they owned—during the cold of the night.

The Bible still enjoins believers to treat one another with compassion and love. From the very beginning, God intended for those who belong to Him to be different from those around them, and one of those differences is spelled out wonderfully in these words of Jesus: "By this everyone will know that you are my disciples, if you love one another" (John 13:35 NIV).

A Christian is someone who loves fellow believers, and that love is demonstrated not just in words but in actions.

NEVER FORGET GOD'S GOODNESS

*Did I not rescue you from the Egyptians, the Amorites, the Ammonites,
the Philistines, the Sidonians, the Amalekites, and the Maonites?*
JUDGES 10:11–12 NLT

Judges 10:6–18 is another chapter in a recurring story in the lives of the people of Israel. This one took place during the time of the Judges. The people had seen the hand of God deliver and protect them time after time, yet they seemed to quickly forget His goodness and might and turn away from Him to a number of false "gods."

It's easy to turn up our noses at the Israelites for their lack of faithfulness to their God. But we modern-day Christians are faced with—and, far too often, fall for—the same kinds of temptations the people of Israel faced in the days of the Judges. Sure, we may not turn to and worship another god in the most literal sense. And we don't completely abandon the true and living God. But we're still prone to turning to other "gods"—such as our own talents and abilities, our own knowledge, or our own strength—in order to find the security God Himself wants to provide us.

There is no better or more secure place for a believer to live than under the protective hand of the heavenly Father. Remind yourself daily of all that God has done for you in the past, and know that He's still bigger than any problem or temptation you may face.

BY WHATEVER MEANS HE CHOOSES

By what means?
I KINGS 22:22 NIV

Ahab, the evil king of the Northern Kingdom of Israel, had gone too far, and God was about to carry out His death sentence upon the wicked monarch (1 Kings 20:42; 21:19).

Micaiah, a true prophet of God, had warned Ahab that he was about to die, but Ahab continued planning his war with Syria. At this point, Micaiah received a vision of God in heaven asking for volunteers to draw Ahab into this battle in which he would die. A spirit (apparently a deceptive demonic being) stepped forward and volunteered to deceive Ahab by causing his prophets to lie to him (1 Kings 22:21). In the end, Ahab listened to his prophets' lies, and it led to his death in battle.

It might seem strange to us that God would make use of a deceiver to carry out His divine plan. The Bible teaches that God by His very nature can't deceive anyone (Numbers 23:19; Titus 1:2). However, it also teaches that God can use any means He chooses to bring His plans to fruition.

We can take comfort in the fact that God asked the spirit, "By what means?" before allowing it to work its deception. This shows us that the Lord has complete authority over everything in creation and that no thing or no one—even evil spirits—can do anything without God allowing it.

Count on it—our God is in complete control!

GRATEFUL FOR EACH NEW DAY

Have you ever given orders to the morning,
or shown the dawn its place, that it might take the
earth by the edges and shake the wicked out of it?
JOB 38:12–13 NIV

As God dialogued with Job, He cited examples from His creation to remind Job of how wise and powerful He was—and how small, limited in understanding, and powerless Job was.

In this verse, the Lord asked Job if it was he who caused the sun to rise over creation every day—and in the exact same position each day. Of course it wasn't Job who created the earth or who caused it to rotate and orbit the sun in such a way that the sun actually rises in *different* places on the horizon, depending on the time of year. Only God Himself has the power and the wisdom to cause these things to happen.

When we awake each morning, we can rejoice and thank our heavenly Father not just for the amazing creativity, power, and wisdom it takes to guide our planet's rotation and orbit, but also for giving us each day of the year.

One of the psalmists gave voice to the wonder of a God so powerful, yet so loving, that He not only gives us each new day, but also gives each day of the year its own identity: "This is the day the LORD has made; we will rejoice and be glad in it" (Psalm 118:24 NKJV).

FEELING SMALL ENOUGH?

Can you bind the cluster of the Pleiades,
or loose the belt of Orion?
JOB 38:31 NKJV

In Job 38:31, God challenges Job, asking him if he had the power to change the movement of the stars in the sky. Pleiades is a constellation of many stars, only a few of which are visible to the naked eye. Orion is one of the most prominent constellations in the nighttime sky.

In other words, God was telling Job, "You don't have near the power it would take to alter what I've placed in the sky, but I do. I can do that and much, much more."

King David didn't have nearly the scientific knowledge we have today, but he was able to look into the darkened sky and recognize that the countless visible stars and constellations were evidence of the greatness of God: "The heavens declare the glory of God; the skies proclaim the work of his hands" (Psalm 19:1 NIV).

The next time you get away from the city lights on a clear, moonless night, take some time to marvel at the power and creativity of a God who put those stars in their place and keeps them there year after year, century after century. Marvel at the fact that a God who made it all still cares so deeply and passionately about you, a microscopic being living on a tiny speck of dust that revolves around one of trillions of stars in the universe.

CARING FOR HIS CREATION

Do you know the month when mountain goats give birth?
Have you ever watched a doe bear her fawn?
JOB 39:1 MSG

In that part of the world, and in that point of human history, people were much more aware of the natural world around them than we are today. So it's very likely that Job *had* observed mountain goats and does giving birth and that he knew those things happened at roughly the same time every year.

While Job may have had some general knowledge of the fact that wild animals reproduced at the same time of year, each year, he seemed to need to be reminded that those things took place away from the protection or care of any human shepherd. Rather, they occurred under the watchful eye of the God who created them.

Jesus once spoke about the wonder of wild birds finding enough food to sustain themselves, and that apart from any human intervention on their part: "Look at the birds of the air, for they neither sow nor reap nor gather into barns; yet your heavenly Father feeds them. Are you not of more value than they?" (Matthew 6:26 NKJV).

Nature is filled with many wonderful examples of the creativity and care of our heavenly Father. The next time you observe the wonders of the natural world, stop and ponder this amazing truth: "God has made all this and provides for His creations. And He does the same thing for me!"

LIMITED IN OUR HUMANITY

Can anyone capture it by the eyes,
or trap it and pierce its nose?
JOB 40:24 NIV

The identity of the beast called "Behemoth" (Job 40:15–24) is a matter of debate among Bible scholars. Some identify it as an elephant or a hippopotamus. Some believe the animal was a dinosaur like a gigantic brontosaurus, while others believe it was another enormous animal that has since become extinct.

Whatever Behemoth was, it was an amazing, powerful creature—so powerful that God challenged Job to think about what it would take to tame it. God wanted Job to understand that Behemoth, like humans, was one of His creations (verse 15) and therefore under His control and dominion (verse 19).

There's a lesson for each of us in God's discussion of Behemoth: There is nothing this world can throw at us—in the natural realm or the supernatural—that God can't handle. Apart from the protection and empowerment of our Creator, can we have victory over this world and over the enemy of our souls, the devil? No, we can't. Jesus told His followers, "Apart from me you can do nothing" (John 15:5 NIV).

As created beings, we're limited by our humanity. But our God, "who made the world and everything in it" (Acts 17:24 NIV), is bound by no such limitations. While the world we live in can be a frightening and dangerous place, our God can handle even the worst we have to face.

GOD UP CLOSE AND PERSONAL

You asked, "Who is this that obscures
my plans without knowledge?"
JOB 42:3 NIV

In Job 42:3, the title character repeated a question God had asked him in Job 38:2. Job, in questioning God about his terrible pain and suffering, had asked Him some very pointed questions—questions that showed Job's limited, flawed understanding of his heavenly Father.

Job had come to a point many Christians come to during difficult times—namely, that while they may not understand the reasons for their suffering, God does. . .and He knows what He's doing.

"Surely I spoke of things I did not understand, things too wonderful for me to know," Job admitted. "My ears had heard of you but now my eyes have seen you" (Job 42:3, 5 NIV).

In his misery, Job had made some wrong assumptions about God. But as he spent time with Him, he realized how presumptuous and wrong he had been. In the end, Job was a changed man, and that was because his notions of God and his relationship with Him had deepened and broadened. "Therefore I despise myself and repent in dust and ashes," he said (verse 6).

When you're experiencing a time of difficulty, don't be afraid to ask God the tough questions. You may not get clear answers as to why you're enduring such difficulties, but it's possible that He'll open your eyes to some truths about Himself, truths that will enable you to experience Him in a new and wonderful way.

HE'S IN COMPLETE CONTROL

Haven't you gotten the news that
I've been behind this all along?
ISAIAH 37:26 MSG

Hezekiah, the godly king of Judah, knew he and his people were in deep trouble. Sennacherib, the powerful and ruthless Assyrian king whose army had already conquered dozens of strongholds in Judah, had his sights on the capital city, Jerusalem.

Blinded by his arrogance, Sennacherib sent envoys to demand surrender. Sure that his soldiers would easily take Jerusalem, he openly mocked the people for trusting in their God.

Speaking through the prophet Isaiah, God assured the king that He would protect the city. Then God had a message for Sennacherib, one of doom and judgment, because he had attempted to contend not just with God's people but with God Himself.

"Haven't you gotten the news that I've been behind this all along?" In other words, God told Sennacherib, "Since you're too blind to see it, I'll tell you: There is only one God, and you're not Him. I have always been in control of the affairs of My people, and I always will be."

Though the Lord's message was spoken to the evil Assyrian king, it has application to our lives today. It's easy to forget that no matter how out-of-control and crazy our world seems to be, no matter how terrible current events may look, we can always take comfort in this simple truth: Our God is behind how things turn out. He's always in control, always working behind the scenes on our behalf.

BLIND AND DEAF SERVANTS

Who is blind but my servant,
and deaf like the messenger I send?
ISAIAH 42:19 NIV

The message in Isaiah 42:18–20 was directed toward a truly blessed people—the people of Israel and their national leaders. Over time, however, they had developed a problem with their ability to see and hear the Lord.

The problem was that God's servants, the messengers He had chosen to use to communicate salvation to the world, had become spiritually blind and deaf. As God's own people, the Jews of Isaiah's day had every advantage and privilege over those around them. Yet they had become so hard-hearted and complacent toward their God that they could no longer see what He had done for them or hear what He had to say to them.

In New Testament times, God identifies His chosen people as those who follow Jesus Christ. The apostle Peter wrote to Christians living in his day, "You are a chosen people, a royal priesthood, a holy nation, God's special possession, that you may declare the praises of him who called you out of darkness into his wonderful light" (1 Peter 2:9 NIV).

God saw the people of Israel in the time of the prophet Isaiah the same way. Yet they had become blind to who they were and deaf toward the One who called them His own possession. As Christians living in the twenty-first century, let's never forget who we are—or *whose* we are.

GOD CHOOSES THE HOWS

Does clay talk back to the potter:
"What are you doing?"
ISAIAH 45:9 MSG

———————

Cyrus the Great reigned over Persia from 539 to 530 BC. Though he wasn't one of God's people, he's remembered in history as the one who allowed—even assisted—the Jews to return to Israel after seventy years in captivity.

Isaiah's prophecies regarding Cyrus were astonishing because they were written about 150 years before he was even born. Yet God called him by name!

Isaiah 45:8–13 was addressed to the Jewish captives who may have chafed at the idea of God using a pagan ruler to deliver them. When God asked, "Does the clay talk back to the potter: 'What are you doing?' " He was reminding Israel that He made them, that He was with them, and that He alone could choose the means He'd use for their deliverance.

God's message in Isaiah 45 still applies to His people today. We are sometimes like Israel in Isaiah's day in that we love the idea of God doing great works of healing, cleansing, and change in our lives, but we'd prefer to reserve the right to tell Him *how* we want those things done.

As God's adopted children, we have received the right to ask anything in Jesus' name, and He will do it. As clay in our Maker's hands, however, we do well to let Him accomplish what we ask in the way He chooses to do it. . .and when He chooses to do it.

A DEBT FULLY PAID

To which of my creditors did I sell you?
Isaiah 50:1 NIV

―――――――――

In the days of the prophet Isaiah, the people familiar with the law of Moses would have known that God allowed a man who was hopelessly in debt to another man to sell himself, or one of his children, to be that man's slave. This was a very difficult experience to have to go through.

The above verse is a rhetorical question—a question with an obvious "no" answer—from God to His people. They had sinned grievously against their God, but He wanted them to know that He had not "sold" them, that they still belonged to Him. Rather, it was their own willful sin that had caused all their troubles.

The Bible teaches that there is a relationship of indebtedness between God and humankind, but it's not a debt *God* owes anyone. Rather, it is *we* who are hopelessly indebted to our heavenly Father because of our own sin. No amount of work or payment on our behalf can get us on equal footing again.

But the good news is that God Himself has paid that debt for us. The apostle Paul wrote, "There is one God and one Mediator who can reconcile God and humanity—the man Christ Jesus. He gave his life to purchase freedom for everyone" (1 Timothy 2:5–6 NLT).

God has stamped on our debt *Paid in Full*.

TOUGH LOVE FROM ABOVE

Are you not a brood of rebels, the offspring of liars?
ISAIAH 57:4 NIV

⸻

The fifty-seventh chapter of Isaiah opens with God speaking to His people in language that can be described as blunt and to the point. God saw the sin of the people, and He very directly called them out for failing to live up to their own professions—both in their dealings with Him and with other people.

When God asked the people, "Are you not a brood of rebels, the offspring of liars?" there was only one acceptable answer, and that was to agree with the One who knows all and sees all.

Thankfully, it didn't end there! Isaiah is commonly referred to as "the Prophet of Redemption," and while he records some of God's most pointed messages toward His people's sinfulness, he also records a message of restoration.

That reflects perfectly a God who is willing both to demonstrate some tough love as He calls out His people when they stray, and to cleanse them and restore them when they heed His message.

The God who so forcefully and bluntly—even harshly—chided His people for their sin is the same God who also spoke this amazing promise of forgiveness and redemption: "I live in a high and holy place, but also with the one who is contrite and lowly in spirit, to revive the spirit of the lowly and to revive the heart of the contrite" (Isaiah 57:15 NIV).

A GOD OF THE IMPOSSIBLE

Has anyone ever heard of such a thing?
Has anyone seen anything like this?
ISAIAH 66:8 MSG

Isaiah 66 is a message of judgment on those who refused to hear the words of the Lord. . .and of hope for those who had the courage to trust Him and cling to His promises. In this chapter, God promised that the Israelites' return to their homeland of Judah after the Babylonian captivity would be so swift that it could only be understood to be the work of the God who still worked miracles, who made possible what was physically and humanly impossible.

When God said, "Before she went into labor, she had the baby. Before the birth pangs hit, she delivered a son" (Isaiah 66:7 MSG), He was likening Israel's deliverance to a woman suddenly giving birth without experiencing labor pains—something just about anyone knows is an impossibility.

God's promises of restoration for the people of Israel are an amazing reflection of His promises to us Christians today. While we spend our earthly lives in bodies that break down over time, God promises that one day we'll be miraculously changed, that we'll become eternal beings whose bodies will never die or get sick: It will happen "in a flash, in the twinkling of an eye, at the last trumpet. For the trumpet will sound, the dead will be raised imperishable, and we will be changed" (1 Corinthians 15:52 NIV).

Has anyone ever heard of such a thing?

FRIENDSHIP WITH THE WORLD

And why go to Assyria to drink water from the Euphrates?
JEREMIAH 2:18 NIV

In the second chapter of Jeremiah, the prophet recorded God's case against His people in great detail. God loved the Jews, and He had called them to be devoted to and dependent upon Him. But instead of clinging to God, they turned from Him and chose instead to enter into alliance with two nations—Egypt and Assyria—who were, in reality, their enemies.

When God asked, "Why go to Assyria to drink water from the Euphrates?" He was pointing out to them that though they had the best of everything when they remained true to Him, they would lose it all if they turned from Him to make alliances with ungodly nations.

In the New Testament, the apostle James had a similar message when he wrote, "Do you not know that friendship with the world is enmity with God? Whoever therefore wants to be a friend of the world makes himself an enemy of God" (James 4:4 NKJV).

Among the many sins of Judah in the days of Jeremiah was entering into friendships with those who didn't know God or honor Him. We face those same temptations in our world today. This is why the apostle Paul wrote, "Do not conform to the pattern of this world, but be transformed by the renewing of your mind" (Romans 12:2 NIV). When we do that, he wrote, we'll know God's perfect will, which is to be completely devoted to Him.

YET RETURN TO ME

They say, "If a man divorces his wife, and she goes from
him and becomes another man's, may he return to her again?"
Would not that land be greatly polluted?
JEREMIAH 3:1 NKJV

According to the law of Moses (Deuteronomy 24:1–4), if a man divorced his wife and she married another who then divorced her also, husband number one was forbidden from remarrying her after her latest divorce.

In the third chapter of Jeremiah, God posed a question of the legality of remarriage in such circumstances, asking, "May he return to her again?" The answer, of course, was, "No, he may not."

God was making a point in posing this question, and each of us must consider it today also. Like those people thousands of years ago, we have sinned against God, and we have no right to presume He must forgive and restore us. God, on the other hand, has every right to "divorce" us and send us away forever.

From the beginning of time, God intended that He and His people share an intimate Creator/creation relationship. When sin entered into the human experience, death followed—physical death, emotional death, and, worst of all, spiritual death. We were eternally separated from God, and there was nothing we could do to be reunited with Him.

But God, in His undying love for His people, sent His Son to pay the legal price for our sins, in effect offering us this amazing invitation: "Yet return to Me" (Jeremiah 3:1 NKJV).

A NEW CONSCIENCE

Are they ashamed of their detestable conduct?
JEREMIAH 6:15 NIV

God sent the prophet Jeremiah to speak out to a people whose hearts were so hard, who had drifted so far away from their God, who had become so entrenched in their sinful behavior that their consciences were no longer piqued over their sin. They had become so comfortable in their wrongdoing that they couldn't even remember how to blush when confronted about it.

The consequences for this loss of conscience would be dreadful.

We live today in a world that is very much like the one in Jeremiah's day. The idea of shame or guilt over sinful behavior is no longer in vogue; many prefer to focus instead on justifying or excusing a bad lifestyle.

Even as Christians, it can be too easy to excuse sinful habits and to allow our hearts to become hard and our consciences to become deadened. The good news is that God has given us a path to a softened heart and a new conscience. It starts with first confessing known sin and then asking God to reveal things within us that are not pleasing to Him.

When we do that, we'll find that God will keep the promise He delivered through Ezekiel thousands of years ago: "I will give you a new heart and put a new spirit within you; I will take the heart of stone out of your flesh and give you a heart of flesh" (Ezekiel 36:26 NKJV).

THE SOURCE OF TRUE WISDOM

These wise teachers will fall into the trap of their own foolishness,
for they have rejected the word of the LORD. Are they so wise after all?
JEREMIAH 8:9 NLT

Solomon, the man the Bible calls the wisest person who ever lived (1 Kings 4:30), wrote: "The fear of the LORD is the beginning of wisdom, and knowledge of the Holy One is understanding" (Proverbs 9:10 NIV).

If you were to turn Solomon's words around, you'd have an apt word picture of the people of the Southern Kingdom of Judah in the days of the prophet Jeremiah. God had put up with these people for many years, and He had spoken to them through His prophets of their need to turn away from their wicked deeds. Yet they refused to listen to and act on His words, trusting in their own wisdom and in the deceitful words of false teachers.

Today, those who follow Jesus Christ need godly wisdom to navigate through a world that has its own brand of wisdom—one that seems to change almost daily.

God calls His people to live in the wisdom He has provided through His written Word. Not only that, He promises to freely give us wisdom if we simply ask for it: "If any of you lacks wisdom, you should ask God, who gives generously to all without finding fault, and it will be given to you" (James 1:5 NIV).

That's a beautiful promise we should daily claim as our own.

VESSELS TO BE FILLED

And they will say to you, "Do we not certainly
know that every bottle will be filled with wine?"
JEREMIAH 13:12 NKJV

At a glance, today's question looks like a positive promise from God. The people of Judah certainly saw it that way. But taken in context, we can see that the "wine" mentioned in this question is actually the judgment of God on a rebellious people.

Many commentators believe that the bottles in this passage (which were actually the clay pots or wineskins of the day) represented the people themselves. God wanted Jeremiah to understand that the people—even the national leaders—would be so intoxicated that they would be at the mercy of their enemies. The result would be the eventual destruction of Judah.

Hundreds of years after this prophecy, the apostle Paul wrote, "Do not get drunk on wine, which leads to debauchery. Instead, be filled with the Spirit" (Ephesians 5:18 NIV).

God had intended that the people of Judah find their satisfaction in being filled with Him and Him alone. He wants the same thing for us today. He wants us to understand that to be filled with His Spirit is to experience all the good things about Him— His love, His mercy, His forgiveness, and His provision.

The passage that includes today's question is a great reminder to make sure we let God fill us so that there's no room for anything this world has to offer.

OUR MASTER POTTER

Can I not do with you, Israel, as this potter does?
JEREMIAH 18:6 NIV

In the days of the prophet Jeremiah, Judah was a mess. The people were broken, lost, filled with sin and idolatry. . .and they didn't even seem to know it. But God hadn't given up on them, and speaking through the prophet, He begged them to turn back to Him so He could heal them, forgive them, and restore them.

God led Jeremiah to a potter's house and showed him a man working at a pottery wheel, taking a marred, imperfect vessel and re-forming it so it could be made into something beautiful and useful. God then showed Jeremiah what this scene meant, namely that He wanted to do the same with the people of Israel. He even instructed Jeremiah to go to the people and ask them, "Can I not do with you, Israel, as this potter does?"

Our heavenly Father asks us the same question today. He wants to take all of us—including our messes, our mistakes, and our ugliness—and remold us into beautiful vessels He can use for His glory and for the good of those around us.

Our part in that equation is to answer "Yes!" when He asks us whether He can mold us into what He knows each of us can be. That is, in the words of the apostle Paul, "a vessel for honor, sanctified and useful for the Master, prepared for every good work" (2 Timothy 2:21 NKJV).

THE SOURCE OF LIVING WATERS

Does the snow of Lebanon ever vanish from its rocky slopes?
Do its cool waters from distant sources ever stop flowing?
JEREMIAH 18:14 NIV

Today's question focuses on the unchanging beauty and blessings of the snow on the summits of Lebanon, which provides runoffs of cool, clean, life-sustaining water. When God delivered the message of Jeremiah 18, He was speaking figuratively—He was Israel's Rock and the Source of a never-ending flow of water.

The point of all this is that no reasonable person would think of abandoning such a rich supply of clean, cold water and instead resort to laboring to find an inferior water supply. Yet, that's exactly what the people of Israel did when they abandoned God and turned to idols.

Fast-forward some six centuries, and another great prophet—the Son of God, Jesus Christ—spoke to a thirsty woman seeking water at a well and referred to Himself as the Source of eternal, life-giving water: "Everyone who drinks this water will be thirsty again, but whoever drinks the water I give them will never thirst. Indeed, the water I give them will become in them a spring of water welling up to eternal life" (John 4:13–14 NIV).

Though few know it, we live in a world that is desperately thirsty for the water of life that Jesus freely offers. Let us never forget to ask God to bring these people into our sphere of influence and then make sure to lead them to the place where they can freely drink.

INTERACTING WITH GOD

What do you see, Jeremiah?
JEREMIAH 24:3 NKJV

Jeremiah 24 begins with God showing the prophet two baskets—one filled with good, delicious fruit and the other filled with worthless, inedible fruit. The Lord, apparently wanting Jeremiah to know the importance of the vision He'd given him, asked, "What do you see, Jeremiah?"

God went on to explain to Jeremiah the significance of the vision: He would bless the "good" exiles who had been led out of Judah to the land of the Babylonians. On the other hand, He would judge those in Judah who had led the people into sin and idolatry and had brought judgment on the nation.

Why did God ask Jeremiah what he saw? Perhaps it is because God knows that His communication with His people is best received when He interacts with them. From the time of creation, God wanted fellowship with us humans. He wanted us to give ourselves to Him, and He wanted to share Himself with us. In other words, He desired close, personal, Creator/creation interaction with us.

Prayer is more than just speaking words of praise, thanksgiving, and request to your God—as important as those things are. Prayer also involves listening when He speaks to you, to give you the wisdom, encouragement, or teaching you need.

When you spend time praying and reading your Bible, stop and ask yourself what God wants you to see and hear—what He's saying to you personally.

A TEACHABLE SPIRIT

Will ye not receive instruction to hearken to my words?
JEREMIAH 35:13 KJV

In Jeremiah 35, God addressed the Jews using a contrast between the Rechabites—a clan that closely followed the instructions of their father—and the nation of Judah, which had refused to listen to and obey the words of their God.

God instructed Jeremiah to tell the people, "I have spoken to you again and again, yet you have not obeyed me. Again and again I sent all my servants the prophets to you" (35:14–15 NIV).

God had sent messenger after messenger—men like Moses, Isaiah, and others—to speak warnings to His people. He was about to speak a message of judgment through Jeremiah, not because He didn't love and value His people (He most certainly did), but because they refused to hear and act on what He'd already told them.

The Bible is filled with examples of the blessings God's people received when they obeyed their heavenly Father. But it also contains many examples of those who failed to listen to Him when He spoke.

If you want to be among those who hear and act on God's Word, ask yourself how you should respond when you're confronted with an uncomfortable biblical truth or word of instruction. Ask yourself what your attitude should be when a Christian brother or sister lovingly points out something in you that needs to change, or when God Himself speaks to you in His still, small voice.

RESPONDING TO YOUR BROTHER'S DOWNFALL

*Was she caught among thieves, that you shake
your head in scorn whenever you speak of her?*
JEREMIAH 48:27 NIV

God directed this question to the Moabites, a people who had celebrated Israel's fate when its people were taken into captivity because of their sin against the Lord (2 Kings 17:6). God warned the Moabites that there would be severe consequences for them celebrating the calamity Israel had suffered (Jeremiah 48:26–46).

The Bible teaches that God watches over His people when others mistreat or bad-mouth them (Obadiah 1:13–18). But His people must allow God to deal with those offenses. "Do not take revenge, my dear friends, but leave room for God's wrath, for it is written: 'It is mine to avenge; I will repay,' says the Lord" (Romans 12:19 NIV).

There's another lesson we can take from God's pronouncement of judgment against the Moabites, and it's this: the Lord is very concerned when people—even fellow believers—speak ill or celebrate the downfall of one of His people.

It can be tempting to think thoughts and speak words of derision toward a fellow believer who is going through a self-inflicted season of misery. So search your heart when you see another Christian suffering because of sin and wrongdoing. Make sure you don't fall into the temptation to do anything but pray for (and help to bring about, when it's appropriate) that person's full restoration.

LIVING IN INTEGRITY

*Son of man, have you seen what the elders of Israel are
doing in the darkness, each at the shrine of his own idol?*
EZEKIEL 8:12 NIV

In Ezekiel 8, God showed the prophet vivid pictures of the behavior of the leaders of both Judah and Israel, the two kingdoms that had at one time comprised the nation of Israel.

It was far from a pretty picture.

The leaders of Israel had begun engaging in terrible, sinful behavior, all the while convinced that God was no longer watching: "They say, 'The LORD does not see us; the LORD has forsaken the land'" (Ezekiel 8:12 NIV). In other words, they were more concerned about their reputations than about their character. That's the nature of "hidden sin," isn't it? It's too easy sometimes to excuse our sin, convinced that since no one knows about it, we must be doing all right.

When we believe we can do whatever we want in private, even when it contradicts what we profess in public, we violate what God has called us to be. God wants us to commit ourselves to integrity, even when it comes to the things we do when no one else is present.

Integrity has been defined as always doing the right thing, even when no one is observing. As followers of Jesus Christ, we should always remember that there is never a moment when our heavenly Father isn't watching us—and we should always do what is right.

FRUIT-BEARING VINES

When it was whole it wasn't good for anything.
Half-burned is no improvement. What's it good for?
EZEKIEL 15:5 MSG

Ezekiel 15 records God's words concerning a people whose way-wardness and rebellion made them useless to Him. God likened the people to the useless wood of grapevines (Ezekiel 15:1–5) and told the prophet that those useless vines would be cast away and devoured by fire.

The idea of Christians bearing good fruit is an important theme in the New Testament as well. Jesus taught that we could know people who faithfully follow Him by the "good fruit" their lives produced (Matthew 17:17–20).

Later, the apostle Paul wrote that the key to producing good fruit is living under the influence of God's Holy Spirit: "But the fruit of the Spirit is love, joy, peace, forbearance, kindness, goodness, faithfulness, gentleness and self-control" (Galatians 5:22–23 NIV).

God wants each of us, His beloved, to bear fruit, the kind of fruit that both glorifies Him and influences those around us. We do that when we allow Him to fill us, when we learn to obey Christ's commands. He says, "Remain in me, as I also remain in you. No branch can bear fruit by itself; it must remain in the vine. Neither can you bear fruit unless you remain in me" (John 15:4 NIV).

Without Jesus living in us through the Holy Spirit, there's no way we can bear the kind of fruit God wants to see in us. With Him, though, there's nothing we can't do.

PERSONALLY RESPONSIBLE

Will such a man live?
EZEKIEL 18:13 NIV

━━━━━━━━━━

Ezekiel 18 is an account of God refuting a proverb the Jewish people quoted during Ezekiel's day. This saying strongly implied that the people weren't guilty and paying for their *own* sins but were innocently suffering for the sins of their ancestors.

God laid out the charges against a hypothetical man, the son of a righteous father who committed all manner of sin against the Lord and against the people around him. He listed the charges against this man and then asked Ezekiel if that man would live— followed by an answer to the question: "No," God told Ezekiel. "He will not! Because he has done all these detestable things, he is to be put to death" (Ezekiel 18:13 NIV).

True, the Bible teaches that our personal sin can carry with it consequences for our children (Exodus 20:5; Jeremiah 32:18), but it also teaches that each of us is responsible for our own actions. Furthermore, it tells us that none of us is without sin and that none of us can escape the consequences of that sin—at least not on our own.

The apostle Paul wrote, "All have sinned and fall short of the glory of God" (Romans 3:23 NIV). But he continued with the "good news" part of that equation when he wrote, "And all are justified freely by his grace through the redemption that came by Christ Jesus" (verse 24).

GENTLY SPEAKING THE TRUTH

Will you judge them, son of man,
will you judge them?
EZEKIEL 20:4 NKJV

When God called the prophet Ezekiel to judge the people of Israel, He was in effect saying, "Bring to their attention their sin and the sins of their fathers before them. Point them out to them. Let them know that I will hold them accountable for their sin if they don't change course."

Ezekiel ministered during a very difficult time in the history of Israel. The people's hearts had grown hard, and they had abandoned their devotion to God. While the Lord still loved these people, He wanted them to know that they'd place themselves in grave danger if they refused to repent and turn back to Him.

The prophet spoke to a people who bore a resemblance to so many individuals living today. They didn't want to hear what God had to say but preferred to remain in their complacency and sin.

God doesn't call us as modern believers to speak words of condemnation to those around us. However, He does call us to speak honestly (and lovingly) and to confront sin where we see it. We are not to pass judgment on others but instead seek to gently bring them into fellowship with our loving heavenly Father.

As the apostle Paul wrote, "If someone is caught in a sin, you who live by the Spirit should restore that person gently" (Galatians 6:1 NIV).

CHOOSE HUMILITY

Is no secret hidden from you?
EZEKIEL 28:3 NIV

———————

The king of Tyre was filled with pride and arrogance. He believed that his kingdom's riches were the result of his own wisdom and strength. He was such a stark picture of conceit that many believe Ezekiel 28 refers to the devil himself. His vanity and his greed for material wealth and power motivated him to exploit nations around his kingdom, leading to God's proclamation of doom against him (Ezekiel 28:11–19).

One of the Bible's overarching messages is that God hates human pride and that He will deal firmly with those who refuse to humble themselves. The pages of the scriptures are filled with accounts of people who allowed sinful egotism to destroy them. That's the way it works: "Pride goes before destruction, a haughty spirit before a fall" (Proverbs 16:18 NIV).

But that message has a wonderfully hopeful opposite, and it's summarized perfectly in the writings of the apostle James: "Humble yourselves before the Lord, and he will lift you up" (James 4:10 NIV).

The king of Tyre had the opportunity to humble himself and to put God in His rightful place in his heart. He chose instead to exalt himself, leading to his fall. Likewise, God calls each and every one of us to humble ourselves and allow Him to lift us up in His time.

OUR HEAVENLY SHEPHERD

Should not shepherds take care of the flock?
EZEKIEL 34:2 NIV

In Ezekiel 34, the prophet addressed the irresponsible and ineffective leadership of the kings and rulers of Israel. These national authorities didn't lead with an eye toward what was best for the people, and God let them know He wasn't pleased with their behavior.

Speaking through Ezekiel, God went on to communicate the wonderful truth that He was not like an earthly ruler or leader but was His people's loving heavenly Shepherd, who would do what they had failed to: "Indeed I Myself will search for My sheep and seek them out. As a shepherd seeks out his flock on the day he is among his scattered sheep, so will I seek out My sheep and deliver them from all the places where they were scattered on a cloudy and dark day" (Ezekiel 34:11–12 NKJV).

There are several great lessons to take from this passage of God's Word, one of them being this: People, even the best of them, will fail in performing their "shepherdly" duties. But our Father in heaven will never fail to seek us out, to deliver us, to feed us, to provide for us, to heal us, and to strengthen us.

King David beautifully acknowledged the sufficiency of his heavenly Keeper when he wrote, "The LORD is my shepherd; I have all that I need" (Psalm 23:1 NLT). Indeed, with a heavenly Father/Shepherd like our God, we truly don't lack anything.

THE PATIENCE OF GOD

O Ephraim, what shall I do to you?
HOSEA 6:4 NKJV

God's words to Ephraim (Israel)—"What shall I do to you?"—weren't those of an angry God asking Israel what punishment He should mete out but of a heavenly Father who asked what He needed to do to bring His wayward child back into fellowship with Himself.

By this time in Israel's history, God had shown His people incredible mercy and blessings. He had sent His prophets to correct them and had even disciplined them. So far, nothing had worked; the people were still in sin and rebellion.

Yet God, in His amazing, self-sacrificial love, hadn't given up on His people. This is a picture of an incredibly patient God, of whom the apostle Peter wrote, "The Lord is not slow in keeping his promise, as some understand slowness. Instead he is patient with you, not wanting anyone to perish, but everyone to come to repentance" (2 Peter 3:9 NIV).

Has God ever laid on your heart His desire for you to pray for and witness to someone you know needs Jesus, yet months or even years go by, and you don't see any change? If so, don't lose heart. Instead, focus on the patience and promises of God for that person's salvation. Keep praying, keep witnessing, and keep living out the life of Christ in front of that person. And as you do, take this heart attitude:

God hasn't given up on this person, and neither will I.

TURNING FROM IDOLS

Ephraim, what more have I to do with idols?
HOSEA 14:8 NIV

━━━━━━━━

In the book of Hosea, the name "Ephraim" refers to the ten tribes that comprised the Northern Kingdom of Israel (Hosea 5:3). This prophetic writing is a picture of God's undying love for His people, even when they strayed from Him to follow other "gods."

The Lord said to His people, "I know all about Ephraim; Israel is not hidden from me. Ephraim, you have now turned to prostitution; Israel is corrupt" (Hosea 5:3 NIV). The people of Israel had fallen into willful sin (Hosea 2:5), and they would suffer the consequences.

The bad news is that all of humanity is in the same situation as Israel in Hosea's day. All people are in rebellion against God and attempt to fill the void made for Him alone with other things.

But the good news is that God has brought us into fellowship with Himself through His Son, Jesus Christ. God promises us new life in Him, and though we're all still prone to wander from the love and security of our heavenly Father, He has promised us great blessing and life when we turn our focus from the things of this world back to Him alone.

As the apostle Paul wrote, "Since you have been raised to new life with Christ, set your sights on the realities of heaven, where Christ sits in the place of honor at God's right hand" (Colossians 3:1 NLT).

JUSTICE, MERCY, HUMILITY

Shall I acquit someone with dishonest scales,
with a bag of false weights?
MICAH 6:11 NIV

In the time of the prophet Micah (around the mid-eighth century BC), the people of Judah had a problem—a *huge* problem—with focusing on the wrong things. The people were big on the religious rites and ceremonies laid out in the law of Moses, but they were very lacking in applying God's principles for living in love toward others.

Speaking through the prophet, God let His people know that external acts of religion—though the Law called for these things—meant nothing unless their hearts were filled with genuine love for God and they treated their earthly brothers and sisters right.

In the same chapter of the book of Micah, God gave His people this vitally important and timeless message: "He has shown you, O mortal, what is good. And what does the LORD require of you? To act justly and to love mercy and to walk humbly with your God" (Micah 6:8 NIV).

Justice, mercy, and humility. Those are bedrock principles for living the Christian life. That was part of Jesus' message when He said this of the greatest commandment: " 'Love the Lord your God with all your heart and with all your soul and with all your mind.' This is the first and greatest commandment. And the second is like it: 'Love your neighbor as yourself.' All the Law and the Prophets hang on these two commandments" (Matthew 22:37–40 NIV).

SATAN'S ACCUSATIONS. . .AND GOD'S ANSWER

Is not this man a burning stick snatched from the fire?
ZECHARIAH 3:2 NIV

Joshua was the high priest in the days of Nehemiah and Ezra. This was during the rebuilding of God's temple after the Jewish people's return from their decades of captivity in Babylonia. In Zechariah's vision, he saw Joshua wearing filthy clothes as he stood before the angel of the Lord. Satan, meanwhile, accused Joshua right to God's face.

But God wasn't having it. "The LORD rebuke you, Satan!" He exclaimed. "The LORD, who has chosen Jerusalem, rebuke you! Is not this man a burning stick snatched from the fire?" (Zechariah 3:2 NIV).

The angel then ordered the dirty rags to be removed from Joshua and replaced with clean clothes—a beautiful picture of God's forgiveness and cleansing (verses 3–5).

In a very real way, we are all Joshua—fallible, sinful beings who have nothing to offer God but our filthy garments (Isaiah 64:6). But God will no longer entertain Satan's accusations against us—not because we have reached sinless perfection, but because God Himself has done what we could never do for ourselves: cleansed us, forgiven us, and snatched us from the fires of hell through the work of His Son, Jesus Christ.

So when the devil sidles up to you and begins whispering accusations against you, don't listen. After all, God doesn't. Not only that, when the accuser dares speak a word against you, the angel simply says, "The LORD rebuke you!"

GIVING GOD YOUR BEST

With such offerings from your hands,
will he accept you?
MALACHI 1:9 NIV

The book of Malachi opens with the prophet chastising the people of his day for their dishonest and ungrateful hearts. He also chided the priests for their unfaithfulness in carrying out their duties as representatives of God—specifically by offering less than the best they had when they brought their sacrifices to the altar.

God's message through the prophet was a simple but vitally important one, and one that applies to His people today: *"I love you and have chosen you, but you've grown cold in your love for Me. You're not giving me the best you have, which is My due as your Father in heaven. Honor Me with the very best you have, and I'll protect and bless you."*

Jesus taught this very same message when He said, "He who has My commandments and keeps them, it is he who loves Me. And he who loves Me will be loved by My Father, and I will love him and manifest Myself to him" (John 14:21 NKJV).

That sounds like a great heavenly Father/earthly child relationship, doesn't it?

When God came to earth in the person of Jesus Christ, it was a picture of ultimate love, of a gracious Creator giving His prized creation the very best He had to offer. We honor Him, and open ourselves for His blessings, when we give Him the very best we have in return.

THE FIG LEAF FAIL

Who told you that you were naked?
Genesis 3:11 niv

In the beginning, "Adam and his wife were both naked, and they felt no shame" (Genesis 2:25 niv). However, once they ate the forbidden fruit, they became aware of their appearance. They felt inadequate, and this brought on shame, so they sewed fig leaves together. But when God showed up in the garden later, they were *again* naked. Adam said, "I was afraid because I was naked" (Genesis 3:10 niv). Apparently their hastily sewn coverings had quickly broken apart. They had then resorted to hiding.

God wasn't impressed by their cover-up or their hiding. He wanted Adam to confess why he felt the need to do so in the first place. It's the same today. If you disobey God, you get a guilty conscience, but He isn't interested in you trying to "fix" the situation. And He certainly isn't impressed if you smooth things over and act like nothing's wrong. He wants you to own up to the disobedience that caused your mess and trust Him to forgive and restore you. "He who covers his sins will not prosper, but whoever confesses and forsakes them will have mercy" (Proverbs 28:13 nkjv).

God's solution was to give Adam and Eve animal skins as coverings. This involved sacrificing the beasts and shedding their blood. Likewise, God has also provided forgiveness and restoration today: if you trust that Jesus' blood, shed for you, washes away your sin, you're forgiven.

KNOWING GOD'S IDENTITY

Why do you want to know my name?
GENESIS 32:29 NLT

The Angel of the Lord—a representation of God Himself—wrestled with Jacob all night and, just before dawn, asked him, "What is your name?" "Jacob," he answered. Now, *Jacob* meant "supplanter, deceiver." That wasn't just his name; it was his identity, who he was. So God gave him a new name—*Israel* ("he struggles with God")—because he had struggled and now had a *new* identity (verse 28).

But when Jacob asked what *His* name was, the Lord didn't tell him. Centuries later, God answered the same question, saying, "Why do you ask My name, seeing it is wonderful [incomprehensible]?" (Judges 13:18 NKJV).

The Old Testament saints knew that God's name was Yahweh (written "LORD" throughout the scriptures), but they didn't truly know His identity, who He fully was. No person, even today, can begin to comprehend the eternal, almighty, omniscient God. He's incomprehensible, beyond our ability to grasp. However, to varying degrees, Christians can experience and know His power and goodness and grasp His mysterious ways.

God told David He would deliver the righteous "because he has set his love upon Me. . .because he has known My name" (Psalm 91:14 NKJV). How well do *you* know the Lord? The closer you walk to God in love and obedience, the more you understand His heart, and the more this transforms you inside, giving you a new God-centered identity.

MALIGNING GOD'S ANOINTED

*Why then were you not afraid to
speak against My servant Moses?*
NUMBERS 12:8 NKJV

Many Ethiopians (Kushites) lived in Egypt, and when the Israelites left Egypt, a number of these went with them. One dark-skinned Kushite beauty caught Moses' eye, so he took her for a wife. But Aaron and Miriam didn't approve—perhaps because this was his *second* non-Hebrew wife—and publicly criticized him. How could they challenge God's prophet? Easy. Aaron and Miriam asked, "Has the LORD spoken only through Moses? . . . Hasn't he also spoken through us?" (Numbers 12:2 NIV).

Their intention was not simply to have equal authority, but to undermine Moses' authority and take over leadership. God was upset. Hence His question.

He had already told the Israelites, "Do not. . .curse the ruler of your people" (Exodus 22:28 NIV). This command still applies to Christians today. God still cautions, "Do not touch My anointed ones" (1 Chronicles 16:22 NKJV), and in the New Testament God instructed, "Do not listen to an accusation against an elder unless it is confirmed by two or three witnesses" (1 Timothy 5:19 NLT).

This doesn't mean you should take loyalty to leaders to an extreme and overlook glaring sins and faults, or be afraid to ask legitimate questions, but you should have a respectful attitude toward those who have oversight in your life. Before you listen to accusations against leaders—and certainly before you pass them on to others—check thoroughly to make sure that they're true.

ABUSING SACRED PRIVILEGES

Did I not clearly reveal myself to your ancestor's
family when they were in Egypt under Pharaoh?
1 SAMUEL 2:27 NIV

The tribe of Levi had special privileges: because they had been chosen to serve God, they lived off of the tithes that the other eleven tribes gave, and they were entitled to a share of the meat sacrificed to God, and other offerings.

However, the priest Eli had allowed his sons to run amok, to abuse the privileges of the priesthood, and to offend the Israelites who had come to sacrifice. So God asked him the above question then went on to declare, " 'I promised that members of your family would minister before me forever.' But now the LORD declares: 'Far be it from me! Those who honor me I will honor, but those who despise me will be disdained'" (1 Samuel 2:30 NIV).

When you come to faith in Christ, God gives you full access to the richness of His mercy. He gives you the right to approach His throne and ask Him for help during your times of need. He gives you many promises of protection and provision. Yet some believers are so ungrateful and disrespectful that they "have treated the blood of the covenant, which made [them] holy, as if it were common and unholy, and have insulted and disdained the Holy Spirit who brings God's mercy to us" (Hebrews 10:29 NLT).

Don't let this be you. Keep a tender heart and stay close to God.

PROUD BLASPHEMERS

Who do you think it is you've insulted? Who do you think you've been bad-mouthing? Before whom do you suppose you've been strutting?
2 Kings 19:22 msg

Sennacherib, the king of Assyria, had sent his armies to conquer Judah and instructed his field commander to ridicule Yahweh, the God of Israel. Decked in gleaming armor, the commander strutted before the walls of Jerusalem. He boasted that none of the gods of any *other* peoples had saved them from him, so why did the Jews hope that their God would deliver them? He mocked, "Do not let Hezekiah persuade you to trust in the Lord when he says, 'The Lord will surely deliver us'" (2 Kings 18:30 niv). He assured them that God could *not*.

There are many people in the world today like King Sennacherib. They loudly tell you that there is no God, and even if He does exist, He's too weak, distant, or uncaring to help you. But King Hezekiah trusted in the Lord and prayed desperately to Him. He reminded God of the Assyrian king's insults and pleaded with Him to take action. And God did.

God is still just as powerful today. He says, "I am the Lord, I change not" (Malachi 3:6 kjv). If you find yourself in a hopeless predicament, look to the Lord. Your situation may be a disaster, but God is able to save you. . .if you cry out to Him with your whole heart.

SPRINGS OF THE SEA

Hast thou entered into the springs of the sea?
or hast thou walked in the search of the depth?
JOB 38:16 KJV

———————

This is a beautiful passage, but what does it mean? It's more than just lofty poetry. Let's look at it from a few other translations. The NLT asks, "Have you explored the springs from which the seas come? Have you explored their depths?" and the NIV questions, "Have you. . .walked in the recesses of the deep?" God was trying to impress Job with his weakness and ignorance compared to God's vast power and wisdom.

Many modern scientists believe that all water on earth came from outer space, brought courtesy of comets. (That would be a whole *lot* of comets!) The Bible, however, indicates that water surged up from within our planet. In fact, in June 2014, scientists announced that there are immense amounts of water below the earth's crust, inside rocks that are 255 to 410 miles deep. There is as much water down there as there is in all the oceans on the surface of the world. Scientists now believe that it may still be cycling between Earth's interior and surface through the action of plate tectonics—seeping up through deep ocean trenches.

God's mysterious workings in nature often remain enigmas for millennia, only to be unlocked by startling scientific discoveries. Job was unable to explore the deep recesses of the oceans, and even today, with our most amazing submersible vehicles, this remains beyond man's ability.

GUIDING THE CONSTELLATIONS

Can you bring out Mazzaroth in its season?
Or can you guide the Great Bear with its cubs?
Job 38:32 nkjv

M azzaroth is Hebrew for "constellations," so Job 38:32 (nlt) words this, "Can you direct the constellations through the seasons. . . ?" As the seasons change during the year, the constellations slowly rotate around the North Star. The Great Bear and her cubs is the constellation Ursa Major (Latin for "Great Bear"). The Big Dipper is in its center, and the square ladle is considered the Bear's body. Jewish astronomers said Alioth, Mizar, and Alkaid (the stars forming the handle) were three cubs following their mother.

When God was challenging Job's wisdom and power, He asked Job whether he could direct the stars as they wheeled across the heavens. Of course he couldn't. Only God can do that. Job admitted, "He designed the Big Dipper and Orion, the Pleiades and Alpha Centauri. We'll never comprehend all the great things he does" (Job 9:9–10 msg).

You'll never be even a tiny fraction as powerful as God, and you can't comprehend more than a minute portion of all His mysterious doings. God is immeasurably greater than you. This should not only put you in awe of your almighty Creator, but be a tremendous comfort. The God who designed and guides distant stars is looking after you and guiding you as well. "The steps of a good man are ordered by the Lord: and he delighteth in his way" (Psalm 37:23 kjv).

ASKING THE RIGHT QUESTIONS

Who let the wild donkey go free? Who untied its ropes?
JOB 39:5 NIV

———————

The domestic donkey is descended from the African wild ass, *E. africanus*, and has been used as a work animal, pulling carts and carrying loads, since 3000 BC. In Job's day, men used them as pack animals in caravans, and as far as people knew, donkeys had always been tame. So when their donkey caravans passed asses running wild in the deserts and salt flats (Job 24:5; 39:6), they asked, "Who let the wild donkey go free? Who untied its ropes?"

God repeated these questions to Job. He wasn't saying that the wild ass was originally a domestic donkey that had gone feral—although a few had likely done so. God created the African wild ass free in the beginning, and there were no ropes to untie at creation.

Likewise, Christians don't always ask the right questions. For example, if you get into an automobile accident, your first impulse might be to question, "God, why did You let this happen? I thought You would protect me." Whereas the *right* question might be, "God, what did I do wrong here?" You might have been speeding, distracted, or breaking some other traffic rule.

Many Christians also jump to conclusions when they come across a seeming contradiction in the Bible. They assume that God made a mistake. It's much better to study the matter and research the historical, social, religious, and geographical context. Don't ask the wrong questions.

RESTRAINING POWERFUL BEASTS

Can you catch Leviathan with a hook or put a
noose around its jaw? Can you tie it with a rope
through the nose or pierce its jaw with a spike?
JOB 41:1–2 NLT

According to the Bible, there was a gigantic monster inhabiting the oceans of the ancient world. It was known as "Leviathan, the swiftly moving serpent, the coiling, writhing serpent. . .the dragon of the sea" (Isaiah 27:1 NLT). It sometimes ventured into swamps on land (Job 41:30–32). Read a full description of this amazing monster in Job 41.

Now, the ancient peoples were used to harnessing great power. They had domesticated the wild ox and put ropes through its nostrils to lead it along. But God questioned Job as to whether he was up to doing such a thing with Leviathan.

But there's a beast that's as difficult to control as this primordial sea monster—your own tongue. "People can tame all kinds of animals, birds, reptiles, and fish, but no one can tame the tongue. It is restless and evil, full of deadly poison" (James 3:7–8 NLT). Bottom line: "If we could control our tongues, we would. . .also control ourselves in every other way" (James 3:2 NLT).

You might not be able to control a Leviathan, no more than the keepers of *Jurassic World* could control the enormous Mosasaurus. But good news! If you yield to the power of God's Spirit, you *can* control your tongue. The things that are impossible with men are possible with God.

LOVE ME, LOVE MY KIDS

*What are you up to, quoting my laws,
talking like we are good friends?*
PSALM 50:16 MSG

———

Many scribes and Pharisees in Jesus' day had practically memorized the five books of Moses and were constantly teaching God's Word to others. They acted like they were faithful, devoted followers. But they were just putting on a hypocritical show. Though they worshipped God with their lips, their hearts were far from Him. They made public displays of prayer but oppressed their fellow Jews. It was the same with many people in David's day.

To the righteous, God says, "Call upon Me in the day of trouble; I will deliver you," because they had a close relationship with Him. But of the wicked, He asked, "What right have you to declare My statutes. . .seeing you hate instruction and cast My words behind you?" (Psalm 50:15–17 NKJV). Christians today can fall into the same trap if they don't watch out. For example, you know that the two greatest commands are to love God with all your heart and love your neighbor as yourself (Mark 12:29–31), but how easy is it to *live* these basic commands? It's sometimes difficult.

Yet obeying them is vitally important. As the apostle John brings out, if you say you love God but hate your fellow man, you're lying that you love God (1 John 4:20). The surest proof that you love God is if you love your fellow man.

OUR INCOMPARABLE GOD

So—who is like me?
ISAIAH 40:25 MSG

Once God wanted to give the Israelites a very clear idea of how incomparable He was, how exalted He was above anything they could possibly imagine. He asked them, "To whom will you compare me?" (Isaiah 40:25 NIV). If they imagined that a majestic king was like Him, well, God routinely reduced the rulers of this world to nothing. At His command they became like flecks of chaff blown in the wind (verses 23–24).

Did the Israelites think that any of the great empires around them could match God in splendor and magnificence? To God, all the nations of the world were like one small drop of water clinging to the side of a very large bucket. Or, to use another comparison, He considered them of no more importance than dust on a set of scales; if He wanted to weigh something valuable, He wouldn't even bother to blow the dust off first, because it wouldn't affect the weight at all. To put it bluntly, "before him all the nations are as nothing; they are regarded by him as worthless and less than nothing" (verse 17).

Did they think that the stars of the heavens above could compare to God? Hardly. He was the One who *created* every star they could see, including millions of enormous galaxies too distant for them to see (verse 26).

Our God is utterly incomparable. Nothing can match Him.

PAYING ATTENTION

Who is blind like the one in covenant with me,
blind like the servant of the LORD?
ISAIAH 42:19 NIV

‎———

Many people wonder how a servant of God, living in a relation-ship with Him, could be said to be blind. But this verse isn't talking about the ideal believer but about someone with plenty of room for improvement. Obviously. The very next verse describes the problem. The person isn't literally blind, because God states, "You have seen many things, but you pay no attention; your ears are open, but you do not listen" (verse 20).

It's not that they can't see. In fact, they see "*many* things," but they simply aren't paying attention and soon forgot what is revealed to them. This is why Moses warned, "Take heed to yourself, and dil-igently keep yourself, lest you forget the things your eyes have seen, and lest they depart from your heart" (Deuteronomy 4:9 NKJV). If you quickly forget the things you've seen, it's as if you never saw them to begin with.

Jesus said, "The hearts of this people have grown dull. Their ears are hard of hearing, and their eyes they have closed" (Mat-thew 13:15 NKJV). Spiritual blindness comes from deliberately closing your eyes. You're not interested, so you don't pay attention and the truth doesn't register. What's the solution? "We ought to give the more earnest heed to the things which we have heard, lest at any time we should let them slip" (Hebrews 2:1 KJV).

THE HANDS OF GOD

Shall the clay say to him that fashioneth it. . .He hath no hands?
ISAIAH 45:9 KJV

It's a delight to watch a skilled potter at work, cupping both hands around a clay vase rapidly spinning on his wheel. He knows exactly what he's doing, and his fingers nimbly work the clay, a touch here, a touch there, applying sustained pressure to form a ridge, then a depression, patiently fashioning the vessel into an exquisite work of art.

Now imagine for a brief second that the clay could actually think and speak. Would it be inclined to say, "The potter has no hands?" No, that should be about the *last* thing the clay would say. If clay could feel, it would sense every slight variation in the pressure of his fingers. The vessel owes its very shape and style— everything that makes it unique—to the fact that the potter *has* hands and that he uses them skillfully.

Yet many people today, even if they acknowledge that God exists, think that He has no means of influencing events in the world. They think, *He has no hands.* But two verses earlier in Isaiah, God said, "I am the LORD. . .I form the light and create darkness, I make peace and create calamity; I, the LORD, do all these things" (Isaiah 45:6–7 NKJV).

God can not only influence major world events, but He can touch your personal circumstances lightly with His fingers to form them into the exact pattern and shape that He desires.

GOD NEVER CASTS YOU OUT

*Where is your mother's certificate of
divorce with which I sent her away?*
ISAIAH 50:1 NIV

Under the law of Moses, a man could write his wife a certificate
of divorce, give it to her, and send her away (Deuteronomy
24:1). Spiritually, God was married to His people. He *did* give the
Northern Kingdom, Israel, such a certificate (Jeremiah 3:8), but
to His chosen people in Judah, He implored, "Return, O backslid-
ing children. . .for I am married to you" (Jeremiah 3:14 NKJV), and
explained, "For a brief moment I abandoned you, but with deep
compassion I will bring you back" (Isaiah 54:7 NIV). Judah's seventy-
year exile was not a divorce but a temporary separation.

Sometimes you may get so down and discouraged that you
feel God has rejected you and cast you out. What you're basically
saying is that He has divorced you and sent you away from His
presence. Although it's true that He may *feel* distant at times, do
you really think that He has ended His relationship with you? His
challenge is "If you think that's the case, produce the certificate of
divorce that I gave you."

The Judeans couldn't produce it, and neither can you, "because
God has said, 'Never will I leave you; never will I forsake you'"
(Hebrews 13:5 NIV). And Jesus promised, "All that the Father
gives Me will come to Me, and the one who comes to Me I will
by no means cast out" (John 6:37 NKJV).

IDOLATRY GRIEVES GOD

Do you think all this makes me happy?
ISAIAH 57:6 NLT

━━━━━━━━━

In the verses before His question, God described the Israelites' licentious idolatry, how they engaged in sex with shrine prostitutes in hilltop groves, sacrificed children on bloodstained stones, and poured out drink offerings to pagan gods. Then God asked, "Do you think all this makes me happy?" Clearly, such activities grieved His heart.

Judah's history was filled with such idolatry, however, and God's chosen people repeatedly turned away from Him to engage in idol worship. You understand why worship of Baal and Asherah upset God so deeply. The Israelites weren't simply choosing an alternate religion that they felt made more sense than faith in God. They were indulging in selfish, carnal acts, gleefully reveling in depraved activities.

You may be relieved that you aren't involved in idolatry, but Samuel told Saul that "stubbornness is as iniquity and idolatry" (1 Samuel 15:23 KJV). And Paul said, "Put to death your members which are on the earth: fornication, uncleanness, passion, evil desire, and covetousness, which is idolatry" (Colossians 3:5 NKJV). What is covetousness? It's greed and a desire for something that doesn't belong to you.

Are there areas in your life in which you're stubbornly resisting God? Do you act selfish or greedy at times? Do you think covetous thoughts? Psalm 19:14 (NLT) says, "May. . .the meditation of my heart be pleasing to you, O LORD." Be sure to think thoughts that God finds pleasing. Live in such a way as to make Him happy.

JERUSALEM, OUR MOTHER

Shall the earth be made to bring forth in one day?
or shall a nation be born at once?
ISAIAH 66:8 KJV

————

The Lord goes on to say that "no sooner is Zion in labor than she gives birth to her children" (Isaiah 66:8 NIV). He then paints a tender picture of a mother with her newborn child. "Rejoice with Jerusalem and be glad for her, all you who love her. . . . You will nurse and be satisfied at her comforting breasts. . . . You will nurse and be carried on her arm and dandled on her knees" (verses 10–12).

God was describing the restoration of Jerusalem and the return of the Jewish exiles. Their beloved city was about to be destroyed by the Babylonians, and its people carried off to a distant land. But God described their nation reborn and its people back in their homeland.

Many people believe this verse also describes the birth of modern Israel on May 14, 1948, when David Ben-Gurion declared the establishment of the state of Israel. It's also a picture of the eternal city of God in the heavenlies, because "the Jerusalem above is free, which is the mother of us all" (Galatians 4:26 NKJV). As believers, we long to join God in the eternal New Jerusalem.

You can even apply it to your life now. When major dreams have died, or important relationships have become estranged, but then God restores them, He comforts you and brings you joy. . . just like a mother with her child.

FRANKENSTEIN VINE

How did you grow into this corrupt wild vine?
JEREMIAH 2:21 NLT

God told the Israelites, "I was the one who planted you, choosing a vine of the purest stock—the very best. How did you grow into this corrupt wild vine?" In the beginning, Israel had been "a royal priesthood, an holy nation" (1 Peter 2:9 KJV), a people dedicated to obeying God. Yet instead of staying faithful and bearing the fruit of righteousness, they had degenerated into a vine of inferior quality. The word translated "wild" literally means "foreign." In other words, a grapevine of a different, foreign stock.

How did they grow into a different vine? Owners of vineyards do this all the time in a process called "head grafting." They cut away most of the trunk of a vine and graft a foreign vine in its place to take advantage of the existing extensive root system. The original vine is called the rootstock; the engrafted vine is called the scion. Now, God had planted "a vine of the purest stock," but the Israelites, by grafting foreign gods into their spiritual lives, had transformed themselves into something utterly foreign.

If you aren't careful, you can be guilty of similar spiritual grafting. If you accept the scions of secular worldviews, moral compromises, and selfish attitudes and graft them into your rootstock, don't be surprised if you end up producing bitter, inferior fruit, not what God intended. Don't even graft *small* corrupt branches into your spiritual trunk.

TRULY RETURNING

Would you now return to me?
JEREMIAH 3:1 NIV

The law of Moses said that if a man divorced his wife and she married another man, if the second man also divorced her, the first man was not to marry her again (Deuteronomy 24:1–4). God reminded the Jews of this then asked, "You have prostituted yourself with many lovers, so why are you trying to come back to me?" (Jeremiah 3:1 NLT). Didn't God *want* His people to return? Yes, He did. But as He pointed out a few verses later, "Judah has never sincerely returned to me. She has only pretended to be sorry" (Jeremiah 3:10 NLT).

God told the prophet Hosea, "Go and love your wife again, even though she commits adultery with another lover. This will illustrate that the LORD still loves Israel, even though the people have turned to other gods and love to worship them" (Hosea 3:1 NLT).

If you've strayed from the Lord, know that your Father in heaven longs for you to return and will welcome you back with open arms, like the prodigal son. He will see you returning from afar off, will run to meet you, and will throw His arms around you (Luke 15:11–24). But you have to be *actually* returning, not simply toying with the idea or pretending to be sorry.

Hosea said, "Come, and let us return unto the LORD" (Hosea 6:1 KJV). Return to God today.

SPICE AND SINCERE WORSHIP

*What would I want with incense brought
in from Sheba, rare spices from exotic places?*
JEREMIAH 6:20 MSG

The Law stipulated that incense made from the rare and costly
spices stacte, onycha, galbanum, and frankincense was to be
burned in the temple (Exodus 30:7–8, 34). And calamus in verse
20, translated above as "rare spices," which probably came from
India, was a required ingredient in the holy anointing oil used in
God's worship (Exodus 30:23).

So, why did the Lord ask the Israelites why they were going to
the trouble of acquiring such spices and then state that they were
no use to Him? Because mere legalistic worship wasn't acceptable
to God. The spiritual stench of His backslidden people couldn't be
covered by sweet-smelling incense. God didn't want the wicked
to come pretending to worship Him. "Religious performance by
the wicked stinks" (Proverbs 21:27 MSG). Or as the NLT says, "The
sacrifice of an evil person is detestable, especially when it is offered
with wrong motives."

Speaking of motives, Jesus said, "If you bring your gift to the
altar, and there remember that your brother has something against
you, leave your gift there before the altar, and go your way. First
be reconciled to your brother, and then come and offer your gift"
(Matthew 5:23–24 NKJV). Whatever you decide to do for God,
first make sure there's not hypocrisy, hateful thoughts, or unfor-
giveness in your heart.

ABOMINABLE ACTS

Were they ashamed when they had committed abomination?
JEREMIAH 8:12 KJV

An *abomination* is something that causes disgust, horror, or hatred. Words with a similar meaning are *outrage, disgrace, evil, crime,* and *anathema.* Another way of asking the above question is "Were they ashamed of these disgusting actions?" God was talking about the Israelites' depraved worship of Baal, Asherah, and other obscene Canaanite gods. God then answered this question: "Not at all—they don't even know how to blush!" (Jeremiah 8:12 NLT).

Christians are washed by the blood of Jesus and, thankfully, aren't usually guilty of disgusting or outrageous actions. But they sometimes turn away from God. This is why scripture warns, "Take heed, brethren, lest there be in any of you an evil heart of unbelief, in departing from the living God" (Hebrews 3:12 KJV). When believers harden their hearts toward God, He considers them to have "an *evil heart* of unbelief."

How do you avoid this? By listening to God. "To day if ye will hear his voice, harden not your hearts" (verse 15). You also do so by listening to other believers when they speak into your life. "Exhort one another. . .lest any of you be hardened through the deceitfulness of sin" (verse 13).

You may ask how believers can become cold and distant from God, but all Christians must daily fight sin and hypocrisy to prevent these things from taking root in their lives. If you've turned from God, ask Him to forgive you today.

CLEANSED BY GOD

Will you still not be made clean?
JEREMIAH 13:27 NKJV

To give this question context, let's look at the full verse: "I have seen your adulteries and your lustful neighings, the lewdness of your harlotry, your abominations on the hills in the fields. Woe to you, O Jerusalem! Will you still not be made clean?" (Jeremiah 13:27 NKJV). Canaanite worship involved sex with shrine prostitutes on high places (hills). This lascivious "worship" inevitably led to a breakdown of societal restraints, with the Israelites feeling free to consort with harlots and commit adultery. About their "lustful neighings," Jeremiah 5:8 (KJV) says, "They were as fed horses in the morning: every one neighed after his neighbour's wife."

A similar acceptance of sexual promiscuousness permeates modern society and has even seeped into the thinking of many believers and churches. They don't really see anything wrong with premarital or extramarital sex, or in Christians cohabiting with their boyfriends or girlfriends. Even if they don't personally indulge in such things, they may fantasize about them. But what you think reveals your core values and is the precursor of your actions. Jude warns, "These filthy dreamers defile the flesh" (Jude 1:8 KJV).

But the good news is God longs for His people to repent and be cleansed of their sins—both of the heart and of the body. He promises, "If we confess our sins, he is faithful and just to forgive us our sins, and to cleanse us from all unrighteousness" (1 John 1:9 KJV).

PERKS OF THE JOB

So, that makes you a king—living in a fancy palace?
JEREMIAH 22:15 MSG

The NKJV has a more literal translation, asking, "Shall you reign because you enclose yourself in cedar?" When building their palaces, Israelite kings prized wood from cedar trees of Lebanon. Cedar is a beautiful reddish-brown color, is very durable, and is resistant to rot. It also has a long-lasting, sweet scent. David had a modest palace with an interior of cedar panels (2 Samuel 5:11), but Solomon built a new, extravagant palace and called it "the House of the Forest of Lebanon" (1 Kings 7:2 NKJV). Later kings also only felt truly royal when surrounded by excessive amounts of cedar panels.

Then as now, God cares little for outward trappings. He's more concerned with the state of people's hearts—who you are inside—and your resulting actions. You may not be a king, but if God has entrusted you with a position of leadership or authority, however small, let your focus be on serving God and others, on carrying out your duties and responsibilities. Don't get your eyes on the perks that go with the title.

God doesn't mind you enjoying a few benefits. In fact, His Word says, "Let the elders who rule well be counted worthy of double honor" (1 Timothy 5:17 NKJV). It only becomes a problem if you get your sense of security and identity from the frills—or if you allow yourself to get a feeling of entitlement. Avoid these and you'll be okay.

GOD IS JUST

*For behold, I begin to bring calamity on the city which is
called by My name, and should you be utterly unpunished?*
JEREMIAH 25:29 NKJV

Judah was a nation of divine, just laws, and its people lived in
covenant with God. So when they habitually disobeyed, He
prepared to punish them. But what about the pagan nations
surrounding Judah? They had *never* obeyed God. They worshipped
idols and oppressed their people instead of providing justice.
That's why God asked them, if He was about to punish His own
children, could the truly guilty nations hope to escape? No, they
couldn't.

God is fair, even if it sometimes doesn't seem like it. You
may look at unscrupulous people who have become wealthy and
successful, and wonder why the Lord lets them get away with so
much, while you endure trouble. David explored this in the first
twelve verses of Psalm 37. But after describing the man "who
brings wicked schemes to pass," he concluded, "The Lord laughs
at him, for He sees that his day is coming" (Psalm 37:7, 13 NKJV).

Corrupt, worldly people will eventually get their just dues.
You can be sure of that—if not in this life, then in the next.
Meanwhile, God tells you, His child, "I will discipline you but
only in due measure; I will not let you go entirely unpunished"
(Jeremiah 30:11 NIV). God chastises you because He loves you
(Revelation 3:19), and His punishment is designed to bring about
good in your life.

HAVEN'T YOU HAD ENOUGH?

*Why bring such great disaster on yourselves by cutting off
from Judah the men and women, the children and infants,
and so leave yourselves without a remnant?*
JEREMIAH 44:7 NIV

Despite being warned for years to repent, the Jews had stubbornly persisted in idolatry, so God had finally brought judgment on their nation. The Babylonians had besieged and conquered Jerusalem, and now a handful of shell-shocked Jewish survivors fled south to Egypt. Considering the extraordinary calamity they'd just suffered, you'd think that they'd have been convinced of the evils of idol worship. But though they were impoverished refugees in Egypt, they still refused to change their ways. Hence God's question.

Can you identify with this? It may be painful to admit, but probably at some point in your life you have failed to learn a much-needed lesson—even after God knocked you flat on your face in the mud to get you to stop. God's question to you, as it was to the Jews of Jeremiah's time, is "Haven't you had enough? You're bringing yourself to the brink of utter ruin!"

God often complained that the Jews were unreasonably obstinate, saying, "I know how stubborn and obstinate you are. Your necks are as unbending as iron. Your heads are as hard as bronze" (Isaiah 48:4 NLT). Some people actually take pride in being stubborn, but there is a high price tag for pigheadedness. Don't lose everything by failing to repent. Don't resist God.

YOU DON'T BELONG HERE

Are there no descendants of Israel to inherit the land of Gad?
Why are you, who worship Molech, living in its towns?
JEREMIAH 49:1 NLT

In 734–732 BC, the armies of the Assyrian king, Tiglath-Pileser III, overran the land east of the Jordan River—the Israelite territory of Gad, as well as the nation of the Ammonites. The Ammonites hunkered down in their cities and rode out the storm. The Israelites, however, in their smaller, less-fortified towns, were battered. After the Assyrians left, the Ammonites marched into Gad's territory, driving out the survivors, who fled across the Jordan into Israelite territory. Then the Ammonites praised their god, Molech, for the victory. But God warned that one day "Israel will drive out those who drove her out" (Jeremiah 49:2 NIV).

You may have been brought low due to catastrophes and setbacks and suffered further humiliation at the hands of others—who, emboldened by your defeat and weakness, took advantage of you and further robbed you. You may have endured injustice upon injustice. But God is watching over you; He's aware of the wrongs you've suffered and is determined to set things right.

"To crush under one's feet all the prisoners of the earth, to turn aside the justice due a man. . .or subvert a man in his cause— the Lord does not approve" (Lamentations 3:34–36 NKJV). Hang in there. Don't become bitter. Cast your troubles upon the Lord in prayer. Turn to Him in your desperate need. He can help you.

FROM BAD TO WORSE

Do you see this, son of man?
EZEKIEL 8:15 NIV

n a vision, God showed Ezekiel Israelite elders worshipping
pagan gods, and warned, "You will see them doing things that are
even more detestable" (verse 13). He then showed Ezekiel women
mourning the "death" of the god Tammuz. They believed that the
annual fading of the vegetation was due to the Babylonian fertility
god dying. The Lord said to Ezekiel, "Do you see this, son of man?
You will see things that are even more detestable than this" (verse
15). God was basically saying, "You think this is bad? You ain't
seen nothing yet."

Idol worship often leads to depraved lifestyles. Paul wrote,
"Just as they did not think it worthwhile to retain the knowledge
of God, so God gave them over to a depraved mind, so that they
do what ought not to be done. They have become filled with every
kind of wickedness, evil, greed and depravity" (Romans 1:28–29
NIV). Modern people are just as guilty. They often choose to
believe in evolution because it teaches that there is no God, no
moral absolutes, and no rules. Therefore, they can live however
they please.

But once all moral restraint is gone, it doesn't take long before
people are way, way out of bounds. So it matters very much what
you believe. Jesus told people to base their lives on the solid rock.
You do this by hearing, believing, and obeying His Word (Matthew
7:24–27).

GOING TO THE DARK SIDE

*Did you not add lewdness to all
your other detestable practices?*
EZEKIEL 16:43 NIV

The Lord described Jerusalem as a beautiful virgin to whom
He had joined Himself in a holy covenant. But when she gave
herself over to the licentious worship of the Canaanite gods Baal
and Asherah, God said, "You trusted in your beauty. . .to become
a prostitute" (verse 15). Soon Jerusalem was giving herself "to anyone who passed by" (verse 25), so that even the pagan Philistines
"were shocked by [her] lewd conduct" (verse 27). God concluded,
"You not only. . .copied their [Israel's and Judah's] detestable practices, but in all your ways you soon became more depraved than
they" (verse 47).

Sometimes children raised in Christian homes, when they
grow up, not only turn from their parents' faith, but go out of their
way to flaunt their lack of morals. This can also happen to adults
who have a conversion experience, are zealous for a few years,
but burn out and crash. They sometimes end up kicking over all
moral restraints and completely yield to temptations they once
resisted. "Having lost all sensitivity, they [give] themselves over to
sensuality so as to indulge in every kind of impurity" (Ephesians
4:19 NIV).

Succumbing to your flesh may be easier and more pleasurable,
but it bears bitter fruit in the end. If you find yourself getting
frustrated with God, pray desperately that He will give you a
tender heart and keep you true to Him.

STOP QUOTING THAT PROVERB

Why do you quote this proverb concerning the land of Israel:
"The parents have eaten sour grapes, but their
children's mouths pucker at the taste"?
Ezekiel 18:2 NLT

Ezekiel was prophesying in Babylon while Jeremiah was prophesying in Judah, and during those years there was a clever proverb circulating among the Jews: "The parents have eaten sour grapes, but their children's mouths pucker at the taste" (Jeremiah 31:29 NLT). What they meant was: "We're not responsible for the mess we're in. We're simply suffering for our parents' sins." God told Jeremiah, "The people will no longer quote this proverb," so when He heard Ezekiel quoting it, He called *him* to task as well.

Of course, children learn bad habits from their parents, and certain proclivities and weaknesses are genetically passed down—but that doesn't make them a fulfillment of Deuteronomy 5:9 (NKJV), which says, "I, the LORD your God, am a jealous God, visiting the iniquity of the fathers upon the children to the third and fourth generations of those who hate Me." God was talking about those who hated Him and worshipped idols. When "their eyes lusted after their parents' idols" (Ezekiel 20:24 NIV), they, too, were cursed.

Unfortunately, many people today still hold to the premise of this proverb by believing in the doctrine of "generational curses." According to this, God curses everyone—including redeemed believers—with a whole host of curses, all because their parents sinned. But as God explained to Ezekiel in chapter 18, people suffer for their *own* sins.

HIGH PLACES, LOW SPACES

What is this high place you go to?
EZEKIEL 20:29 NIV

In the ancient Near East, pagans commonly worshipped their gods on hilltops. They believed that their gods lived in the sky, so by climbing to the top of a hill, they got closer to them. The Bible calls these "high places," and this term came to mean any hilltop where licentious pagan worship and sacrifices took place. Many Israelites sacrificed to God on the same high places where Baal and Asherah had been worshipped. And often they ended up worshipping Asherah together with the Lord, since they believed she was His divine consort.

Today, "high things," not "high places," compete with your love for God. Paul wrote, "The weapons of our warfare are not carnal but mighty in God for pulling down strongholds, casting down arguments and every high thing that exalts itself against the knowledge of God" (2 Corinthians 10:4–5 NKJV). "High things" can be ungodly philosophies, atheistic worldviews, pride, obsessions, sinful habits, and other things that seek to displace knowing God.

God's eternal question is "What is this high place you go to?" What thing or mind-set or habit do you exalt above intimately knowing the Lord? What stronghold do you rely on to defend yourself from God? What tower of Babel are you building that displeases the Almighty?

The meaning behind His question is "Why *would* you choose some other god instead of Me?" God is the One who gives you life, after all.

CONCEITED LITTLE PSEUDO-DEITY

Will you still say before him who slays you, "I am a god"?
EZEKIEL 28:9 NKJV

King Ittobaal was the wealthy, renowned ruler of Tyre and, like many other leaders in the Levant, was concerned by the rapidly expanding Babylonian empire. He gathered with his allies to discuss plans (Jeremiah 27:3). Ittobaal was convinced that, united, they could stave off the Babylonians. He had a backup plan, too: if the Babylonians *did* invade, he would simply move his court and riches to an island off the coast. (This is what he ended up doing.) Ittobaal believed he was invincible, a god on earth, and that his splendor would endure forever.

Like Ittobaal, many people today believe that whatever trouble comes, they've got all the bases covered. They've got insurance. They've got backup plans. They're so conceited that they don't think anything can touch them. But like the rich, self-absorbed man in Jesus' parable, God tells them, "Fool! This night your soul will be required of you" (Luke 12:20 NKJV).

You would do well to recognize that you're merely a limited mortal, not a living legend or a godlike being. After all, you will die one day, won't you? Be aware that riches can seduce you and give you a distorted sense of privilege and power. Paul advised, "Command those who are rich in this present age not to be haughty, nor to trust in uncertain riches but in the living God" (1 Timothy 6:17 NKJV).

SELFISH SHEPHERDS

Isn't it enough for you to keep the best of the pastures for yourselves?
Must you also trample down the rest?
EZEKIEL 34:18 NLT

God gave a scathing denunciation of Israel's spiritual leaders. He asked, "Shouldn't shepherds feed their sheep?" (verse 2). The priests and Levites enjoyed the benefits of the people's tithes and offerings but failed to fulfill their obligations as shepherds. They didn't care for the weak, didn't look after the sick, didn't tend to their wounds, and didn't seek out those who'd gone astray. They had been entrusted with the riches of God's Word, but they couldn't be bothered to feed the people. They let them starve.

This condemnation holds true for modern pastors and leaders who fail to spiritually feed people. But it can apply to any of us if we become self-serving and covetous, seeking only the blessings and benefits that come from being a Christian but failing to have compassion on our fellow believers who are needy, weak, or stumbling.

You can keep the best pasture for yourself and trample the rest with your feet, in a literal sense. "If someone has enough money to live well and sees a brother or sister in need but shows no compassion—how can God's love be in that person?" (1 John 3:17 NLT). Jesus also said that you are not to withhold compassion or fail to show hospitality and consideration to the lonely and neglected people God puts across your path (Matthew 25:31–45).

RAIN VERSUS DEW

O Judah, what shall I do unto thee?
HOSEA 6:4 KJV

Hosea prophesied, "Let us pursue the knowledge of the LORD. His going forth is established as the morning; He will come to us. . .like the latter and former rain" (Hosea 6:3 NKJV). God had assured His people that if they'd seek Him, He would answer as faithfully as the sunrise. He would reveal Himself to them as dependably as the former rains that fell every autumn and the latter rains that fell every spring. By contrast, however, the Jews' faithfulness was "like a morning cloud, and like the early dew it goes away" (verse 4).

God still asks believers today, "What shall I do with you?" He longs to bless you, to protect you, to lead you into all that He has for you, but if you fail to pray, if you fail to "pursue the knowledge of the LORD" and fail to be true to Him, He's unable to bless you.

Many people promise to follow the Lord, and at first, like drops of dew that blanket the ground, they seem to be carrying through with their promise. But no sooner does the heat of the sun arise—symbolic of difficulty and persecution (Mark 4:5–6, 16–17)—than the dew evaporates. The morning clouds that promise life-giving rain likewise dissipate.

God is faithful. He has promised that if you seek Him with all your heart, you'll find Him (Jeremiah 29:13). So faithfully and sincerely seek Him.

BLAMING GOD

Now what have you against me, Tyre and Sidon and all you regions of Philistia? Are you repaying me for something I have done?
JOEL 3:4 NIV

The events in the book of Joel describe not only a devastating locust plague, but an invasion by Israel's enemies—the Philistines from the west, and the Phoenicians of Tyre and Sidon from the north. God informed these nations that when they had carried off His people and sold them as slaves and stole the silver and gold and treasures of the Lord, they'd personally attacked Him. He asked what He had ever done to them to cause them to act so viciously. He had done nothing to provoke them.

In fact, God shows all nations on earth His love throughout the year: "He has shown kindness by giving you rain from heaven and crops in their seasons; he provides you with plenty of food and fills your hearts with joy" (Acts 14:17 NIV).

Yet instead of being grateful, people often blame God for all the evil that happens in the world. Whenever there's an earthquake, a plague, or a natural disaster of some kind, they accuse God. They show their bitterness to Him in many small ways—by disrespecting His name and by taking every opportunity to be cruel to His people. Yet God is the One showing them kindness and filling their hearts with joy, and He asks, "What have you against Me?" It's time to stop blaming God and be grateful instead.

FOOLISH WISDOM

"Will I not in that day," says the LORD, "even destroy the wise men
from Edom, and understanding from the mountains of Esau?"
OBADIAH 1:8 NKJV

Since ancient times, the land of Edom was famous for its wise
men. Teman was a chief region of Edom, and one of Job's counselors came from there (Job 2:11). Jeremiah asked, "Is wisdom
no more in Teman? Has counsel perished from the prudent? Has
their wisdom vanished?" (Jeremiah 49:7 NKJV). Edom, for all its
wisdom, had made a very foolish decision in aligning itself against
God's people, and God promised that as a result He would drive
out its people—including its celebrated wise men.

In the New Testament, Paul asks, "Where is the wise? . . .
Where is the disputer of this age? Has not God made foolish
the wisdom of this world?" (1 Corinthians 1:20 NKJV). Like the
ancient Edomites, many worldly wise people today set themselves against the Lord, ridiculing faith in Him, disputing biblical truth, and arguing that His Word is full of contradictions and
therefore untrustworthy.

To God, the vaunted wisdom of such people is foolishness,
and when He brings judgment and humiliates the so-called wise
men, they won't be found anymore. It doesn't pay to trust in your
own wisdom and set yourself against the Lord. You may be very
smart and able to figure out many things, but God is the One
who holds the power of life and death. So the beginning of true
wisdom is to fear Him (Proverbs 9:10).

BILLS COMING DUE

Will not your creditors suddenly arise?
Will they not wake up and make you tremble?
HABAKKUK 2:7 NIV

As the mighty Babylonian military machine crushed nations across the ancient Near East, they pillaged cities and plundered their treasuries. God stated, "Woe to him who piles up stolen goods and makes himself wealthy by extortion!" (verse 6). He added, "Woe to him who builds his house by unjust gain" (verse 9). Then God uttered this startling warning: "Because you have plundered many nations, the peoples who are left will plunder you" (verse 8).

It was against this background that He asked, "Will not your creditors suddenly arise? Will they not wake up and make you tremble?"

Sometimes evil people cruise to victory after victory and seem utterly unstoppable. But God has the long view, and He knows how things will turn out when the dust finally settles. The ruthless may seem to be winning for now, but they're also making lots of enemies, enemies whom God will one day cause to rise up and overthrow them.

It's important to be aware that those who are making your life miserable will eventually tremble with fear. It may not seem likely right now, but it will happen. God judges evil, even though He takes His time. It's as if your enemies are borrowing from the future and running up a huge moral deficit, which they will one day have to pay. But they won't be *able* to pay, and down they will go.

EMPTY OBEDIENCE

When you held days of fasting every fifth and seventh
month all these seventy years, were you doing it for me?
ZECHARIAH 7:5 MSG

After Jerusalem fell and the temple was burned, the Jews observed solemn fasts twice a year. Now that the temple was rebuilt, they wondered whether they should have days of mourning anymore. God asked, "When you held days of fasting. . .were you doing it for me?" Then He answered, "Hardly. You're interested in religion, I'm interested in people" (verse 6). They had simply been going through the motions.

The reason they'd been judged was because they'd treated one another unjustly, hated their neighbors, and took advantage of widows, orphans, strangers, and the poor. And they were *still* doing these things.

Believers today sometimes go through the motions of obeying God and doing all the right, Christian things outwardly, but they fail to truly love God, fail to *prove* their love for Him by loving their fellow man. It's a good thing if you pray daily and read your Bible, it's a good thing to faithfully attend church, and it's a good thing to fast, but if your heart is full of selfishness and hatred and you treat your fellow man badly, your good works are in vain.

James advises Christians what to do: "Let there be tears for what you have done. Let there be sorrow and deep grief" (James 4:9 NLT). Repent and change your ways. Then God will restore you.

OFFERING GIFTS WITHOUT OFFENSE

Should I accept this from your hand?
MALACHI 1:13 NKJV

God's people went through the motions of honoring Him by sacrificing sheep, goats, and bulls to Him, but they acted like He was a blind and dumb deity. God had specified that whether they brought a sheep, a goat, or a bull to sacrifice, it should be "without blemish" (Exodus 12:5; 29:1; Leviticus 1:10; 3:1 NKJV). But the people were presenting lame and sick animals to Him—even animals they had stolen from others! God's question was "Should I accept this from your hand?" Not likely!

God still asks this question of believers. You aren't bringing sacrificial animals to the altar, but you *do* bring tithes and offerings to God and expect Him to bless you for your giving. But Jesus said, "If you bring your gift to the altar, and there remember that your brother has something against you, leave your gift there before the altar, and go your way. *First* be reconciled to your brother, and *then* come and offer your gift" (Matthew 5:23–24 NKJV, emphasis added).

The clear implication is that God won't accept your gift otherwise—at least not with intent to bless you.

The Lord doesn't expect you to be perfect, but He does expect you to sincerely love your fellow human beings (Matthew 22:39). This, together with loving God, is one of the two greatest commandments in the Bible. Obey these and God will bless you.

THE GREAT HOLDOUT

Have you eaten from the tree that I commanded you not to eat from?
GENESIS 3:11 NIV

Sometimes we get stuck on the idea of the forbidden fruit—the things that God has forbidden—and we forget the reasons why. Like any good father, God is protecting us from our worst impulses—impetuous desires that burn so brightly in our eyes that we can't possibly see their consequences. In that sense, we're like children playing with a live wire, wondering what's so bad about touching our tongues to its tip.

Somewhere in our hearts is wedged the sliver of a dangerous thought: *God is holding out on me.* Adam and Eve had everything anyone could ever want—each other, a beautiful home, meaningful work, and a literal daily walk with God—but they still chose to eat the fruit. Satan deceived them, yes, but he played off a basic human fear, that they were missing out on something.

God didn't set the tree apart to tempt Adam and Eve. That's not how He operates: "Let no one say when he is tempted, 'I am tempted by God'. . . . But each one is tempted when he is drawn away by his own desires and enticed" (James 1:13–14 NKJV).

We must learn to stop and think about our choices and their ramifications, but more than that, we must learn to trust God with our whole heart. If He has told us not to do something, it really is for our best and highest good.

THE JOB AT HAND IS IN YOUR HANDS

What is that in your hand?
EXODUS 4:2 NKJV

―――――――

God often uses resources already at your disposal to accomplish His work in and through you. He didn't tell Moses, "You're going to need a special kind of staff, so head over to Sharper Image and check out their upper-end supplies." Instead, He used what Moses had literally on hand—his trusty shepherd's staff.

Admittedly, God was rather poetic about His choice: "You've used that staff to guide and protect sheep, but now I'm going to use it to shepherd My people out from slavery." But He was also reminding Moses not of *what* he had to help him, but whom. In effect, God was saying, "Check this out. I'm going to do a MacGyver with that walking stick you've got there and put Pharaoh on alert."

God loves to take the unlikeliest path to achieve His purposes. He regularly chooses "the weak things of the world to shame the strong" (1 Corinthians 1:27 NIV). What matters most is your willingness to be available to Him.

If you want to be a part of what God is doing, tell Him so each day. The opportunities will come, and God will use what is on hand to do the work—you, your skills and talents, and even your weaknesses and shortcomings. Your part is to do what God told Moses to do: "Reach out your hand and take it by the tail" (Exodus 4:4 NKJV).

SIN WILL HOG THE SPOTLIGHT

If her father had spat in her face,
wouldn't she be ostracized for seven days?
NUMBERS 12:14 MSG

You never sin in isolation. In Miriam's case, when she spoke out against Moses, the ramifications were twofold: she got hit with a nasty skin disease for a week, and the whole nation was immobilized while she was out of commission.

God's response to Moses' plea to heal his sister was met with a reminder: just as a father would show his disgust with a child's wicked behavior, God demonstrated that her words were actually questioning His provision—in this case, of His chosen leader.

"Your sin will find you out" (Numbers 32:23 KJV), and one way or another, God will call you out on it. Sin is like a publicity-hungry celebrity with the philosophy *There's no such thing as bad press*. It will go public somehow—physical consequences, as with Miriam; psychological ramifications, as shame and guilt consume your peace of mind; or spiritual ones, as your separation from God leads you to treat others poorly.

Anyone you care about and everyone you'd rather didn't know about it will likely be pulled into the drama—family, friends, and coworkers who are affected directly or indirectly. You've always got a choice, though: "You become the slave of whatever you choose to obey. . . . You can be a slave to sin, which leads to death, or you can choose to obey God, which leads to righteous living" (Romans 6:16 NLT).

HEARTFELT WORSHIP

*Why do you now treat as mere loot these very
sacrificial offerings that I commanded for my worship?*
1 Samuel 2:29 msg

Eli's sons didn't fear God—and they were His priests! They failed
to appreciate their sacred duty and presumed on their father's relationship with God, rather than cultivating one for themselves. No
one gets grandfathered into God's kingdom. The beauty and great
challenge of God's gift of free will is that He wants you to choose
to love Him and follow Him—but you can also choose not to.

And no amount of religious dressing-up can cover that missing element of relationship. That starts with a healthy fear and
respect of the Lord.

One of the first places a calloused heart manifests is in
worship. You go through the motions, but your heart's not in it.
Your attention turns from sharing a moment with the God who
loves you dearly to what's next—football or brunch or tomorrow's
meeting—or to nitpicking others—*She's wearing that? Look at him,
raising his hands. What a poser!*

When you look away from God, it's too easy to get plank-
eyed (Matthew 7:1–5). Eli's sons filled their bellies with burnt offerings and their pockets with loot, rather than filling their hearts
with praise for the One who provided for them. True worship is a
way of life. And no one is more worthy than God to receive your
best efforts in all you say and do.

LOOK PAST YOUR TROUBLES—LOOK UP!

Did you not hear long ago how I made it,
from ancient times that I formed it?
2 KINGS 19:25 NKJV

God was fed up with the arrogant bragging of the Assyrian king Sennacherib. God had used him to punish Israel's sins, but now the Assyrian tyrant was taking all the credit for his accomplishments. God fed his list back to him—the might of his army, the pride he took in harnessing the assets of the lands he conquered—and basically told him, "Didn't anyone tell you? You're just My tool." Assyria, for all its might, was nothing more than a cog in God's wheelhouse, turning only at God's pleasure and for His purposes.

It's easy to get fixed on your circumstances and lose sight of God's sovereign care. After all, the world is pretty scary—terrorism, political unrest, financial woes. But when things seem to be spinning out of control all around you—in other words, most days—remember that you are God's. You are in His hands, under His protection, and part of His plans.

No matter what you're facing in life—joblessness, loneliness, sickness—God is there, and He will never abandon you. Look for Him. Ask Him to let you see Him at work all around you. Let the knowledge of His presence cheer you up and anchor you in your trials. "For God has not given us a spirit of fear, but of power and of love and of a sound mind" (2 Timothy 1:7 NKJV).

PEACE IN THE UNDISCOVERED COUNTRY

Have the gates of death been opened unto thee?
or hast thou seen the doors of the shadow of death?
JOB 38:17 KJV

Death is, in John Wesley's words, an "undiscovered region." Among the things we don't know about it are how, when, and where we will leave this mortal plane. The only thing we know for sure is that, barring the Rapture or some Elijah-like fiery chariot getaway, we all will die.

God's question offered Job a few crucial reminders—first and foremost that God is not like us. He knows far more than we do. Regarding death, He has all the answers we think we crave, but He has, in His wisdom, hidden them from us. How awful it would be to know the details of your own death—or anyone else's, for that matter.

God permitted Satan to bring death to Job's doorstep. He did kill his children, his servants, and his livestock, yet God forbade the devil to take Job's life. Why? To show Satan that true faith can handle devastating loss.

All your comings and goings are largely hidden from you but not from your Maker. As long as you live, your life resonates with God's good purposes and plans. And when your time is up, you can leave without fear, knowing that the best is yet to come— meeting your Father, your Savior, reuniting with loved ones, meeting heroes of the faith, relieved forever of sorrow and pain.

THE PARADOX OF CONTROL

Do you know the laws of the heavens?
Can you set up God's dominion over the earth?
JOB 38:33 NIV

God set the universe in motion, countless galaxies spinning with design and purpose beyond our reckoning. Astronomers and astrophysicists work diligently to uncover a fraction of the wonders of the cosmos, and the wisest are humbled by their discoveries. God was reminding Job that even though his life had changed, he still worshipped the One who never changes.

Far too often, people twist that proper perspective into something idolatrous. Astrology is one example. People put a ridiculous amount of time and effort into reading the stars, looking for direction and meaning in their lives based on alignments of constellations and planets. They want to know the "laws of heaven" without having to recognize the Lawmaker.

In contrast, astronomy is legitimate science, the precise and quantifiable study of space and stars, systems and planets—one that, through a proper lens, points the observer to the magnificence and order of God's creation. Neither of them, however, offers the control over our own lives that so many crave.

In God's economy, control is a paradox: To gain it, you must give it up. You gain your true eternal life in Christ when you give Him your sin-riddled, death-addled experience (Luke 9:24). Though God alone is sovereign over all of time, space, and all that lies beyond, He has given you control over the most important decision in your life: where you will spend eternity.

THE BIRTH OF TRUSTING FAITH

Do you know how many months they carry their young?
Are you aware of the time of their delivery?
JOB 39:2 NLT

Nowadays, wildlife biologists can answer God's questions to Job with factual data. Wild goats, for instance, mate between the end of October and early December, giving birth six months later. Most species of deer gestate for about seven months and bring little Bambis into the world, one to three at a time, in May or June.

What they can't answer, though, is *why*. Why six months? Why June? Everything seems to be happening at the right time. It all points to design and order—and if you're willing to believe, to the Designer Himself.

At this point in God's "because-I'm-God-that's-why" discourse with Job, He wasn't quizzing Job on his zoological competency but on his willingness to submit in all the seasons of his life. And birth is often messy and painful. Wendell Berry wrote, "For parents, the only way is hard. We who give life give pain. . . . Yet we who give pain give love; by pain we learn the extremity of love."

God knows your pain and fear as you struggle to figure out your life, to find your way through hardship, to remember that you are loved by your Father. What your Father knows best, though, is the big picture and your place in it. Your "whys" need to become "whats"—not, *Why is this happening to me?* but, *What are You doing in this season, Lord?*

TRUST GOD, NOT YOUR EXPECTATIONS

*Will the wild ox be willing to serve you? Will he bed
by your manger? . . . Will you trust him because his
strength is great? Or will you leave your labor to him?*

JOB 39:9, 11 NKJV

When God reproved Job, His response was pretty hot at first, but by the time He asked Job about this wild ox, His amusement seems evident: "Go ahead, Job—get Ferdinand's uncle to do the work you normally reserve for donkeys. And then see if you can get him to cuddle up next to your feed trough at night."

The King James Version translates the Hebrew word for "wild ox" as "unicorn," but most commentators figure it was probably a now-extinct species of wild bull like the great aurochs. Whatever it was, it wasn't domesticated. Job's expectations, however, were.

Job expected his life to go a certain way, the way he was used to, the way he wanted it to. He figured since he had honored God wholeheartedly that things would always go his way. But if you've ever gotten comfortable in your faith, you know that's when God is most likely to shake things up.

You must learn to recognize when God is working to mature your faith and accept that. When fear and anger threaten to run wild during a trial in life, you will be able to say—and mean—the remarkable words Job uttered: "The LORD gave, and the LORD has taken away; blessed be the name of the LORD" (Job 1:21 NKJV).

YOUR MONSTERS ARE GOD'S GOLDFISH

Will it beg you for mercy or implore you for pity?
Will it agree to work for you, to be your slave for life?
JOB 41:3–4 NLT

The language used to describe the futility of controlling a massive monster like Leviathan could well be used to portray the foolishness of putting powerful things in the place of God in your life. Even when He breaks through your stubbornness and pride, you often bear the scars of the idols you've worshipped: addictions, careers, even love.

In fact, you will become an even greater target for the devil once he sees that you've switched to God's side. And even though "He who is in you is greater than he who is in the world" (1 John 4:4 NKJV), temptations remain to go back to your old life.

But those old habits, those old acquaintances, those old haunts are all much too Leviathan-like for you to return to them. Would you make your alcoholism beg for mercy by going back to a bar as a child of God? Would you work out an arrangement with pornography or enslave the corporate ladder for your purposes?

If any such things tempt you, remember why you came to the cross: You recognized that you were powerless to save yourself from the greatest temptation to turn from God you'll ever face, your own selfish desires. Your monsters, though, are just goldfish to God, so trust in His power to deal with them.

THE ONE THING

Why this frenzy of sacrifices?
ISAIAH 1:11 MSG

God was sick and tired of His people's hypocrisy. They put on a great religious show but didn't share God's concerns. Their hearts were cold toward Him because they had fallen in love with their rituals; they thought what they *did* saved them. It was a reminder they still needed centuries after Isaiah, when Jesus said, "Go and learn what this means: 'I desire mercy and not sacrifice.' For I did not come to call the righteous, but sinners, to repentance" (Matthew 9:13 NKJV).

Jesus is all we need and the Source of "every spiritual blessing" (Ephesians 1:3 NKJV). Paul said all the things that he once valued —education, status, human authority—were garbage compared to knowing Christ (Philippians 3:8).

And yet, so many times, we embrace a different message— that, as Christians, we have the right to a problem-free, healthy, and wealthy life. Or that we need Christ plus something else— Christianity, the Church, evangelism, missions, spiritual gifts, and so on. This frenzy of sacrifices blinds us to the simplicity of the only sacrifice we require.

Embrace this simple truth: "You are complete in Him" (Colossians 2:10 NKJV). Then you can act with the freedom of one who has been given real and lasting life. Then you can serve God with the heart He was looking for in Isaiah's day, a heart willing to learn "to do good; seek justice; rebuke the oppressor; defend the fatherless, plead for the widow" (Isaiah 1:17 NKJV).

NONPAREIL

Who is my equal?
ISAIAH 40:25 NIV

God asked this question after offering Israel another of His reminders that no one is like Him. No one can create an image that depicts Him, and no one can offer Him counsel as a mentor or a peer. The rulers of this world judge and act to gain power, and plan and scheme to keep it—but they're chaff, dispersed by God's merest breath. There is no one like Him, and He is not like us.

No one sees the big picture like God does. Even mankind's best and brightest cannot take in a broad enough view to offer more than a limited take. We require lenses through which to view the vast panorama of life; we need political, economic, religious, philosophical, anthropological, and legal filters to be able to get a toehold on everything. Our vision needs correction, in other words.

God sees clearly—and someday we will, too. "Now we see things imperfectly, like puzzling reflections in a mirror, but then we will see everything with perfect clarity. All that I know now is partial and incomplete, but then I will know everything completely, just as God now knows me completely" (1 Corinthians 13:12 NLT). His power and perfection should inspire awe in you but also comfort and peace.

Today and each day afterward, you can place yourself in the hands of the God who has perfect vision and clarity about everything going on in the world and in your life.

UNBREAKABLE

When I act, who can reverse it?
ISAIAH 43:13 NIV

God spoke to Israel of His power to deliver and His power to uphold His deliverance. "Besides Me there is no savior. . . . And there is no one who can deliver out of My hand" (Isaiah 43:11, 13 NKJV). For eternity, you are safe in God's hand. Nothing and no one can undo the salvation to which you cling.

If you are His, it means you reached a point where the immensity of your sin overwhelmed you. You surrendered your broken life to Christ and received the free gift His blood earned for you on the cross. That work can never be undone, that sacrifice never unmade. You are His child, now and always.

In this world you are safe in God's hands. As His child, nothing can separate you from His love (Romans 8:39), and as a member of His Church, you are part of a fellowship against which the gates of hell will not prevail (Matthew 16:18).

All around you are opportunities to lose sight of this truth—both in the world and in your own life. But cheer up! From the global to the personal, from terrorism and political upheaval to illness and joblessness, God has you in mind. You can trust Him with anything you are facing because "all the promises of God in [Jesus] are Yes, and in Him Amen, to the glory of God through us" (2 Corinthians 1:20 NKJV). You are secure because His promises are unbreakable.

TURNING WOE TO WOW!

GOD, The Holy of Israel, Israel's Maker, says: "Do you question who or what I'm making? Are you telling me what I can or cannot do?"
ISAIAH 45:11 MSG

The Bible tells of many unlikely individuals whom God guided and guarded so that they could serve Him. One example is Cyrus the Great, ruler of the Persian Empire. Despite his conquests, he was known even by his enemies as an ethical and tolerant ruler. But God had a bigger picture in mind than Cyrus's victories. He was reminding Cyrus in advance that even at his mightiest, he was only playing his part in God's plan.

It's easy to look around and think, *The world is getting darker every day*. Even for the believer, doubt creeps in. Calling evil good and good evil seems to be the rule of the day, and that means one thing: *woe* (Isaiah 5:20). But even in His just judgments, God is good. His purposes include using people who don't acknowledge Him for who He is.

If God could use Cyrus to defeat Babylon and liberate Israel, turning the greatest world leader of his day into another cog in the machinery of salvation, He can protect you in a world that rejects Him more each day. No world leader has ever existed who could question God or reject His will. You are His child, in His hands, for His purposes. Say *Whoa!* to your *Woe* and watch God turn it into a *Wow!*

SPECIAL DELIVERY

Have I no power to deliver?
ISAIAH 50:2 KJV

Isaiah knew God had called him "to speak a word in season to him who is weary" (Isaiah 50:4 NKJV), and he stuck with it because he trusted that God was able to deliver him from whatever trouble resulted. God is in the business of deliverance. He wants to see people saved, but He has a peculiar system of reaching out to them: He delights in using *you*.

People grow weary, but God doesn't. He's willing to do the heavy lifting—the actual saving work in an individual's heart—but you have to present the information (Romans 10:14).

When He asks you to take that message of relief to your neighbors and coworkers—and, yes, even total strangers—He is fully aware of your worries over being rejected or harassed. Hence the question He asked through Isaiah: Can He not deliver *both* of you—you from your anxiety and the other person from death's grip?

The same power that saved you fills and fuels you as you share who God is and what He has done for you. Yes, you might get grief from a hardened heart, but what if there's a chance God has an appointment of salvation with someone today and He wants you to keep it? Ask God to fill you with His Spirit today, and pray for the opportunity to speak a word to a weary soul.

TAKE IT TO HEART

Of whom have you been afraid, or feared, that you have. . .
not remembered Me, nor taken it to your heart?
ISAIAH 57:11 NKJV

─────────────

Isaiah expressed God's displeasure with those who put all their energy into worshipping idols. "You're afraid of these guys? They're not even real. Me? I'm real." What an infuriating thought: all that time and effort spent fearing idols—as if these little carved figures had incriminating evidence that they would use if their followers failed to appease them!

Idolatry includes things that in and of themselves are good but are easily sullied when you elevate them in priority over God. Your decisions aren't often as simple as good versus bad—you must choose between good, better, and best.

It sounds harsh when Jesus said that putting even your parents or children above Him made you unworthy of Him (Matthew 10:37), but won't He care for them through you if you put Him first (Matthew 6:33)? That's taking Him to heart.

Anticipate a moment when you'll reflect on the choices you've made in life. Will they stand up under God's scrutiny? If so, choose that path of peace and take comfort that, in the long run, "those who follow godly paths will rest in peace when they die" (Isaiah 57:2 NLT). God is willing to lead, heal, and comfort those who have strayed (Isaiah 57:15–21), so how much more will He do so when you make it your goal to seek Him in all you do?

FINISHING WHAT HE STARTED

Do I bring to the moment of birth and not give delivery? . . .
Do I close up the womb when I bring to delivery?
ISAIAH 66:9 NIV

Isaiah reminded Israel that God finishes what He starts—
something that is true of both natural and spiritual childbirth.
God's plan cannot be thwarted. His creation will be redeemed
through His people and because of His unfailing promises.
Because God will finish what He started, you can follow Him
with confidence. You're not done here on earth until He says so.

Take comfort in your role in God's fulfillment of His promises—both those made to Israel as the future site of His kingdom
on earth and to His Church as ambassadors for that coming kingdom. Take comfort in knowing that He "who began a good work
in you will carry it on to completion until the day of Christ Jesus"
(Philippians 1:6 NIV).

God's efficiency is astonishing. He wastes no experience, no
tear, no drop of blood or sweat shed in loving Him and others.
The gratitude of the entire world is a small measure compared to
the ultimate blessings of bearing your cross. There is no suffering
you're going through that God can't use to improve the world.

You "are His workmanship, created in Christ Jesus for good
works, which God prepared beforehand that [you] should walk
in them" (Ephesians 2:10 NKJV). You are your Savior's handiwork,
brought into this world with foresight and purpose, and God's
purposes won't be thwarted.

FIGHT FOR PURITY

How can you say, "I am not defiled;
I have not run after the Baals"?
JEREMIAH 2:23 NIV

Many of the cultures surrounding Israel incorporated sex into their religious practices. God's strict prohibitions against mingling with those nations came because He knew how difficult it would be to resist taking part in such worship. Unfortunately, many of the Israelites did so and then acted as if they could hide their sin from God.

Clearly, God had grown weary of hearing this excuse, because He anticipated their protest—"*What* sex in the hills? Who, me?"—and responded, "Well, look at the tracks you've left behind in the valley" (Jeremiah 2:23 MSG). He went on to compare them to camels and wild donkeys in heat, "on the hunt for sex, sex, and more sex" (verse 24).

Now, God invented sex. He gave people sex drives and intended them to be a means of intimacy between a husband and wife, a source of shared pleasure. But He also meant for this intimacy to be experienced in its proper place—marriage—and not let loose like a flame outside of the fireplace. So often, God's restrictions are KEEP OUT signs.

There is nothing about sex as God intended that need cause you shame, but if you're burning out of bounds, you're asking for trouble. It's sin against God and destruction in your relationships. Staying off those unholy hilltops is worth the fight. Confess any sexual waywardness to God, and commit to a ruthless fight for purity.

CALMING SIN'S RIPPLES

*Is there any place you have not been
defiled by your adultery with other gods?*
JEREMIAH 3:2 NLT

━━━━━━━━━

When Jeremiah challenged Israel's idolatry, he drew on the Mosaic law's divorce regulations: A man couldn't divorce his wife, watch her get remarried, and then marry her again later. Why not? Because it would "bring sin on the land" (Deuteronomy 24:4 NKJV). One person's sin impacted the whole nation because it pulled one part of a connected community away from God.

That sounds strange to modern ears, the idea that our mistakes could have consequences as broad ranging as to affect our entire nation. It makes sense, though, if you follow the ramifications of original sin. "When Adam sinned, sin entered the world. Adam's sin brought death, so death spread to everyone, for everyone sinned" (Romans 5:12 NLT).

Like a stone in a pond, sin ripples out, affecting not only the one who sinned, but others around them, directly and indirectly. But Jesus more than made up for Adam's sin (Romans 5:15).

If you struggle with the idea that you're not having much effect serving God where you are, think of what it would be like if you weren't there, praying and serving and helping. The world doesn't change because you spearhead some massive global undertaking. Fix your corner of the world. Clean up the places that have been defiled by sin, reconciling with God in that place and encouraging others to do likewise. Honor God with every healed place and heart.

HOME FREE

Do you really think you can steal, murder, commit adultery,
lie, and burn incense to Baal. . .then come here and stand
before me in my Temple and chant, "We are safe!"—
only to go right back to all those evils again?
JEREMIAH 7:9–10 NLT

The idea of being "home free" goes back to childhood games and a designated zone—a tree or a portion of sidewalk—where your opponents couldn't touch you. Similarly, Israelite adults figured they could do whatever they wanted away from the temple and then come in and act the part of God's obedient, holy people.

A great number of Christians behave similarly today. They put in their hour on Sunday morning and act as if following God is the spiritual equivalent of filling up their cars—once a week and they're good to go, with maybe an occasional top-off, a desperate prayer fired off at some time other than at a meal or as they put the kids to bed.

God wants *all* of you because He knows you'll never be satisfied with all of anything else, and you'll just be hypocritical if you try to follow Him piecemeal. Many people like *some* better than *all*. That seems doable. Unfortunately, when you try to have it both your way and God's way, you end up with neither.

Ask God to show you any areas of your life where you're holding back, and then surrender them to Him. Don't settle for less than God's best. That's the only way you'll truly get home free.

FORSAKING STRANGE VANITIES

Why have they provoked me to anger with
their graven images, and with strange vanities?
JEREMIAH 8:19 KJV

Jeremiah faithfully delivered God's messages of warning to Judah for decades, and yet there's no record of even one person responding with a change of heart. His heart broke for his people: "Since my people are crushed, I am crushed; I mourn, and horror grips me" (Jeremiah 8:21 NIV). God's question here echoes that heart-cry. It's less about the anger itself than the heartbreak of their infidelity.

The phrase "strange vanities" is evocative. It refers to the people's idols, but it also suggests the emptiness of any effort to worship anything other than God. The Hebrew word for *vanity* means "vapor" or "breath," something that lasts only for a moment.

All the things you think will give you pleasure—an instant of ecstasy or vengeance that looms large in your mind until it's come and gone—leave you only with a hollow echo. You long for something lasting, the eternity God has put inside you (Ecclesiastes 3:11), and only He can fulfill it.

Your sin causes the disconnect you sometimes feel, not any unfaithfulness on God's part. Any emptiness you experience is a call to come back to Him. Think of what you know to be true of God—His goodness, faithfulness, mercies, steadfastness, patience, love, sovereignty—and let knowledge replace misleading feelings. He is always willing to hear your confession, to forgive when you ask, and to take your need to heart.

LOVING OTHERS IS KNOWING

He defended the cause of the poor and needy, and so
all went well. Is that not what it means to know me?
JEREMIAH 22:16 NIV

Jeremiah spoke on God's behalf to Shallum, the king of Judah whose father, Josiah, had been one of the few righteous rulers Judah would ever know. His question served as an admonition to imitate Josiah's behavior: "He did what was right and just, so all went well with him" (Jeremiah 22:15 NIV). Josiah knew God because he obeyed Him. Shallum's departure from that path would not end well for him. He would die in captivity in Babylon.

How do you get to *know* God? Jesus kept it simple: "We can be sure that we know him if we obey his commandments" (1 John 2:3 NLT). And what are His commandments? To love one another (John 13:34). You've heard this before, read it before, but have you lived it? Its impact is transformative.

You don't have to conquer the world for Christ or accumulate wealth, power, or influence to glorify Him. But you do have to love others. That's not some warm, fuzzy vibe you send out; it's a choice you make each day to look out for others' best interests and highest good. You just have to take your best shot. You might take some shots in return, but so did Jesus. He thought it was worth the risk to love us. With whom can you take that risk today?

GET OUT OF YOUR OWN WAY

*Why provoke my anger by burning incense
to the idols you have made here in Egypt?*
JEREMIAH 44:8 NLT

God called out His people on their persistent idolatry. They knew their history of stubbornness and infidelity, knew that it just flat-out made God mad. He wasn't just randomly angry, either; it was their idol making and incense burning that blazed in His eyes and burned in His nostrils. Disobeying God—whether it's intentional or careless—is like playing with spiritual dynamite; it's a faith killer as well as a reputation crusher. From our perspective, we shake our heads and think, *Really?* This *again?*

But here's the thing: Sin shortens your memory—as surely as if it flicked a switch that shut off your brain's frontal cortex and, with it, your ability to learn from your experiences. You've probably heard how teenagers make those amazing decisions in part because their brains haven't finished maturing yet, but getting off of God's path is a surefire way to stay a spiritually arrested adolescent. You're unwittingly getting in your own way because you won't let God have His way.

Have you considered just how countercultural it is to follow Jesus? You're not swayed by shifting trends but anchored to God's unchanging nature and Word. You lead by serving rather than dominating. You rely on the Holy Spirit's guidance rather than your own understanding.

A spiritually mature Christian learns a single key lesson from mistakes: Christ is our example in everything we do that has lasting value.

RESTORING YOUR PERSPECTIVE

Why do you brag of your once-famous strength?
JEREMIAH 49:4 MSG

Jeremiah recognized a pattern with the nations that God allowed to act as agents of His discipline: They all thought themselves superior not only to Israel but to Israel's God. In many material ways they *were* better, stronger, and richer, but they were only allowed to dominate Israel because God was pushing His people toward something higher and better.

The Lord promised His children all those material blessings if they would focus on the most important things first: honoring Him, building families, and serving others.

God promised judgment on Israel's enemies for their abuse of His chosen, but He also often promised to restore their fortunes. They thought they were more powerful than they really were, but God offered them another chance. His heart is to renew and restore people, and through them the nations in which they live. So many crave fame, control, and influence but lose what really matters along the way.

Let God restore your perspective and renovate your heart. Recognize that "the earth is the LORD's, and everything in it, the world, and all who live in it" (Psalm 24:1 NIV). Rather than constructing your own little kingdom, dedicate yourself to building God's. Care for the people, possessions, and priorities God has given you. Offer Him your hopes and dreams and let Him build your confidence in Him. Step down from the throne of your heart, and let its rightful Ruler take His place there.

THE DANGER OF INFATUATION

*Is it a light thing to the house of Judah that they
commit the abominations which they commit here?*
EZEKIEL 8:17 KJV

There's no such thing as a harmless crush. Israel broke God's
heart repeatedly because they kept chasing after their neighbors'
gods, idols based on things around them—the sun, moon, and
animals—that seemed more important than God because they
were visible.

Have you ever had a proximity crush—an infatuation that
develops just because you're near someone on a regular basis? It
could be a coworker, a classmate, or even a colaborer for Christ,
but suddenly, you're sure that person is the one for you. At some
point, the truth sets in—sharing one aspect of your life with
someone doesn't mean you're ready to share all of it. At that point,
you'd consider yourself fortunate if the fascination faded without
collateral damage to any previously existing relationships.

Social media, for example, can be a great way to keep in touch
with close friends and loved ones, but its flip side is a serious
threat: emotional affairs that are just as real and damaging as physical ones. Don't let "friends" replace true relationship. It's no light
thing to God when you choose a readily available fake over Him.

Trust Him to put the right people in your life at the right
times. He will carry you through the heartache and loneliness
until the day you see Him face-to-face and know He's been close
to you the whole time.

TRUE SUCCESS

Will it thrive?
Ezekiel 17:9 nkjv

God sent His people into exile in Babylon, but He told them to make a life there, because "in its peace you will have peace" (Jeremiah 29:7 nkjv). That wasn't good enough for King Zedekiah, who rebelled against Babylon rather than trust God's promise. For his troubles, he got to witness the execution of his sons before his eyes were put out and he spent the rest of his life in jail (Jeremiah 52:10–11). God used his example to ask His people if anything in their lives could thrive apart from Him.

God alone can consistently make green trees wither and dead trees flourish. He does what is best—in spite of our best-laid plans, with no regard for the power of men and institutions. Human nature persists in demanding rights and counting unhatched chicks, but God's nature is different. He glorifies Himself through the humbled heart, the downtrodden spirit, the surrendered life. Look no further than Jesus for proof of all three.

To follow Jesus, to pick up your cross, means letting go of the rights to your life. Even if you have a wonderful white-picket vision for your life and work with diligence and integrity to carry it out, it will be a dead end without God. Trust the Lord anew with the gifts and desires He has given you, and watch Him bring His plans to fruition for you—a life rekindled with hope for today and purpose that echoes into eternity.

KEEP REAL LIFE REAL

Isn't it my pleasure that they turn around,
no longer living wrong but living right—really living?
EZEKIEL 18:23 MSG

Since God's desire is to see good people follow His ways and wicked people turn from theirs to Him, sometimes a hard conversation is required. There are times when you'll need to have a difficult talk with someone you care about. You have no guarantee what the response will be, but thanks to Ezekiel's report, you know what God wants. Be prayerful about how you approach people in those situations.

You've heard the common argument laid out by nonbelievers, that God is a "cosmic killjoy," intent on ruining any fun anyone might have. You know He isn't, so represent Him with a balance of love and truth. Be real with people.

There are few things less enjoyable than being "Jesus-juked"—Jon Acuff's phrase describing the Christian version of the Debbie Downer moment, where a seriously biblical topic is shoehorned into an inappropriate moment. Have a sense of the moment and respect the person's feelings even if you don't agree.

On the other hand, you should definitely bring Christ into a conversation at the right time. After all, people can't be saved without believing in Jesus, and they can't believe in Him if they've never heard about Him (Romans 10:14). God's pleasure is to see people embrace the rich, full life that only He can give them—and some of your best days will come when you facilitate that.

THE CYCLE BREAKER

*Will you defile yourselves the way your
ancestors did and lust after their vile images?*
EZEKIEL 20:30 NIV

The Israelites had a long history of adopting the sex-based religions of the pagan people around them. They employed sex as worship, defiling themselves, their spouses, and God. Before you think, *Those nasty old ancient-world pagans*, consider the impact of porn in modern times.

Pornography is leaving a terrible legacy. What people used to dismiss as entertainment and harmless itch scratching has become a scourge. Porn is teaching men that women are only objects to be used to satisfy their urges and that, once the initial interest wears off, women can be replaced.

Play that attitude out and you get sexting, date rape, and divorce. You get men who don't know how to love sacrificially and selflessly and, as a result, don't know how to be husbands or fathers.

It doesn't help to couch porn use in the language of addiction, like it's a disease instead of idolatry. The Bible doesn't talk about addiction but slavery to sin (Romans 6). There's no solution for that but the blood of Christ. That's where God's grace comes in. It's His willingness to give us a new heart and a new spirit that gives us a chance to defeat sin.

God can break those harmful cycles, so when He asks the question, "Will you defile yourselves?" He's really asking, "Won't you trust Me to cleanse you of your sin?"

LOVE PEOPLE, NOT PROJECTS

Who do you, astride the world, think you really are?
EZEKIEL 31:2 MSG

God described the beauty and wonders of the kingdoms of Assyria and Egypt, comparing them to a magnificent tree that provided shelter and sustenance. It was God who had blessed these nations. He told Pharaoh, "I made it beautiful" (Ezekiel 31:9 NKJV).

Apparently, Pharaoh needed the reminder. He had made the same mistake so many other leaders had—he took credit for his success instead of giving it to God. God's message? No matter how big you get, you can be cut down to size. In fact, history says you will. God told Pharaoh, "You're slated to be cut down. . .to be a dead log stacked with all the other dead logs" (Ezekiel 31:18 MSG). If success can't be handled with humility, it will become a curse.

Your best successes involve people, not projects. What you do should bless others; that's the standard. For all the wonders of God's creation, you mean more than gold, stars, or mountains. You bear His image, house His Spirit, carry out His mission.

Compared to that, nothing else matters. When it comes to success, what matters most is your attitude once you've achieved it. God has given you work to do and the ability to do it. Let God vet your dreams and aspirations, and make sure that they have lasting value—which, in God's economy, means they focus on relationships more than revenues.

LEADERSHIP WORTH FOLLOWING

Isn't it enough for you to drink clear water for yourselves?
Must you also muddy the rest with your feet?
EZEKIEL 34:18 NLT

The tribe of Levi had the privilege and responsibility of serving God as priests. However, they had been taking more than their prescribed portion of the offerings and shortchanging their care-taking duties: "The weak you have not strengthened, nor have you healed those who were sick, nor bound up the broken, nor brought back what was driven away, nor sought what was lost" (Ezekiel 34:4 NKJV).

It probably felt to the people that God didn't care about their shepherds' poor performance, but He made it clear that He would step in and hold the leaders accountable, judging "between the fat sheep and the scrawny sheep" (verse 20 NLT).

Even when it seems that God isn't involved or interested in your hardships, His Word reminds you that He cares. You might be stuck with a bad boss, or you might be one. The best way to improve the first situation is to fix the second one. If you're in charge of people, your template is to strengthen the weak, help the struggling, resolve conflicts, and retrieve the lost.

If you're working for someone who isn't interested in doing those things, then your challenge is to respect your boss's authority as God-given (Romans 13) and be the best worker you can. When you're faced with a leader who isn't worth following, remember that God is.

NEITHER FISH NOR FOWL

How long will they be incapable of purity?
HOSEA 8:5 NIV

Hosea addressed God's concern that the Jews were losing their saltiness—their distinctive identity as His people—among the surrounding cultures. Similarly, we live in the era of the "cool Christian." It's easy to look around and see that hipsterism has infected the Church with beards and flannel and skinny jeans—and some would say it's about time we stopped being stodgy, repressed, joyless drudges. To an extent, they're right. God's people should radiate peace, joy, and love with concern for others' problems.

But is the answer to cozy up to trends and fads in order to appeal to fashionable seekers? Are we following Paul's MO, becoming "all things to all men, that [we] might by all means save some" (1 Corinthians 9:22 NKJV)? Or do we just like the semi-intellectual look of prescription-less nerd glasses? Is all this just a sign of your excellent taste, or is it a means of breaking down cultural barriers in order to share about Jesus? Can people actually see a difference in the way you listen, serve, and love?

If you find yourself more concerned with looking cool than representing God, you're being what James called double-minded (James 1:8)—trying to have it your way *and* God's way. You'll be neither fish nor fowl—too righteous for the world to accept, too carnal to be of any use to God. Wear and eat what you want, but don't lose sight of the mission.

MAKE YOURSELF AVAILABLE

Is this not true, people of Israel?
AMOS 2:11 NIV

God was fed up with the bad example being set for the youth. "I raised up some of your young men to be prophets, set aside your best youth for training in holiness. Isn't this so, Israel? . . . But you made the youth-in-training break training, and you told the young prophets, 'Don't prophesy!' You're too much for me" (Amos 2:11–13 MSG).

There's a lot of talk these days about Millennials and "Nones"—those in their twenties and younger who have either grown up without a religion or have chosen not to follow one. Part of their disenchantment falls directly on the nominal, lukewarm faith of previous generations—and they've got a point. Who would want a part of such hypocrisy and wishy-washy uncertainty?

Every mature Christian should be involved with the growth of the next generation of believers. Whether it's parenting, teaching, coaching, or mentoring, you're called to make a difference. While that might put you out of your comfort zone, Jesus never called you to be comfortable.

You don't have to be perfect to be of service to young folks. All you have to be is available. Trust that when you answer God's call, He will give you what you need to do the job. There's a whole generation hungry for something they can't even properly identify—the sense of purpose, joy, and peace that comes from knowing Jesus. Get in on the action now!

CRIME DOESN'T PAY

*What shall I say about the homes of the wicked filled
with treasures gained by cheating? What about the disgusting
practice of measuring out grain with dishonest measures?*
MICAH 6:10 NLT

The adage "crime doesn't pay" sounds like something said in a
pseudo-sage conversation between campy '60s-era Batman and
Robin. But its essence is right at the heart of God's question. The
"short ephah" was a measure of dry goods, and when merchants
weighed out less grain than they should have, they weren't just
ripping off their customers; they were shortchanging themselves,
because such a measurement was "accursed" (Micah 6:10 NIV).
God repaid their dishonesty with bankruptcy and hunger (Micah
6:12–16).

Failing to follow biblical advice guarantees fallout. We don't
really get away with anything. The ridiculous thing is that people
keep trying to—the whole dog-and-vomit thing—as if it were a
matter of bad luck. When God asked His people this question,
He had just finished telling them His expectations for the right
way to conduct themselves: "To act justly and to love mercy and to
walk humbly with your God" (Micah 6:8 NIV).

Given that most of us aren't cat thieves or crooked merchants,
a question still remains: Are there ways you're shortchanging
God, yourself, or others? Do you accumulate resentment, wrongs
endured, forgiveness withheld? Do you hold back worship, service,
or your best efforts? Answer honestly for yourself first, addressing
your sin, your needs, your doubts; then you can be honest with
God, and then, others.

FISH AND CHIPS

Is it right for you to be angry?
JONAH 4:4 NIV

Sometimes we obey God with a chip on our shoulder. After Jonah's famously fishy (and failed) attempt to avoid God's mission for him, he ended up preaching to Nineveh. Then he went outside the city limits and sulked. Why? Because even though Nineveh was like hell's living room, whose gates were stacked with the skulls of their enemies, Jonah knew God would spare the Ninevites if they repented (Jonah 4:2)—and he didn't like it one bit.

Salvation is funny that way. When we became acutely aware of the thin ice we were skating on, we cried out to God to save us—and He did. Our gratitude led us to pray for others. We pray desperately for God to save Uncle Joe from betting on the ponies, our nephew Sammy from his obsession with Xbox, and that gal at work from getting a divorce—because we want God's best for them.

But we're quick to write people off when we judge they're too far gone to redeem. We want the serial killers, the rapists, and the fraudsters to suffer—but God doesn't. He knows how close they are to hell, just as surely as you know Uncle Joe is going to blow his paycheck at the track, and He wants to save them.

God will sort out the redeemed bread thieves and white liars from the redeemed ax murderers and corporate pirates. Isn't your best prayer that they are in heaven for Him to evaluate?

DEBT RELIEF

How long must this go on?
Habakkuk 2:6 NIV

Reaping and sowing is a biblical axiom: Something always grows from your actions; what it is depends on what you've planted. Debt is the specific context of Habakkuk's words—being weighed down with what the King James Version, in this verse, calls the "thick clay" of money owed for unnecessary goods and services. God called to account those who had made themselves wealthy by extortion and theft.

What was true then is true now: Keeping up with the Joneses will always leave you jonesing for more. The average American carries about $15,000 of credit card debt, burying financial daylight under high interest rates and minimum payments. Once we see everything as God's (Psalm 24:1) and our role as stewards and not owners, we begin to view financial responsibility as part of our Christian witness.

Similarly, we can take on debt in relationships. When we treat others as a means to an end—a way to gain wealth, popularity, status—we lose sight of their value to God as His beloved children. Obeying our call to love others puts us at a surplus in God's economy.

Christian excellence in all areas of life centers on humility—putting others' needs ahead of our own, trusting that God will take care of us as we care for others. Shortchanging ourselves and others in the name of getting ahead will end when we get low, humbling ourselves and rejoicing in the God who humbled Himself for us.

ALL MEANS ALL

When you eat and when you drink,
do you not eat and drink for yourselves?
ZECHARIAH 7:6 NKJV

Zechariah criticized the folks who gave off the appearance of holiness, pretending to celebrate a holy feast to God, but who were really eating and drinking just to satisfy their appetites. They were finding satisfaction in a shadow of worship and thought they were getting away with it.

How much of your life have you given to God? Matthew 22:37 tells us that the correct answer should be "All," but an honest investigation of your heart may reveal a few dark corners you keep for yourself. Hidden in those nooks and crannies might be old habits or thoughts, or maybe some sinful indulgence. Your attic and basement may store greater excesses—pornography, emotional affairs, financial misdeeds—that you think you've hidden from everyone's prying eyes.

But there's a reckoning coming: "Nothing in all creation is hidden from God's sight. Everything is uncovered and laid bare before the eyes of him to whom we must give account" (Hebrews 4:13 NIV).

If the thought of all the times you've pleased yourself rather than God sends a cold shiver down your spine, take comfort: Jesus knows all about your temptations—even the ones you justify and disguise as what is owed you for your good work in *other* areas of life—and He stands ready to forgive, to flood you with grace and mercy and wash out those cobwebbed crevices in your heart.

GRATITUDE IS THE ATTITUDE

Do honest people rob God?
MALACHI 3:8 MSG

It's easy to look at the back-and-forth between God and Israel in Malachi and think, *Why did God choose for His own special people the most ornery, hardheaded lot in the history of mankind?* Simply put: because if God could keep promises to such a people, He can do it for anyone. No matter your starting point, God has already done His part to bring you into relationship with Himself—but people still have to choose to receive His gift of salvation and, then again, each day, to follow Him.

One of the hardest ways to do this is with your finances. You probably love the idea of God dispensing the cash whenever you have a need, but it chafes a bit when you're told to respond to His gracious provision with the first of your increase. Prioritize your tithe and give it cheerfully (2 Corinthians 9:7). Jesus said it best: God's looking after lilies and sparrows, and you matter more to Him than either (Matthew 6:25–34). Honor Him, and He'll take care of you.

Relying on God's provision also means being able to distinguish between your needs and your wants. Being grateful for what He has given you settles something in your heart and keeps you from striving after or clinging to material goods. You will worship from a truer spirit—a place of peace and contentment that will keep you from robbing God of His due in tithes and praise.

THE FIRST OFFENSE

GOD said to the Woman, "What is this that you've done?"
GENESIS 3:12 MSG

Eve was deceived by the serpent and then she persuaded her husband. A precedent was set the moment the first couple ate the fruit of a tree God had placed off-limits. Guilt overcame them. Embarrassment replaced wonder. Sadness replaced joy. Sin replaced relationship. These feelings were new and life altering. Eve had to answer for the first sin known to mankind. How could she respond? How could anything be made right again? Eve had no suitable defense, only excuses.

The act of breaking God's law is something all of us have in common. Romans 3:9–12 (MSG) sets the record straight: "We all start out as sinners. Scripture leaves no doubt about it: There's nobody living right, not even one. . . . They've all taken the wrong turn. . . . No one's living right; I can't find a single one."

The first sin scarred every human heart with imperfection. But even before God questioned Eve, He had a plan that would reestablish the relationship broken when the first couple thought God's command was simply a suggestion. Romans 5:19 (NLT) says, "Because one person disobeyed God, many became sinners. But because one other person [Jesus] obeyed God, many will be made righteous."

God can, and does, cause all things to work together for good to those who recognize they're wrong. He is the only One who can redeem lives ruined by poor decision-making (Romans 8:28).

PREPARED. AMAZED.

The LORD said to [Moses], "Who gave human beings their mouths?"
EXODUS 4:11 NIV

Moses was God's choice to deliver the people of Israel from bondage in Egypt. Songs would be sung about his deeds. God's question should have led to increased confidence, but for forty years Moses had embraced the role of nomad. He had become comfortable with isolation. Perhaps Moses was so immersed in personal pity he forgot that he was arguing with God.

The Lord didn't need an answer to His question, but He let it linger so Moses would stop and think about how absurd it was to tell God He'd made a mistake. There are lessons to be learned in every question God asks. He doesn't ask because *He* needs to be *instructed*. He asks because *we* need to *think*. We can argue with God, but He's the One who created us, gave us skills, and promises to help us to do what He asks.

Philippians 4:13 (NKJV) says, "I can do all things through Christ who strengthens me." If God's given you an assignment, you can be sure He'll prepare you to do what you thought couldn't be done. Then, when the impossible becomes reality, you'll know the Source of your success.

Admit what you can't do, and be prepared to be amazed at what God can do. Remember, God doesn't need your list of excuses; He just needs you to be willing to join Him in the adventure.

WHERE HE LEADS

The LORD said to Moses, "How long will
these people treat me with contempt?"
NUMBERS 14:11 NLT

For years God's people prayed for rescue. Their hopes rose as
Moses began exit negotiations with Pharaoh. When they finally
left, the Red Sea split so they could walk forward in freedom.
Hadn't the people moved from hardship to miraculous relief?
Where there should have been celebration, the new burdens
of liberty seemed more troublesome than God's provision. The
people were promised freedom and a home, but popular opinion
suggested giving up on God's gift in favor of a return to bondage
and a familiar meal plan.

If you've read the story, you know how it ends—with God's
people occupying the Promised Land—but you also understand
that change can be painful; it takes you from your comfort zone
and leaves you uneasy. You may be thinking of a time when God's
plan meant an unwelcome move, a job you never intended to like,
or people who got on your nerves.

Could it be that freedom brings a sense of fear when you're
all too familiar and comfortable with bondage? After all, freedom
brings personal responsibility, alterations in the way you think, and
a difference in how you relate to others. Be encouraged. "Christ
has set us free to live a free life. So take your stand! Never again
let anyone put a harness of slavery on you" (Galatians 5:1 MSG).

Accept the challenge—and blessing—of freedom.

WITHOUT A CHALLENGE

*Why do you treat your sons better than me, turning them
loose to get fat on these offerings, and ignoring me?*
1 SAMUEL 2:29 MSG

The priest Eli served in the temple of God. He knew how a priest
should behave. He knew the rules of service and the customs of
preparation. Eli had two sons who served in the temple also, but
they treated sacrifices to God as a personal entitlement to a divine
buffet. They took what belonged to God and demanded the choice
meat of sacrifice for their personal meals.

Eli knew his sons were entrenched in their sinful behavior,
but he did nothing to stop them. That's why God confronted Eli
before dealing with Hophni and Phinehas. It shouldn't surprise us
that God frowns on enabling sin within our families and sphere
of influence. Eli knew what God commanded, yet he was more
than willing to give his sons a proverbial "get out of jail free" card
(something he had no right to offer).

By overlooking their sin, Eli was essentially telling his sons
that their behavior wouldn't be challenged. They moved from what
might have been viewed as simple indiscretion to blatant disregard
for God's law. There was no remorse, desire to change their behavior, or plan to restore what was taken.

Do we care enough about our families to lovingly challenge
bad behavior? We may not be able to change their minds, but they
need to know what's on our hearts.

BEHIND THE SCENES

The LORD said to Satan, "Where have you come from?"
JOB 1:7 NIV

———

He was an efficient intelligence gatherer. He used his information to devise plans to destroy those who swore allegiance to his enemy. On one side stood God the Creator. On the other, Satan the Destroyer. This enemy's place of operation was *behind the scenes*. His target was a man named Job. Satan had finished his fact-finding mission, and he'd learned a lot. Satan believed Job had several vulnerabilities: his children, his riches, and his health. Satan thought he had enough intel to wage a winning battle, but in order to put his plan in place, he needed permission from God.

Does it ever seem that when you do your best to follow God, you encounter opposition? Even now, you might be experiencing a taste of what Job went through. If your spiritual adversary can't defeat you outright, then perhaps his best tool is distraction. He'll try to shift your focus to comfort, personal plans, and feelings, and you'll find less time for God.

We may have an enemy that is the prince of distraction, but we serve a God who provided the perfect remedy. We are asked to keep "our eyes on Jesus, the champion who initiates and perfects our faith" (Hebrews 12:2 NLT).

When our life vision is focused on God's plans, then there will be fewer opportunities for deceptive distractions and greater opportunities to serve Him well.

LIFE'S FRUSTRATIONS

Have you comprehended the vast expanses of the earth?
JOB 38:18 NIV

Job found himself in a courtroom drama. He asked God to answer for decisions that affected him. Yes, Job had suffered, and he felt his suffering was unjust. But when God spoke, His defense was in the form of rhetorical questions, one after the other. Job had no reply because God's questions were spoken by One who knows all, has seen all, and can do all. Silence or repentance were Job's only appropriate responses.

We can ask God why we must endure life's frustrations, but we can never fully understand His perspective on our personal discomfort. He loves us, but we live in an imperfect world. There's so much outside our control. The sin of Adam and Eve ushered in the worst in human decision-making. Then there's the added negative influence of our determined and devious adversary, Satan.

The question God asked Job is something none of us can answer. Canyons, waterfalls, caves, and mountains are only a part of the vastness of the earth. We may believe we know more about the world than Job did, but as much as we think we understand, there's always more to learn. God, on the other hand, has never needed to know more than He did the moment He called the earth forth from His imagination.

If God can be trusted to imagine oceans and jungles, He can be trusted with everything we don't understand. The only thing we can really control is our own response.

GRATITUDE AND RESPECT

Can you lift up your voice to the clouds,
that an abundance of water may cover you?
JOB 38:34 NKJV

———————

Job enjoyed rain. It caused crops to grow, which fed his livestock. Rain brought rivers and streams to life. Job had used the waters to quench thirst and wash the dust from his face. Water was important, but Job couldn't create water. He couldn't command the sky to provide it. All he really could do was express gratitude when God sent the rain.

The prophet Elijah once prayed for the clouds to come and the rain to fall. His answer came as the result of a faith-filled *request* and not a belligerent *demand*. We can't *tell* God what we want and insist He approve our ultimatum. God made the clouds. He made the rain, and He tells it when to fall. Matthew 5:45 (MSG) says, "This is what God does. He gives his best—the sun to warm and the rain to nourish—to everyone, regardless: the good and bad, the nice and nasty."

God's not a genie in a bottle, a cosmic vending machine, or even a rich grandfather. He can be trusted to take care of us, but He's *not* someone we control.

God has removed the barriers to relationship. There are some resources, like rain, that He gives to everyone. There are some resources, like grace and forgiveness, that He only offers to family. Gratitude and respect should always be our first response to God's great gifts.

THE VALUE OF STORIES

Can you hitch a wild ox to a plow? Will it plow
a field for you? . . .Can you rely on it to bring home
your grain and deliver it to your threshing floor?
JOB 39:10, 12 NLT

With each new question God asked, Job had more to consider. In his mind, Job likely envisioned a wild ox being placed in a harness. It must have seemed absurd. Even a man with little farming knowledge would recognize that a wild beast wouldn't do the work of a tame farm animal.

Was this question designed to indicate the weakness of man? Was it to prove the power of God? Perhaps either answer can lead us to personal humility and the worship of God.

God understands the value of using word pictures to teach. Job worked with livestock, so when God asked His questions, this man was aware that a wild ox couldn't be trusted to plow a field or safely bring a wagon back to the barn. The wild ox would resist the use of a harness, bit, and plow. This animal had the power a farmer needed but not the willingness to follow directions.

Job must have been overwhelmed. God had asked so many questions, and the only thing Job really knew for sure was that God was God—and he was not. Yet, somehow in the midst of the questioning, Job was beginning to remember that the God who had all the answers was worth listening to.

ABSURD COMPARISONS

*Can you make a pet of it like a bird or put
it on a leash for the young women in your house?*
JOB 41:5 NIV

⸻

Compare the docile nature of a tame bird with that of a ferocious, wild beast, then ask yourself whether the beast would make a good pet. This is the picture God painted for Job. It would be like asking whether we could capture a grizzly bear and house-train it, put a shark in a swimming pool to play with, or invite a wolf to be a sheepdog. It's not likely the analogy was lost on Job. Whatever beast God might have been referring to, Job knew it couldn't be tamed.

Perhaps the absurd comparison might have brought a smile if the situation hadn't been so life defining. We each have those moments—times when we learn something about God and it causes awe and wonder. God is so much more of everything we're not, yet even in the midst of being overwhelmed with questions he couldn't answer, Job found a sense of worship rising steadily in his heart.

The awesome nature of God can instill a sense of fear, but the God in charge of everything has at His core a desire to have a relationship with you. The relationship shouldn't be casual. Like the grizzly, shark, and wolf, God has incredible power, but He harnesses infinite power to demonstrate that we're loved. Every gift is delivered with strength under control. We worship a big, big God.

CALM DOWN, LISTEN UP

*When you come before me, whoever gave you the idea of
acting like this, running here and there, doing this and that—
all this sheer commotion in the place provided for worship?*

ISAIAH 1:12 MSG

God's temple had become a sideshow. The people embraced God *culture* without embracing God. They fell in love with the ritual and called it worship. They substituted communion with God for a busy schedule. There was no time for relationship because they were too busy seeking brownie points. Those who needed help would look to God's people, but the people were too busy doing church.

It sounds like this question could have been posed today. We live in a culture that's elevated a worship service to a media experience that can be emotional, entertaining, and worthy of watercooler conversation.

While there's nothing wrong with delivering the message in a new way, there *can* be misunderstanding. Some may view a "worship experience" as the gold standard in how you meet God. This can leave us feeling as if a building visited one day a week is the only place and time where worship can occur. Unintentional? Perhaps, but when the focus moves from real relationship to worship entertainment, we've missed the point.

Worship doesn't have to be a sideshow, but it should be a profound beginning for something greater. God can make an impact—He just needs a little room. Sometimes we might need to move out of His way, calm down, and listen up. He has a message.

SELF-IMPORTANT FORGETFULNESS

Lift up your eyes and look to the heavens: Who created all these?
ISAIAH 40:26 NIV

Moses transcribed the first four words of the Bible, "In the beginning God. . . ." God existed before the heavens and the earth. He lived before the stars. "He determines the number of the stars and calls them each by name" (Psalm 147:4 NIV). However, the people of Israel seemed to have lapses in memory and impaired judgment. Hadn't the people done "whatever seemed right in their own eyes" (Judges 17:6 NLT)? They needed a refresher in *who* had created what. They were left with a familiar reminder: "In the beginning God. . . ."

John 1:3 (MSG) tells us, "Everything was created through him; nothing—not one thing!—came into being without him." We can look to the skies, the valleys, the oceans, the caves, and the faces of other humans, but when we fail to recognize the God behind the beauty, we can easily worship the creation while disregarding the Creator (Romans 1:25).

God was dealing with the self-importance of His people. He deals with the same issues in us. Whenever we think God must be pretty lucky to have us on His side, we need to remember that "he made us; we didn't make him" (Psalm 100:3 MSG).

He made us because He loves us. He loved us enough to send His Son, Jesus, to reestablish relationship. We should be quick to remember that "In the beginning *God*. . . ."

SOMETHING NEW

I am about to do something new.
See, I have already begun! Do you not see it?
ISAIAH 43:19 NLT

God was about to bring His people home from an extended exile in Babylon. We don't know exactly what *new thing* God was doing, but the path home would be through the desert. Perhaps the new thing included increased rain, plant growth, and an abundance of wild game. This would meet their needs as they traveled. Whatever God did for His people, His question suggested it should be obvious to them.

God can make a way when all other options prove impossible. He can lead you forward when you thought you had to stay. He can abundantly provide when you planned to do without. We can get so wrapped up in the logistics of life we forget that if God leads, He can easily supply our need. He's not constrained by a checkbook. He doesn't have to broker any deals. He can do exactly what He wants, when He wants, and in any way He chooses.

This verse suggests a promise of mercy, an act of love, and an offer of blessing. The Lord can do the same for you today. Each of us can return from our personal exile after living apart from God, and we have the same offer of mercy, love, and blessing because of the work Jesus finished on the cross. However, if you never leave where you've been, how can you experience the joy of *coming home*?

THE UNLIKELY RESCUE PLAN

Who told you, and a long time ago, what's going on here?
Who made sense of things for you? Wasn't I the one? GOD?
ISAIAH 45:21 MSG

God had a plan to rescue His people from Babylon. They'd been captive long enough. However, much to their surprise, their rescue would come at the command of a Gentile. Cyrus the Persian was the new leader in Babylon. The forty-fifth chapter of Isaiah includes instructions from God, who placed His plan in the mind and heart of Cyrus. As his reign began, this king obeyed God's plan and released the people of Israel to return home to rebuild the temple in Jerusalem.

God can use anyone with any background to do anything— even those things no one expects or believes possible. God is quick to rescue broken people, and not just *repurpose* our lives but *change* our minds, hearts, actions, and responses. "This means that anyone who belongs to Christ has become a new person. The old life is gone; a new life has begun!" (2 Corinthians 5:17 NLT).

If we take the time to inspect what God said, we begin to understand that God can save anyone. His love is for all humans, not just a few. His salvation is offered to everyone, not just those with the right ethnic background. His forgiveness is for all, not just those who have done the most *right* things.

Good news: God came to rescue you.

SUPERSIZED BAD DAYS

Was my arm too short to deliver you?
ISAIAH 50:2 NIV

The people of Israel had short-term memory loss. God had rescued them before, but they'd shown poor judgment and poor leadership and were reaping the result of their own sin. And they wanted a sequel. Wasn't God strong enough? Maybe they just needed to discover that "the arm of the LORD is not too short to save" (Isaiah 59:1 NIV).

Hadn't God promised King David, "With my powerful arm I will make [you] strong" (Psalm 89:21 NLT)? Had the people so quickly forgotten that "the strong right arm of the LORD has done glorious things" (Psalm 118:16 NLT)?

The answer to God's first question provides a powerful reminder that He understands the difficulties we face and can be counted on to help us during supersized bad days. If the arms of the Lord can make mountains, divide seas, and place a gray blanket of rain clouds over the sky, aren't they strong enough to carry us when we're weak, afraid, and lonely? Isn't the answer obvious?

God owns all the power that will ever be. There's no one equal to Him. While He could use those strong arms to crush our world and destroy sin once and for all, His Son used His strong arms to die a death of torture as the only perfect sacrifice for the sin that kept us distant from God. Jesus is *alive*, and God is *strong*.

AN IMPRESSIVE DISPLAY OF QUIET

*Because I don't yell and make a
scene do you think I don't exist?*
ISAIAH 57:11 MSG

———————

The people of Israel faced a long-standing issue. They wanted to hear from God, but they didn't recognize His voice. They expected an impressive, public display of God's power, but in the silence they were left confused, not listening. They weren't alone. It wasn't in the wind, earthquake, or fire that God spoke to Elijah. It was in a whisper. God doesn't shout to get attention. His "still small voice" (1 Kings 19:12 KJV) invites us to lean in and really listen.

God is often a late-night guest who speaks when we can't sleep, an early-morning friend when we're trying to plan our day, and a companion on the road when we find we have time to think—and listen.

We may not hear His audible voice, but in those quiet moments we'll begin to understand that God is leading us through the things we're learning in His Word. While we want absolute proof that God exists, Jesus said to those who saw Him physically, "You believe because you have seen me. Blessed are those who believe without seeing me" (John 20:29 NLT).

Faith isn't as concerned with proof as it is trust. Some might foolishly say that everything is a result of time and chance and nothing more. Even with such blatant disregard for God's handiwork we find Him whispering, and those who trust will *listen*.

NO FAN OF CONFRONTATION

The word of the LORD came to me:
"What do you see, Jeremiah?"
JEREMIAH 1:11 NIV

This is one of the rare questions for which God actually required an answer. God needed to be sure young Jeremiah was both listening and willing to obey difficult commands. The time God spent with Jeremiah was like a prophet's boot camp. God was instructing him, and they needed to be on the same page.

The things Jeremiah saw were illustrations of future events. Before the first chapter of Jeremiah's story was complete, he would be told that the message he had to share wouldn't be one that others wanted to hear, but God was in control.

Most of us aren't fans of confrontation. Sometimes we'll say what we need to say to make things seem acceptable to the greatest number of people. We don't want to rock the boat, invade someone's personal space, or be misunderstood. The end result of this walking-on-eggshells approach to life is that someone who needed us to love them enough to be honest is left to continue doing things that are counterproductive at the least, or sinful and destructive at the worst.

Like Jeremiah, we might be asked to share a message that feels awkward and leaves us uncomfortable. However, if God is asking us to share, then there's a reason. We may not be sure why we need to speak up, but obedience is better than having an explanation for why.

PASSIONATE PURSUITS

[You are] a wild donkey accustomed to the desert, sniffing the
wind in her craving—in her heat who can restrain her?
JEREMIAH 2:24 NIV

Jeremiah lived in difficult times. The Israelites seemed to have great passion in life, but their pursuits were far different from God's best dreams for His people. Their track record was littered with one bad king after another, one broken promise followed by thousands more, and the rare good choice left to die a lonely death. The God of their fathers didn't seem to hold their attention in the wake of a lifetime of unreasonable pursuits and unhealthy options.

We might like to think we're somehow better and more enlightened than that, but we, too, will often choose personal interests over God's will. Personal satisfaction can become our passionate pursuit, and God's commands are forgotten in our race to get what we want. Most will discover that their personal satisfaction is a mirage. As soon as they get close to what they want, the satisfaction begins to slip away. They try again and again, but happiness dissipates like morning fog.

God has given us desires that match His purpose for our lives, but we exist in a society where there is an infinite number of substitutes to consider. When we consider the options too long, it becomes easier to forget God.

God's call to the Israelites is similar to the call He makes to us today. We're invited to follow His plan and discover real life.

BACKWARD THINKING

Have you not just called to me: "My Father, my friend from my youth,
will you always be angry? Will your wrath continue forever?"
JEREMIAH 3:4–5 NIV

God repeated a question the Israelites had asked, and He recited it word for word. Perhaps He wanted them to really listen to their own question. Sure, they'd paid Him respect by calling Him "Father," they reminded Him of the relationship He'd always had with Israel, then they ended by questioning Him during His wrath.

It's almost as if God couldn't believe what He'd heard. There was no mention of sorrow for wrongdoing. There was no apology. There was no repentance. It was as if the people thought, *We understand You're mad, but can You get over it so we can get on with life?*

Is it possible our actions are similar? We sin and we want the Lord to forget the event when we should be seeking forgiveness. We should be agreeing with Him that what we've done breaks His law, but we show no signs that sin has affected us at all.

Sin separates us from God. We miss out on relationship. We miss out on communication with God. We miss out on His plan for our future. When we fail to admit we've sinned, we treat God's commands as optional while clinging to a sense of inflated superiority.

God chooses to forget our forgiven sin. Sometimes we expect Him to forgive without our having to admit we've sinned. No wonder that sounds backward to God.

THE SIN ACCELERATOR?

Don't you yourselves admit that this Temple,
which bears my name, has become a den of thieves?
JEREMIAH 7:11 NLT

God was worshipped in the temple. It was a place set apart to meet with Him. This was where people could be trained to share His love with others. However, the temple's function had systematically been repurposed. It had become a social club lacking positive cultural impact. God was fed up. "Clean up your act—the way you live, the things you do—so I can make my home with you in this place" (Jeremiah 7:3 MSG).

Today it can seem like the only rule is *There are no rules*. It can be frustrating when people who identify with Christ seem comfortable with sin. Underhanded deals, sexual sin, gossip, and lying are given a green light, while grace is embraced during a weekend church service. The apostle Paul said in Romans 6:1–2 (NLT), "Should we keep on sinning so that God can show us more and more of his wonderful grace? Of course not!"

Grace should never be used as a sin accelerator. We abuse grace when we accept it with no intention of allowing God to transform our character. God's grace forgives our sin, but He doesn't want us to misunderstand His intent. Sin should be the exception to our new way of living, not a welcome part of it. Sin should be avoided, not embraced like an old friend. Sin should leave us sad, not anticipating the next wrong choice.

A PLAN TO REFINE

Watch this! I'll melt them down and see what they're made of.
What else can I do with a people this wicked?
JEREMIAH 9:7 MSG

Smelt silver ore and two things become clear: The first is that there is silver within the stone. The second is that there are a lot of impurities that must be removed before the silver can be useful. This is the likely picture Jeremiah had in mind when God asked this question. To symbolically melt down the people meant that God recognized the wicked hearts within His people, but to refine meant He was willing to do that hard work of purifying polluted minds, hearts, and dispositions.

A smelter does the hard work of refining because he knows his efforts will result in something valuable once the work's done. While this question suggests that God was angry with His people (and He was), there's also the inference that the people were worth the effort it would take to move them from rebellion to purity (and they were).

God has always found His people worth the trouble. There's never been a generation of people who've been 100 percent pure according to God's standard. It's because of His profound love for humanity that He draws them away from sin and toward transformation. His love for the lost means those of us who follow Him must represent Him accurately. His love for His children means He cannot leave us to embrace our impurity with no plan to refine us.

JUSTICE AND DIVINE ACCOUNTING

Who do you think will feel sorry for you, Jerusalem?
JEREMIAH 15:5 MSG

To say God was angry would be a colossal understatement. His was a righteous anger that placed the nation of Israel on notice. They were corrupt and spiritually broken. Their heart, or spiritual core, was hard and unyielding. Their spiritual bank account was bankrupt. Judgment was on its way. The people should have willingly called on God for help. They could have turned their backs on sin. They would have avoided so much pain if they had.

Whenever you're tempted to say, "They got what they deserved," you're contemplating justice. This happens because you recognize, and even agree, that there must be punishment for wrong choices and behavior.

Without the perfect sacrifice of Jesus, the idea of getting what we deserve would always place us on the penalty side of a divine ledger. Why? "For everyone has sinned; we all fall short of God's glorious standard" (Romans 3:23 NLT).

God has given humanity so many chances to do the right thing. He lets us try as hard as we can to meet His standard. The basic human response is either, "I can't, so why even try?" or "I'm better than other people, so God should be happy with me." Both responses deny the power of God to rescue, restore, and revive. Our relationship with God hinges on accepting what Jesus has done for us. Then we'll find ourselves grateful for His grace and mercy.

CONNECT WITH THE SOURCE

Which of them has stood in the council
of the LORD to see or to hear his word?
JEREMIAH 23:18 NIV

Wrong thinking was leading to a radical reset for God's people. It wasn't just that the people were bent on their own spiritual destruction, but those who were called to lead others spiritually were becoming gifted in the creative interpretation of God's Word.

You can sense the exasperation and judgment of God when He told Jeremiah, "My heart is broken within me," "Both prophet and priest are godless," and "I will bring disaster on them" (verses 9, 11, 12). These were men who should have known better but willingly turned the living organism of their faith into a decaying organization that they manipulated for their own benefit.

We get into trouble by accepting what we hear or read without question. First John 4:1 (MSG) says, "Not everyone who talks about God comes from God. There are a lot of lying preachers loose in the world." We shouldn't make it a goal to prove a pastor wrong, but we should investigate to see if what's being said matches God's Word. Remember, pastors are human and can make mistakes. This should give us even more reason to pray for them. It should also give us more of a motivation to study God's Word.

Learn all you can from preachers, but look to the Bible to define truth. Search the scriptures to check whether what people say is accurate (Acts 17:11).

IT SERVED A PURPOSE

Can a man bear children? Then why do I see every
strong man with his hands on his stomach like a
woman in labor, every face turned deathly pale?
JEREMIAH 30:6 NIV

———————

The case against Israel had been presented. Guilt was not in dispute. The sentencing phase was near. There were no national efforts at spiritual reform. Punishment was assured.

God chose to use this description of painful labor to help the people understand that what they would face wouldn't be easy. However, by using this picture there was the inference of hope—there would be new life after the pain. "Writhe in agony, Daughter Zion, like a woman in labor, for. . .you will go to Babylon; there you will be rescued. There the LORD will redeem you out of the hand of your enemies" (Micah 4:10 NIV).

Was God to blame for the punishment His people endured? Is God to blame when we suffer for the consequences of *our* sin? No.

Sometimes God chooses to withhold punishment we deserve, but other times we must endure pain for a season. Like the prodigal son, we may need a stay in a proverbial *pigpen* to remember where we came from and to whom we need to return. We need time to deal with our pride.

No one enjoys punishment, but if it can be used to restore relationship between God and man, then it has not only served its purpose, but it can restore hope to a new generation.

REPRESENT CHRIST

*Have you so soon forgotten the evil lives of your ancestors,
the evil lives of the kings of Judah and their wives, to say
nothing of your own evil lives, you and your wives, the evil
you flaunted in the land of Judah and the streets of Jerusalem?*
JEREMIAH 44:9 MSG

God's people lived lives that were overflowing with corruption, self-reliance, and outright rebellion. Knowing this, God sent prophets to explain that punishment was coming. God urged the people to turn from their habitual choice of sin and come back to Him. However, the people treated God's messengers shamefully and slipped further into rebellion.

It was almost as if they believed that if their parents and grandparents were a little evil, they would demonstrate what *real* evil looked like. They chose to live life as if God was powerless.

Second Corinthians 5:20 (MSG) reminds us, "We're Christ's representatives. God uses us to persuade men and women to drop their differences and enter into God's work of making things right between them." In some ways, we're to do the work of a prophet like Jeremiah. We're to help people see that seeking to *out-evil* others is counterproductive and ruins futures.

Even if no one pays attention to the warning, we're still urged to share the message. God's more concerned with people becoming accountable for their personal response than our ability to change minds. If you are called to speak up, do it, even if no one listens. You represent Christ.

THE COMPARISON CONSPIRACY

*Is there no longer wisdom in Teman? Has counsel
perished from the prudent? Has their wisdom decayed?*
JEREMIAH 49:7 NIV

The punishment for Israel was certain. Justice would result in reforming the thinking of those who endured the punishment to come. However, God knew that other nations who looked at the doom coming to Israel either celebrated or patted themselves on the back. They were comparing themselves with Israel and felt no sadness for the people, just a profound sense of pride, because they wrongly concluded they must be better than Israel. God was not amused.

James 4:16 (NKJV) says, "But now you boast in your arrogance. All such boasting is evil." All of us have some level of insecurity, so it's actually pretty normal for human beings to compare themselves with someone who seems in worse shape. We often boast in an attempt to improve our own sense of worth. The above questions suggest that putting others down to inflate our own worth is not wise or prudent.

When you find yourself interested in comparing yourself favorably to someone in difficulty, spend some time thinking about the following: "Put yourself aside, and help others get ahead. Don't be obsessed with getting your own advantage. Forget yourselves long enough to lend a helping hand" (Philippians 2:3–4 MSG).

Comparison is not about who's *better*, but rather who's *best*. That distinction goes to God, who gave all humanity the opportunity to love others equally and follow Him faithfully.

BENT THINKING

Is it nothing to the people of Judah that they commit these
detestable sins, leading the whole nation into violence,
thumbing their noses at me, and provoking my anger?
EZEKIEL 8:17 NLT

It was as if the fire of Old West lawlessness had originated in
Judah and was spreading. It seemed like the world had gone
crazy. One thing hadn't changed—the lawbreaking choices of the
people. They may have felt that since things were already so bad,
who would notice one more poor choice, but it was just such lawbreaking that had brought them to a place of *outlaw culture*.

God wanted to know whether the sins the people committed
had moved them to a sense of personal responsibility and remorse.
The answer was a resounding "No!"

If you've detected sin as a theme over many of these devo-
tionals, there's good reason. The prophets were those called upon
to speak God's message, and the core message God typically sent
was "Stop breaking My law and come back to Me." His questions
about sin were to invite the hearer to spend time thinking about
both the question and the One asking.

It was clear that God's people often forgot His holiness in
their thinking. When it becomes common for people to believe
their actions mean nothing to God, then the depravity of human
decision-making leads to increasingly dishonorable choices.

Walk with God, understand His commands, and honor Him
by choosing to obey.

THE WITHERING VINE

This is what the Sovereign LORD says: Will it thrive?
Will it not be uprooted and stripped of its fruit so that it withers?
EZEKIEL 17:9 NIV

God used the picture of a vine to indicate the way in which His people gained life and nourishment from Him. It was a word picture that Jesus would use in the New Testament (John 15:5). In Ezekiel's case, it described the people being uprooted and moved away from their homeland because of sin. It represented an alienation from God for a time. It was a verdict based on just cause. It would have weakened the knees of all who really *got* what God was saying.

Follow this line of thinking: God's justice demands perfection. Because Adam sinned, we all sin. Sin denies any ability for perfection to exist within man. When men can't be perfect, they may come to a place where they no longer care. When they no longer care, they live however they want. This leads to an abuse of God's patience.

God chose to respond to this downward spiral by doing the unexpected. "[He] showed his great love for us by sending Christ to die for us while we were still sinners" (Romans 5:8 NLT). His anger was righteous in the Old Testament, but the only remedy to help reestablish lost relationship was if the price for *all* sin was paid in full. God still hates sin, and He hates it largely because of how it hurts the sinner and separates people from Him.

OF DEATH—AND LIFE

If righteous people turn from their righteous behavior and start doing
sinful things and act like other sinners, should they be allowed to live?
EZEKIEL 18:24 NLT

The first covenant God made with humanity was filled with rules no one could keep. Moses wrote, "[God extends] the fallout of parents' sins to children into the third, even the fourth generation" (Numbers 14:18 MSG). It seemed mankind was doomed not only to pass along the will to sin, but also the consequences of sin. Then came the book of Ezekiel with something new: "This is my rule: The person who sins is the one who will die" (Ezekiel 18:4 NLT).

God penalizes the choice to sin. Romans 6:23 (MSG) says, "Work hard for sin your whole life and your pension is death." This *death pension* is both physical and spiritual. Each of us will experience physical death, but sin causes spiritual death. Our choices find us walking toward death—separation from God.

God's *New* Covenant began when Jesus died for our sin and rose from the dead. "God's gift is real life, eternal life, delivered by Jesus, our Master" (Romans 6:23 MSG). When God was finally able to forgive sin because of Jesus' sacrifice, God's Son proclaimed, "I came so they can have real and eternal life, more and better life than they ever dreamed of" (John 10:10 MSG).

Death (separation from God) is no longer inevitable. Life (relationship with God) is available. God's great rescue plan has been established.

SEEKING WIGGLE ROOM

Am I going to put up with questions from people like you, Israel?
EZEKIEL 20:31 MSG

In a courtroom, a judge has the ultimate authority. Cases are considered. Rulings are made. Sentences are passed down. The bang of a gavel silences all objections. The people of Israel came to the Judge who'd rendered a verdict of guilty, but instead of the remorse expected of a convicted defendant, they effectively maligned the justice of God. It would seem the people were questioning how important God's laws really were.

Could the laws be relaxed and adjusted to meet societal trends? God's response? "As sure as I am the living God, I, GOD, the Master, refuse to be called into question by you!" (Ezekiel 20:31 MSG).

We might be guilty of such belligerence today. We want the wiggle room to do what we want and still be considered sin-free. If we can't find a way to justify our guilt, we grab hold of grace, believing the common but flawed saying "It's better to ask for forgiveness than permission."

Colossians 3:14 (MSG) says, "Regardless of what else you put on, wear love. It's your basic, all-purpose garment. Never be without it." Questioning God often means we are convinced there should be instances when we don't need to show love. God didn't change His *love laws*. His command is obedience. There's no need to question the verdict. God's waiting for our response.

COMPARISONS NEVER BRING PRAISE

O Egypt, to which of the trees of Eden
will you compare your strength and glory?
EZEKIEL 31:18 NLT

Egypt had become one of the most splendid nations in the known world. They had art, culture, and building programs. They were the finest example of self-sufficiency. They acted superior to the nations around them. But God wanted them to understand that all their achievements fell short. God was effectively telling Pharaoh that the most impressive splendor Egypt had ever enjoyed could not compare to the trees found in God's garden, Eden.

We're born with a desire to please and impress our parents. We want the *gold star* stickers, the *good job* stamps, and the public *attaboys*. Parents want to (and should) encourage kids, but spiritual growth means we begin to understand that our best efforts can't compare favorably to a single thing God has done for us.

God warned us about this attitude: "Pride leads to disgrace, but with humility comes wisdom" (Proverbs 11:2 NLT). This isn't just an idea from the Old Testament. James 4:10 (NIV) says, "Humble yourselves before the Lord, and he will lift you up."

If we're to truly praise God for His goodness, we can't compare His goodness with our efforts, His majesty with our intentions, or His perfection with our gold stars. Perhaps that's why God inspired King David to write, "My soul shall make its boast in the LORD; the humble shall hear of it and be glad" (Psalm 34:2 NKJV).

A SHEPHERD'S RESPONSIBILITY

Why do the rest of my sheep have to make do with grass
that's trampled down and water that's been muddied?
EZEKIEL 34:19 MSG

God calls us sheep because we must follow. God called Himself Shepherd and led. King David penned Psalm 23:1–3 (NIV): "The LORD is my shepherd, I lack nothing. He makes me lie down in green pastures, he leads me beside quiet waters, he refreshes my soul. He guides me along the right paths for his name's sake." God's example caused under-shepherds to lead the sheep on His behalf. These spiritual leaders assumed great responsibility, but they failed miserably. God wanted to know why.

In the New Testament, God made it clear what these shepherds were to be like. "It's important that a church leader, responsible for the affairs in God's house, be looked up to—not pushy, not short-tempered, not a drunk, not a bully, not money-hungry. He must welcome people, be helpful, wise, fair, reverent, have a good grip on himself, and have a good grip on the Message" (Titus 1:6–8 MSG).

The spiritual leaders in Ezekiel's day had a blatant disregard for the spiritual health and nourishment of the sheep. To make matters worse, the shepherds were polluting the truth and weakening the spiritual value of anything they taught.

Jesus told His disciples not to take advantage of the sheep. He vowed to notice and respond (Matthew 18:6–7). If you're called to lead, do so with great love, steady patience, and solid truth.

JUSTICE LOGIC

Was it not right that the wicked
men of Gibeah were attacked?
HOSEA 10:9 NLT

A traveler and his concubine stopped in Gibeah and received hospitality by staying with a man in the city. Some other men noticed that the guests had found lodging, and insisted they be allowed to take the guests and treat them any way they chose. They ultimately took the concubine and abused her and left her to die. The nation of Israel was called to avenge this sin, and the tribe of Benjamin was nearly destroyed in the aftermath.

Now, centuries later, God wanted to know whether the people of Israel still viewed this as an appropriate response. The people would've remembered this story as part of their nation's history. To agree meant that they deserved similar punishment for the sin culture that had been allowed to grow in Israel. To disagree meant they had become disconnected from their faith in the God who had chosen to repeatedly rescue them.

We want those we disagree with to keep an appointment with justice. We also want to be free from the consequences of our own sin. Perhaps examples of God's justice can humble us enough to confess our sins and in humility accept God's forgiveness and mercy, knowing it's nothing we deserve.

God loves us enough to provide course corrections when needed. We can resist or even refuse God's plan, but perhaps the worst part of going our own way is the choice to intentionally separate ourselves from God.

GOING THROUGH THE MOTIONS

Was it to me you were bringing sacrifices and offerings
during the forty years in the wilderness, Israel?
AMOS 5:25 NLT

Amos 5 begins with God giving Israel a funeral song. If there was to be a future for the nation, it would require a death to the way things had been, the way the people wanted them to be, and the faulty thinking that got them to the funeral. Amos 5:4–5 (NLT) says, "Come back to me and live! Don't worship at the pagan altars." God's core message to Israel seemed to be, "Quit going through the motions. I'm tired of your pretend worship while your hearts drift far from Me."

The people were bringing sacrifices to God in the wilderness, but they were thinking of someone else. "You served your pagan gods—Sakkuth your king god and Kaiwan your star god—the images you made for yourselves" (Amos 5:26 NLT).

At best, the people viewed God as an add-on to their expanding belief system. At worst, they treated Him as a lesser god.

Worshipping God can move from true love for the Lord to hollow ritual. It can become something no longer representing relationship but obligation. Have we settled for *ho-hum*? We must remember who God is and why He's worth our worship. We should never treat Him casually or disrespectfully but wholeheartedly. Deuteronomy 6:5 (MSG) says, "Love GOD, your God, with your whole heart: love him with all that's in you, love him with all you've got!"

A TIME FOR CHANGE

Then God said to Jonah, "Is it right
for you to be angry about the plant?"
JONAH 4:9 NKJV

Jonah hated the people of Nineveh. Then God told the prophet to go tell them that God wanted them to repent, but Jonah boarded a ship heading in the opposite direction. A severe storm at sea and a quick toss in the ocean led to three days' accommodations in the belly of a big fish. Jonah reevaluated his choices. He told Nineveh to repent. They did.

Jonah 4:3 (NKJV) gives us some insight into how Jonah really felt. He told God, "Please take my life from me, for it is better for me to die than to live!"

When the shade tree Jonah was sitting under wilted and died, he was just as angry (verse 8). Logically, it seemed that this prophet would have been happy if the people of Nineveh had been destroyed. Jonah recognized God was merciful, slow to anger, and kind (verse 2). Knowing this didn't change his heart.

How often do we want bad things to happen to bad people? We understand that God is kind and wants them to repent, but we'd rather grumble within our own unrighteous fish belly, wondering why God has to be kind to *those* people.

God has a plan, and it's good. "He doesn't want anyone lost. He's giving everyone space and time to change" (2 Peter 3:9 MSG). We should be grateful God does this, because there was a time when we were lost, too.

BEYOND THE QUESTIONS

Has not the LORD of Heaven's Armies promised
that the wealth of nations will turn to ashes?
HABAKKUK 2:13 NLT

———————————

The message of Habakkuk is a great lesson in the proper way to ask God questions. Just three chapters long, this book records the prophet asking God questions and then listening. God's answers indicated that the most important nations in the world would fall. The structure of the nations would change, and God's people would need to be patient. This short book recounts the plans God had for this restructuring. Perhaps unexpectedly, the final chapter provides Habakkuk's song of praise: "I will rejoice in the LORD, I will be joyful in God my Savior" (Habakkuk 3:18 NIV).

When we ask God a question, we need to be willing to seek answers in His Word. He may have questions for us.

Children often ask parents questions. Usually one answer leads to five more questions. We can become exasperated with their *why* questions and say something like, "Because I said so." As Christians, we should accept God's answers—even if we don't like them—even if we don't agree with Him, and especially if we're looking for a loophole.

Habakkuk begins by asking God questions like, "Why do you tolerate wrongdoing?" (Habakkuk 1:2 NIV). The prophet ends by singing, "The Sovereign LORD is my strength" (Habakkuk 3:19 NIV). Questions lead to understanding. Understanding leads to acceptance. Acceptance of God's answers leads to a greater relationship with Him.

THE END OF EXILE

Don't you still have the message of the earlier prophets from the time when Jerusalem was still a thriving, bustling city and the outlying countryside, the Negev and Shephelah, was populated?
ZECHARIAH 7:7 MSG

God decreed a seventy-year exile for His people. That exile was coming to an end. The religious leaders wanted to know whether they still needed to fast on the seventieth anniversary of their exile. Seven decades hadn't been enough to move the people from religious obligation to a relationship with God. When God asked His question, He was telling them that He'd made a promise and would keep it.

God reminded the people: "Treat one another justly. Love your neighbors. Be compassionate with each other. Don't take advantage of widows, orphans, visitors, and the poor. Don't plot and scheme against one another—that's evil" (Zechariah 7:9 MSG).

Imagine being freed from prison. Would it be a happily-ever-after? This hadn't been the case when Israel was freed from Egypt. They wanted to return to familiar bondage. Freedom was hard work. They were tempted to return to the same sinful behavior that brought about exile. Maybe that's why God gave His reminder to pay close attention to how they treated each other. The captives were coming home, but the *heart* work would continue.

If you find yourself coming out of a dark period in life, allow God the opportunity to continue the work that leads to restoration and relationship. Hang on. He's not finished yet.

THE TRUST DEPOSIT

Who will get everything you worked for?
LUKE 12:20 NLT

———————

Jesus told the story of a rich man who was a very success-ful farmer. His harvest was so significant that he planned a retirement party, built new grain storage, and was convinced he wouldn't need to work another day in his life. He placed his trust in his ability, his crop, and his understanding of riches. God arrived on the scene and told the man he would die. The farmer was left to wonder whom he'd worked so hard for.

Greed consumes the human soul like a campfire consumes dry pine needles. A little is never enough, and a lot is never too little. Every goal in gaining riches refuses to satisfy the goal maker. It wasn't as if God hadn't made it clear that faith should rest on something more stable than what we see, touch, and hold. "Some trust in chariots and some in horses, but we trust in the name of the LORD our God" (Psalm 20:7 NIV).

The writer of Hebrews put a clear focus on the subject: "Don't love money; be satisfied with what you have" (Hebrews 13:5 NLT). Paul told Timothy, "True godliness with contentment is itself great wealth. After all, we brought nothing with us when we came into the world, and we can't take anything with us when we leave it" (1 Timothy 6:6–7 NLT).

God's great question should impact more than the rich but arrogant farmer. Where have you deposited *your* trust?

A PLEASING SACRIFICE

*"Why are you so angry?" the LORD asked Cain.
"Why do you look so dejected?"*
GENESIS 4:6 NLT

The first record of sibling rivalry ended in tragedy when Cain murdered his brother, Abel. Before that, even though God knew what was in Cain's heart, He asked Cain about his anger and dejection.

Hearing God speak was a natural part of life for Cain and Abel. They recognized His voice and understood what sort of gifts pleased Him. Abel sacrificed the firstborn of his flock—he gave his finest (Genesis 4:4).

Cain's offering is described as being from the fruit of the ground. After asking Cain why he was angry, God said, "You will be accepted if you do what is right" (Genesis 4:7 NLT). Cain knew what was right, but he didn't sacrifice what God had requested.

God expected both men to give their best. Have His expectations changed? We all have opportunities to present excellent gifts to the Lord. It is an honor to give back, by treating those around us the same way we would deal with the Lord Himself. Colossians 3:23 (NLT) says, "Work willingly at whatever you do, as though you were working for the Lord rather than for people." How do we regard family members and coworkers? Whomever we're dealing with, do we sacrifice our own attitudes and behave toward them as we would if it were Jesus?

What can we give to our Savior? In everything we do, He deserves our best.

ARE YOU AVAILABLE?

Who makes them deaf or mute? Who gives them
sight or makes them blind? Is it not I, the LORD?
EXODUS 4:11 NIV

God met Moses at a burning bush and gave him an assignment to lead the children of Israel out of Egypt. Moses recited a litany of excuses for why he wasn't the right choice. He reminded his Creator, "I can't speak well." But the Lord stopped him. "I will help you speak and will teach you what to say" (Exodus 4:12 NIV). All Moses needed to offer was his availability. Everything else comes from God, so it didn't matter that Moses wasn't eloquent.

The Lord invited Moses to be the middleman for incredible miracles during the next forty years. God loves it when we work with Him by doing the natural things He asks us to, while He takes care of the supernatural.

Because Moses was willing (after he stopped trying to avoid the mission), we associate him with the wonders recorded in Exodus. After the plagues that decimated Egypt, God parted the waters of the Red Sea to save Israel and destroy Pharaoh's army. Yahweh provided manna, water, a cloud to lead Israel, a fiery night-light, victory over enemies, and all the other miraculous events. He could have done everything by Himself, but He chose to involve Moses.

The only thing God needs from us is a willing heart. When we're available, He allows us to be a part of His phenomenal handiwork.

RESOLUTE FAITH

And the LORD said to Moses, "How long will these people treat
me with contempt? Will they never believe me, even after
all the miraculous signs I have done among them?"
NUMBERS 14:11 NLT

God didn't expect an answer to this question. Moses had dis-
patched twelve spies to Canaan. They returned with stories about
the bountiful land and even brought back samples of the fruit.
However, ten of them reported, "The people living there are powerful, and their towns are large and fortified" (Numbers 13:28 NLT).

They described the Canaanite giants, saying, "We felt like
grasshoppers next to them. No way can we conquer those people!"
Their dire report set off another round of grumbling from the
Israelites: "If only we had died in Egypt" (Numbers 14:2 NLT).

Though the complaints were aimed at Moses, the words
showed their lack of faith in God. He had already performed
multiple miracles, but in spite of everything He had done for
them, they doubted His ability to overcome the giants in the land.
Only two of the spies gave a positive report. Joshua and Caleb saw
the potential and wanted to go quickly and take possession of the
land. Their attitude was *"We can conquer it!"*

Hebrews 11:6 (NIV) says, "Without faith it is impossible to
please God." Because Joshua and Caleb trusted Him, they were
able to enter the Promised Land. Just two people from that huge
multitude had the kind of faith God looks for.

Is *our* faith delightful to Him?

HOW WRONG IS WRONG?

The LORD said to Samuel, "How long will you mourn for Saul,
seeing I have rejected him from reigning over Israel?"
1 SAMUEL 16:1 NKJV

At first glance, this sounds harsh. But King Saul repeatedly rebelled against God's commands. Immediately before this, when the Lord gave Israel victory over the Amalekites, He told Saul to wipe out everything from that ungodly nation. Instead, the army saved the best of the spoils and destroyed the rest.

Saul claimed he had done what God wanted, but Samuel knew they kept the choice livestock. He asked, "What is that bleating I hear?" If we hang on to things God tells us to get rid of, they will cry out against us.

In 1 Samuel 15:11 (NKJV), God said, "I greatly regret that I have set up Saul as king, for he has turned back from following Me, and has not performed My commandments." Although Saul figured it was fine to save the good animals for a sacrifice, that wasn't what God directed. His Word says, "To obey is better than sacrifice" (1 Samuel 15:22). Saul apparently felt justified. However, that didn't change the facts; partial obedience is the same as disobedience. Samuel grieved over Saul's failures and told him, "The LORD has torn the kingdom. . .from you" (verse 28).

We all make choices to obey or fudge a little. "It was just a little white lie." "No one will notice if I take a few items from work." Really? Whom are we fooling?

PLEASE DON'T TALK ABOUT ME

Then the LORD said to Satan,
"Have you considered my servant Job?"
JOB 1:8 NIV

————

Job was the most righteous man alive at that time. This verse
continues, "There is no one on earth like him; he is blame-
less and upright, a man who fears God and shuns evil." We all
want God to see us the way He saw Job—but we tremble at the
thought of our Lord pointing us out to Satan. We'd rather remain
anonymous and unseen. God's approval set Satan's evil nature on
edge, and he was determined to erase Job's spotless record. . .and
his faith.

Not only was Job upstanding, he was also extremely wealthy
and had a large family. The devil figured Job would turn against
God if everything was taken from him, so in one day Satan
destroyed Job's children and everything he owned.

It's interesting to note that God set limits on how much
damage Satan could do: "The LORD said to Satan, 'Very well, then,
everything he has is in your power, but on the man himself do not
lay a finger'" (Job 1:12 NIV).

Job's first response to the disaster was to fall to the ground and
worship God (Job 1:20).

Everyone experiences devastating situations. The way we
choose to respond to them will either strengthen our faith or tear
us apart. An intimate relationship with Jesus equips us to endure
catastrophes when they occur. Will we shake our fist at God or
worship Him?

THE LIGHT OF THE WORLD

Do you know where Light comes from and where Darkness lives so you can take them by the hand and lead them home when they get lost?
JOB 38:19–20 MSG

In the list of impossible-to-answer questions God posed to Job, this one shows a touch of His sense of humor. Try to imagine grabbing Light and Darkness by the hand to take them home. It might make a cute children's picture book, but it's obviously an impossible observation.

The first thing God made when He created the earth was light. "God spoke: 'Light!' and light appeared. God saw that light was good and separated light from dark" (Genesis 1:3–4 MSG). From the beginning, the Lord wanted His people to live lives filled with Light, not trying to hide from Him. Sin wraps us in a shroud of dark despair, but Light reveals everything.

In the New Testament, we read: "Jesus once again addressed them: 'I am the world's Light. No one who follows me stumbles around in the darkness" (John 8:12 MSG). We don't need to worry about being lost in the darkness of sin and shame, because He is Light. He overcomes the evil one, who wants us to stumble.

We can't lead Light and Darkness to their home. Instead, the Lord Jesus leads us out of darkness to our eternal home, where His Light can never be extinguished.

PRIDE MUST GO

Do you send the lightning bolts on their way?
Do they report to you, "Here we are"?
JOB 38:35 NIV

Can you picture how God's relentless questions must have impacted Job? He had lost everything that was precious to him, and later painful boils erupted all over his body, from head to toe. Then his so-called friends made matters worse, accusing him of bringing trouble on himself through sin. Even his wife said, "Are you still maintaining your integrity? Curse God and die!" (Job 2:9 NIV).

Yet through all his distress, Job never faltered in his faith—or in his insistence that he had done nothing wrong. He did wish he'd never been born or had died as soon as he was born, but he never gave up on God's faithfulness. He took a shot at the men who accused him: "Anyone who withholds kindness from a friend forsakes the fear of the Almighty" (Job 6:14 NIV).

Finally, Job's companions gave up their accusations, and Job stopped proclaiming his righteousness.

Because God spoke.

And Job responded, "My ears had heard of you but now my eyes have seen you. Therefore I despise myself" (Job 42:5–6 NIV). When God shows up, there's no room for pride. Listen to what Isaiah said when he saw the Lord: " 'Woe to me!' I cried. 'I am ruined! For I am a man of unclean lips'" (Isaiah 6:5 NIV). When we come face-to-face with God's magnificence, our hearts are humbled, and submission is the only possible response.

GOD'S CRAZY ABOUT YOU

Have you given the horse its strength or clothed its neck
with a flowing mane? Did you give it the ability to
leap like a locust? Its majestic snorting is terrifying!
JOB 39:19–20 NLT

Powerful horses are majestic, with rippling muscles and flowing manes; their strength can be terrifying. The many questions God posed to Job make the Creator's position crystal clear. People might know how to tame some wild creatures, but no human has the ability to create horses, or any other living thing, from the original cosmos. Genesis 1:24 tells us: "Then God said, 'Let the earth produce every sort of animal, each producing offspring of the same kind—livestock, small animals that scurry along the ground, and wild animals.' And that is what happened."

"Then God said"! Think about that. A single utterance from His mouth releases more power than an army or a missile. He spoke, and the entire universe came into existence.

By the time Job was confronted with this question, he had developed a better understanding of who God was. Before this, he had defended his own righteousness to his friends. Even though he knew there was a God worthy of his worship, he didn't actually comprehend the Lord's magnificence. As Job contemplated the questions, he was awed by the Creator.

We worship the same God, and like Job, we feel insignificant by comparison. Yet God loves us beyond our wildest imagination. Each of us is created to be His special masterpiece.

GOD IS LORD OF ALL

*Will you put him on display in the market
and have shoppers haggle over the price?*
JOB 41:6 MSG

An entire chapter in Job is reserved for questions about Leviathan, a massive sea monster. Again, God's sense of humor shows through when we imagine displaying a terrifying brute like that for sale. Even today in Jerusalem's Old City, merchants sell an unbelievable assortment of goods and are very aggressive about luring people into their shops. A vendor would definitely not display something that would scare shoppers away.

Whether the Leviathan was a crocodile or some other monstrosity men can't tame, we get the picture. God shows His power not only to create, but also to control a frightening beast; His supremacy is beyond our feeble comprehension.

By proclaiming His mastery over Leviathan and every other animal on the earth, God also revealed His lordship over Job's trials. Job had complained about God's injustice, but as the Lord questioned him, Job's heart became tender. He chose to see things differently and submit every part of his life to God's authority.

James 4:7 (NKJV) tells us, "Therefore submit to God. Resist the devil and he will flee from you." Satan's plan from the beginning was to destroy God's people. He wrecked Job's life, but when Job submitted to the lordship of God, Satan beat a hasty retreat. It's as true today as it was then. When the enemy tramples on our lives, we must choose to stay very close to our Savior.

IT'S ALL ABOUT LOVE

*"What do you mean by crushing my people and grinding
the faces of the poor?" declares the Lord, the LORD Almighty.*
ISAIAH 3:15 NIV

There is no adequate answer for this question. The words conjure up images of unspeakable treatment. Think about crushing people and grinding their faces. Throughout the generations, the Lord told His people how to treat each other, but selfishness and pride so often stand in the way of kindness. Verse after verse in this portion of Isaiah deals with the ungodly way people treated one another. When we don't allow God to reign as Lord of our lives, every aspect of society suffers, particularly the poor.

In Deuteronomy, God laid out definitive blessings we can depend on if we do His will. He was just as specific about curses on those who ignore Him and do their own thing. His blessings aren't always what we expect or want—He doesn't promise a cushy life with no problems—but we can sense His blessings even when things are tough.

In the New Testament, Jesus quoted from Deuteronomy 6:5 when a lawyer asked about the greatest commandment. "Jesus replied: 'Love the Lord your God with all your heart and with all your soul and with all your mind.' This is the first and greatest commandment. And the second is like it: 'Love your neighbor as yourself'" (Matthew 22:37–39 NIV).

If we could ever master that concept, everything else would fall into place.

HE KNOWS

Why do you say, O Jacob, and speak, O Israel: "My way is hidden from the LORD, and my just claim is passed over by my God"?
ISAIAH 40:27 NKJV

This question is a little confusing without reading more of the chapter. God asked a number of questions, including this one, about why the people thought He wasn't paying attention to them, and why they believed He didn't care when they were treated unfairly.

The Israelites repeatedly disregarded God's law, but they expected His favor despite their behavior. Did they honestly believe He didn't see what was going on? He showed His divine protection over and over in spite of their rebellion. Maybe that explains why they thought He didn't notice.

Although the people ignored God, He promised never to forget them. "See, I have inscribed you on the palms of My hands" (Isaiah 49:16 NKJV). When spikes pierced Jesus' hands, He remembered His people and those to come.

Throughout the book of Isaiah, the prophet's words rang with power from the Holy Spirit as he tried to direct people back to genuine love and compassion. Isaiah knew God was bored with hollow prayers. He wanted holiness.

Do we ever go to church, sing the songs, listen to a sermon, and leave thinking we're good? If our hearts are unchanged—if we just go through the motions—we're like the people of Isaiah's time. Nothing is hidden from God. Let's rejoice that we know Him and stay close all the time.

IS ANYONE EQUAL TO GOD?

Who compares with me? Speak up. See if you measure up.
ISAIAH 44:7 MSG

If God asked you that question, would you say, "Yeah, I'm probably able to do pretty much everything You can!" Surely no one is brazen enough to feel equal with God. The only reasonable response is to fall to our knees in humble worship. Could we speak at all, or would we be mute before the God of the universe?

In Isaiah 44:1-2 (MSG), the Lord spoke through the prophet: "But for now, dear servant Jacob, listen—yes, you, Israel, my personal choice. GOD who made you has something to say to you; the God who formed you in the womb wants to help you." Then in verse 6, God affirmed His sovereignty as Israel's King, Redeemer, and God-of-the-Angel-Armies. He said, "I'm first, I'm last, and everything in between. I'm the only God there is."

The Lord used Isaiah to assure us of God's endless love, power, and faithfulness. No one compares with Him. He is our *Abba*—Father—and our strength, watching over us from the beginning. No matter what foolish things we do, He is always there, ready to rescue us from the muck of whatever pit we slide into.

Just as in Isaiah's day, God still yearns for every one of us to turn to Him, accept His forgiveness, and trust Him to care for us. Then we can enjoy an abundant life as His precious children.

NO OTHER GOD

To whom will you liken Me, and make Me
equal and compare Me, that we should be alike?
Isaiah 46:5 nkjv

God was determined to convince His people that He was the one true God and that there was none like Him. He spoke through Isaiah, saying that idols could do nothing. They were inanimate objects formed by human hands from gold and silver. They couldn't even move from place to place on their own, much less do anything to help anyone else—yet people worshipped them as gods.

The true God, Yahweh, carries and heals and saves His children and never gives up, no matter how stubborn we may be. Isaiah 45:22 (nkjv) tells us: "Look to Me, and be saved, all you ends of the earth! For I am God, and there is no other."

Over and over we hear the Lord declare His unique position. "For thus says the Lord, who created the heavens, who is God, who formed the earth and made it, who has established it, who did not create it in vain, who formed it to be inhabited: I am the Lord, and there is no other" (Isaiah 45:18 nkjv).

The Lord pleads for an intimate relationship. He reminds us of all He has done and keeps doing for us, how He sustained us from our mothers' wombs until our old age. Even if we are willful and disobedient, nothing can separate us from His love (Romans 8:39).

He yearns for us to love Him in return.

ARE WE REAL?

You humble yourselves by going through the motions of penance,
bowing your heads like reeds bending in the wind. You dress in
burlap and cover yourselves with ashes. Is this what you call fasting?
Do you really think this will please the LORD?
ISAIAH 58:5 NLT

In Bible times people wore sackcloth, a burlap-type fabric, and covered their heads with ashes to show great sorrow. Some also went through an elaborate charade, trying to look pious and distressed when they fasted. Though it may have fooled others, did they really think it impressed the Lord?

Jesus addressed this attitude several hundred years after Isaiah: "And when you fast, don't make it obvious, as the hypocrites do, for they try to look miserable and disheveled so people will admire them for their fasting. I tell you the truth, that is the only reward they will ever get" (Matthew 6:16 NLT). He went on to say that when we fast, we should act natural, not trying to impress others, and our heavenly Father, who sees the secrets of our hearts, will reward us.

Later, Paul warned Timothy about similar hypocrisy. He was very firm: "They will act religious, but they will reject the power that could make them godly. Stay away from people like that!" (2 Timothy 3:5 NLT).

God wants us to be genuine in everything we do. Faith is not based on rituals. He longs for us to be one with Him. When our hearts beat with His, something powerful happens.

BE STRONG IN THE LORD

The word of the LORD came to me again: "What do you see?"
JEREMIAH 1:13 NIV

Jeremiah was still young when the Lord commanded him to speak to the children of Israel. He hesitated at first, feeling inadequate, but God's charge stood. Jehovah touched Jeremiah's lips and said, "I have put my words in your mouth" (Jeremiah 1:9 NIV).

Jeremiah prophesied during the reign of four Judean kings and witnessed the ongoing wickedness of the people. His heart ached for them to return to an intimate relationship with their Creator.

When God showed Jeremiah a vision and asked, "What do you see?" Jeremiah answered, "I see a pot that is boiling. It is tilting toward us from the north" (Jeremiah 1:13 NIV). The Lord explained that calamity would come from the north on all the inhabitants. Armies would come against Jerusalem and the cities of Judah because of their evil lives.

The Lord continued to strengthen Jeremiah. He was to warn the people, and though some fought against him, no one could prevail—because God was with him. On our own, we can't stand against the sinful forces of this world, but our God calls each of us to open our mouths. If we speak the Word of God into others' lives when He leads us, we become participants in His divine, eternal plan. He will give us the words, and the Holy Spirit will empower those words to reveal the loving heart of the Father to the lost.

WORTHLESS IDOLS

Why not go to your handcrafted gods you're so fond of?
Rouse them. Let them save you from your bad times.
You've got more gods, Judah, than you know what to do with.
JEREMIAH 2:28 MSG

The wording of this scripture in *The Message* almost makes God sound like He had an attitude. He didn't, but He *was* trying to get a point across. God was always with His people, and for generations, in spite of their rebellion, He had poured out His love to them. No matter what He did, however, they turned their backs on Him and worshipped worthless idols.

From the beginning, the Israelites should have known God's heart. When He gave Moses the Commandments, the very first one was "You must not have any other god but me" (Exodus 20:3 NLT). His second was equally clear: "You must not make for yourself an idol of any kind. . . . You must not bow down to them or worship them, for I, the LORD your God, am a jealous God who will not tolerate your affection for any other gods" (Exodus 20:4 NLT).

As believers, we would never bow down to idols. But wait! Have we carved a place of vital importance in our lives for possessions, achievements, careers, or even ministry? Do we give such things more affection than we should? Everything we have is a gift from our heavenly Father. We must be careful that insignificant things don't take the place of truly worshipping the Lord.

FICKLE ISRAEL

The LORD said to me, "Have you seen what fickle Israel has done?
Like a wife who commits adultery, Israel has worshiped
other gods on every hill and under every green tree."
JEREMIAH 3:6 NLT

God knew Israel was fickle. Even though she was like a wife who had committed adultery, He continued to love her, to woo her back to His heart. The penalty for adultery in the Old Testament was death, yet God refused to destroy His beloved Israel.

Every time the people faced some catastrophe, they cried out to their God and He rescued them. But they were as unstable as waves in the ocean, moving toward Him then drifting away; they mouthed obedience until the next alluring temptation. They continually slipped into sin. They repented, but it didn't last.

Over a hundred years before Jeremiah, God painted a graphic picture of Israel when He told the prophet Hosea to marry a harlot (Hosea 1:2). Hosea found Gomer and did as the Lord directed. They had three children, but in spite of Hosea's tender love, Gomer abandoned her family to go back to her former life. Just as Gomer returned to prostitution, so Israel wouldn't give up her sinful idolatry. Israel was as precious to God as Gomer was to Hosea, and Hosea's anguish exemplified God's own feelings.

No matter how wayward God's people are, His love for us is patient. His love believes, hopes, and endures all things. His love never fails (1 Corinthians 13:4–8).

DON'T LISTEN TO THE LIE

*Do you not see what they do in the cities
of Judah and in the streets of Jerusalem?*
JEREMIAH 7:17 NKJV

God directed this question to the Israelites through Jeremiah. He wanted them to look at themselves, their own lives, and examine their actions. They weren't sneaking around, doing vile deeds in darkness, thinking they could fool their Father. No. They were parading boldly in the streets of Jerusalem with cakes they baked for a Babylonian goddess, the queen of heaven, and they openly poured out drink offerings to other gods (Jeremiah 7:18).

Long before this, the Lord had said to Moses, "Oh, that they had such a heart in them that they would fear Me and always keep all My commandments, that it might be well with them and with their children forever!" (Deuteronomy 5:29 NKJV).

God's covenant with the people didn't change. He was forever faithful. "Yet they did not obey or incline their ear, but followed the counsels and the dictates of their evil hearts, and went backward and not forward" (Jeremiah 7:24 NKJV).

Israel, especially Jerusalem, has always been a sacred place, chosen by God as a site for worship. Satan wants to demolish the Holy City and, even more, to bring an end to the Jewish people. But his fight is useless. He can cause war and rebellion—as he has throughout the ages—but he will never destroy God's love for His chosen people. Those who trust Him are safe in His care.

OBEDIENCE IS SIMPLE

How can you say, "We are wise, for we have the law of the LORD,"
when actually the lying pen of the scribes has handled it falsely?
JEREMIAH 8:8 NIV

The people of Israel were wrapped up in their own things and didn't seem to know they were doing anything wrong. It should have been simple to love the Lord. "He has shown you, O mortal, what is good. And what does the LORD require of you? To act justly and to love mercy and to walk humbly with your God" (Micah 6:8 NIV). God didn't make it difficult to follow Him.

When the Israelites began to settle in the Promised Land, it was lush and fruitful, and the Lord promised to water the land with rain so it would always produce abundantly. But there was a caveat—they needed to obey Him (Deuteronomy 11:10–17).

The children of Israel managed to stray, repeatedly, even before Moses finished explaining the law. Prior to God's question about how they could think they were wise, He reminded them that even birds knew how they should live. But God's chosen people didn't get it.

The fertile land became a wilderness. Sin does that to the earth and to our souls. When we love the Lord and our hearts line up with His, life is rich and full. That doesn't necessarily mean everything works out perfectly, but when He is in charge, love, joy, peace, and the other fruits of the Spirit grow and satisfy our souls.

HIS LOVE REACHES FURTHER

What right do my beloved people have to come to my Temple,
when they have done so many immoral things?
JEREMIAH 11:15 NLT

Do you hear the anguish in the heavenly Father's question? His love is deeper than we can imagine, yet His children turned their backs on Him. They broke their covenant—and broke His heart—though His servants pleaded with them. His anger at their disobedience shows when He said, "Though they beg for mercy, I will not listen to their cries" (Jeremiah 11:11 NLT).

In verse 14, God told Jeremiah, "Do not weep or pray for them, for I will not listen to them when they cry out to me in distress." It's hard to picture God becoming so furious that He wouldn't even listen to the prophet's prayers. Instead, He would allow Israel's enemies to uproot the people. It shows how hideous their sin was.

Yet in spite of His anger, God said in Jeremiah 12:15 (NLT) that His kindness and love would prevail: "But afterward I will return and have compassion on all of them. I will bring them home to their own lands again, each nation to its own possession."

God isn't wishy-washy. His judgments stand. But His righteous anger in no way negates His amazing forgiveness. His Word assures us today, "God showed his great love for us by sending Christ to die for us while we were still sinners" (Romans 5:8 NLT). No sin is beyond the reach of God's tender compassion or His longing to forgive.

CHOOSING WHOM TO SERVE

Who do you think will waste tears on you?
JEREMIAH 15:5 MSG

A dramatic preacher, Jeremiah never married or had a family of his own (Jeremiah 16:2), but he devoted his life to speaking God's Word. That included a commission to tell a sick nation it was dying. He prophesied, warned, and pleaded with Judah's kings to set their hearts on pleasing the Lord before it was too late. Jeremiah told them they were headed for destruction, but no one heeded his warnings. He tried to convince them that God would heal their fatal disease if only they would turn from sin.

When Jeremiah voiced God's question, asking who would even waste their tears on Israel, what could they say? They were tormented by their own ways but refused to listen to wisdom. Arguing with them was like trying to reason with a willful toddler, determined to have his own way even though it inevitably would lead to trouble.

God could have saved Himself a lot of heartache when He created people by making us like puppets, without self-will. But He knew if we couldn't choose whether or not to love Him, it would be an empty relationship. Forced love is not love at all.

Generations earlier, Joshua challenged the people: "If you decide that it's a bad thing to worship GOD, then choose a god you'd rather serve—and do it today. . . . As for me and my family, we'll worship GOD" (Joshua 24:15 MSG).

WE'RE NEVER TOO FAR

"Am I only a God nearby," declares the LORD,
"and not a God far away?"
JEREMIAH 23:23 NIV

God was outraged by false prophets who spoke lies in His name. He said, "They keep saying to those who despise me, 'The LORD says: You will have peace.' And to all who follow the stubbornness of their hearts they say, 'No harm will come to you'" (Jeremiah 23:17 NIV).

These prophets weren't listening to God or trying to turn the hearts of the people to Him; they condoned Israel's evil conduct. Did they think He couldn't hear what they said or see what they were doing? Did they believe they could move so far from Him they'd be hidden? The Lord fills heaven and earth. He knows even our secret thoughts and yearns for us to humbly run into His safe presence.

God is magnificent in His intimate attention and far-reaching knowledge. He planned our lives—even knew where each of us would live. Acts 17:27 (NIV) tells us, "God did this so that they would seek him and perhaps reach out for him and find him, though he is not far from any one of us."

Even if we drift away and think we've gone too far, He is aware of us and draws us back into a close, tender relationship. He is delighted when we stay near Him. "The LORD is near to all who call on him, to all who call on him in truth" (Psalm 145:18 NIV).

GLORIOUS FUTURE

Why do you cry about your affliction?
JEREMIAH 30:15 NKJV

This verse goes on to say, "Your sorrow is incurable. Because of the multitude of your iniquities, because your sins have increased, I have done these things to you."

Though Israel's condition was critical—almost beyond cure—she would eventually be healed. Her oppressors would be plundered, and her adversaries would become captives (Jeremiah 30:16–17). Why? Not because the people were righteous, but because God is full of mercy and He treasures His children. "For you are a holy people to the LORD your God, and the LORD has chosen you to be a people for Himself, a special treasure above all the peoples who are on the face of the earth" (Deuteronomy 14:2 NKJV).

They were certainly not living holy lives when Jeremiah wrote his prophecies. Their failures were devastating, but God saw beyond that. He knew from the beginning that the destructive lies of Satan would cause His people to falter, over and over. But the Lord would ultimately win the battle.

Our lives are a tiny speck of time. We have successes and failures. We're ecstatic and discouraged. Life is wonderful or couldn't get much worse. In the eternal picture, our time is very brief, but we can live each day knowing He has good things planned. "I know the thoughts that I think toward you, says the LORD, thoughts of peace and not of evil, to give you a future and a hope" (Jeremiah 29:11 NKJV).

WHO WINS?

But what do I see?
JEREMIAH 46:5 NLT

God addressed this question to Pharaoh Necho, who ruled Egypt from 610 to 595 BC. In one major battle, his archers killed Judah's King Josiah (2 Chronicles 35:23). The Egyptians then controlled all of Judah until they were defeated by Nebuchadnezzar. Eventually Egypt's powerful army was beaten down and her influence over Israel and the surrounding nations was shattered. The above verse goes on to say, " 'The Egyptian army flees in terror. The bravest of its fighting men run without a backward glance. They are terrorized at every turn,' says the LORD."

God's dominion is unlimited. Every nation must bow to Him. From His heavenly perspective at the time of this prophecy, the Egyptians were already defeated—terrorized and running for their lives—even though Pharaoh thought they were victorious.

In our own nation, political parties vie for prominence, wealthy men and women fight to be on top, and corporations do whatever it takes to mark their place in history. But no matter who is in the White House, or among the top 500 richest people, or which company logos are universally recognized, God is still on His throne.

People who worship the Lord and delight in serving Him never have to be ashamed of their accomplishments or scheme beyond their natural limits to succeed. "God works in different ways, but it is the same God who does the work in all of us" (1 Corinthians 12:6 NLT). Let Him work through you, and enjoy being allowed to participate.

GOD'S BLESSINGS

If grape pickers came to you, would they not leave a few grapes?
JEREMIAH 49:9 NIV

The sovereign God was about to pour out His wrath on the proud and rebellious people of Edom in order to save the Israelites and restore righteous rule to their land.

God cares about the poor, and He expects His people to help provide for them. Biblical law required farmers not to reap their fields completely but to leave some of the crop so poor people could glean enough grain to sustain themselves. The same was true for those who owned vineyards. Leviticus 19:10 (NIV) says: "Do not go over your vineyard a second time or pick up the grapes that have fallen. Leave them for the poor and the foreigner. I am the LORD your God."

This law wasn't designed to encourage laziness; it enabled those who were experiencing hard times to provide for their needs.

Deuteronomy 24:19 (NIV) explains the concept more fully: "When you are harvesting in your field and you overlook a sheaf, do not go back to get it. Leave it for the foreigner, the fatherless and the widow, so that the LORD your God may bless you in all the work of your hands." If we want God's blessings, we must be willing to help those in need.

When we choose to bless others, pride is ousted and we experience God's great goodness. He looks for humble, compassionate people. "Blessed is the one who is kind to the needy" (Proverbs 14:21 NIV).

ABIDE IN JESUS

Son of man, has not the house of Israel,
the rebellious house, said to you, "What are you doing?"
Ezekiel 12:9 nkjv

Ezekiel heard the call to become a prophet to the children of Israel and he obeyed, even though sometimes what the Lord directed him to do seemed extreme. He dramatized what would happen if the people didn't repent.

Chapter 12 tells how Ezekiel symbolically demonstrated the Judeans being taken into captivity. He dug a hole in the wall of his house, covered his face, and carried only a few belongings on his shoulders through the opening. When the people asked, "What are you doing?" he told them that Judah would be carried into captivity and scattered among the nations (Ezekiel 12:11, 15). It should have shaken them out of their sinful, complacent ways.

The Lord allowed catastrophic experiences for the rebellious Israelites for one reason: "Then they will know that I am the Lord" (verse 16). Ezekiel repeated that phrase over fifty times in the pages of his book.

When God's loving care doesn't grab our attention, He disciplines us and does whatever is necessary to prove that He is Lord. He said through Moses, "You shall walk after the Lord your God and fear Him, and keep His commandments and obey His voice; you shall serve Him and hold fast to Him" (Deuteronomy 13:4 nkjv).

If we follow the ways of the world, we miss an intimate friendship with our Lord.

HEALTHY TRANSPLANTS

But when the vine is transplanted, will it thrive?
EZEKIEL 17:10 NLT

The Lord told Ezekiel to pose a riddle and speak a parable to the house of Israel. He could have simply said, "Look, I've put up with your rebellion long enough. You ignored Me and never lived up to My expectations. I planted you in a good place and gave you everything you needed to thrive, but you continually rebelled."

This time, God wanted the people to figure out for themselves what they were facing and why. The riddle involved an eagle that plucked a twig from a large tree and carried it to another city. Then the eagle planted seed in good soil beside water, so it grew into a vine, but the vine stretched its branches toward another great eagle.

God went on to explain. He reminded them how they trusted in the gods and rulers of other lands to provide for them. When they broke their covenant with the Lord and reached out to other gods, they brought about their own destruction. They couldn't thrive like healthy transplants.

In order to flourish, they needed to repent, ask the Lord to renew them, and let Him transform them into godly people. Romans 12:2 (NLT) tells us: "Don't copy the behavior and customs of this world, but let God transform you into a new person by changing the way you think. Then you will learn to know God's will for you, which is good and pleasing and perfect."

NO WHINING ALLOWED!

Do I hear you saying, "That's not fair! God's not fair!"?
Listen, Israel. I'm not fair? You're the ones who aren't fair!
EZEKIEL 18:25 MSG

Have you ever felt like God isn't fair? When life comes crashing down, it's easy to blame Him, but in truth, because of sin, none of us deserves anything good. If someone isn't fair, it's us, as sinful humans, who expect a happy life with no problems.

When we worship the Lord for who He is rather than what He does for us, we see beyond our troubles and are awed by His grace. Even in the midst of trials, His ways are just.

Listen to the victorious saints in heaven who sing, "Great and marvelous are Your works, Lord God Almighty! Just and true are Your ways, O King of the saints!" (Revelation 15:3 NKJV). If we want to sing the victory songs, we must submit to His perfect ways. In the midst of the hardest times, He is still our Lord and He is worthy of praise.

To get a better perspective on how hard life is, think about the early believers. They were thrown in prison and killed for their faith. The apostle Paul relates his trials in 2 Corinthians 11:23–33, yet he considered himself blessed to suffer for Christ. And James tells us to count it all joy when we fall into various trials (James 1:2).

Rather than feeling sorry for ourselves, let's lift our voices in praise!

GLORIOUS JUDGMENT

*Now, son of man, will you judge, will you judge
the bloody city? Yes, show her all her abominations!*
EZEKIEL 22:2 NKJV

O nly God has the authority to judge others, so why would He ask
Ezekiel to do so? Because the Lord knew this was a man He
could trust to speak what He directed. It would be Ezekiel's voice
but God's words of judgment, poured from His heart of love.

The evil actions of the people broke God's heart. Yet He
promised in 2 Chronicles 7:14 (NKJV), "If My people who are
called by My name will humble themselves, and pray and seek
My face, and turn from their wicked ways, then I will hear from
heaven, and will forgive their sin and heal their land." When we
repent, God has a victory celebration!

Have we changed much since Ezekiel's day? People refuse to
live by God's laws. Many think we must tolerate aberrant behavior
rather than speak truth. Some seldom think of God.

Generations before Ezekiel, in a song of thanksgiving, King
David said: "Let the heavens rejoice, and let the earth be glad. . . .
For He is coming to judge the earth" (1 Chronicles 16:31, 33).
David was called a man after God's own heart. Though he sinned,
he repented and rejoiced at God's judgment.

We, too, can rejoice because of Jesus. "For God did not send
His Son into the world to condemn the world, but that the world
through Him might be saved" (John 3:17 NKJV).

HIS FAVORED ONES

Say to them, "Are you more favored than others?
Go down and be laid among the uncircumcised."
EZEKIEL 32:19 NIV

God gave Ezekiel seven oracles, or prophecies, to warn the Egyptian multitude that He would not always tolerate their unrighteousness. The question in this verse was actually a statement: their nation was not more favored than others and would be consigned to the pit, along with the other godless heathens.

The Egyptians thought they were faultless—better than everyone else. They considered their lifestyle as the perfect benchmark. Other nations' leaders were expected to defer to Pharaoh. Egypt was a superpower. The people were haughty, admired, privileged, and self-absorbed. When we look at our own country today, we see some frightening similarities.

Who are the truly favored ones? Who is most beautiful in God's eyes? Those who obey His Word. Proverbs 12:2 (NIV) says, "Good people obtain favor from the LORD, but he condemns those who devise wicked schemes."

The humble—those who know they are nothing without God—reap His bountiful rewards. "It was not by their sword that they won the land, nor did their arm bring them victory; it was your right hand, your arm, and the light of your face, for you loved them" (Psalm 44:3 NIV).

The way to victory is surrender. When we are so proud we don't realize we're displeasing the Lord, we're in a perilous place. But when we bow before Him, we can bask in His favor.

HE BRINGS LIFE

*Then he asked me, "Son of man,
can these bones become living people again?"*
EZEKIEL 37:3 NLT

The Lord took Ezekiel, in the Spirit, to a valley full of bones. When God asked him this question, Ezekiel replied, "O Sovereign LORD, you alone know the answer to that" (verse 3).

Ezekiel had experienced God's power and didn't doubt His ability to make dry bones into living people again, but he wouldn't be presumptuous. God then told him to prophesy to the bones that they would live, so they would know He is the Lord. Knowing Him as Lord was God's intention in everything that happened to the people—and still is.

What does it take to make us realize that the Lord wants to get our attention—and our love? We walk through our daily lives, working hard to keep up an image, but often feel dry and lifeless. We don't want anyone, even God, to see what we're really like. But no matter how hard we try to appear alive, God knows our hearts. He understands our fears, regrets, and insecurity. More than anything else, He wants to show us He is Lord. So surrender everything to Him and live.

Psalm 24:7 (NLT) tells us: "Open up, ancient gates! Open up, ancient doors, and let the King of glory enter." Are there parts of our lives with closed doors—places we've never opened to Him? Throw open the doors and allow Him to bring healing and life to every dry area.

WILL WE TURN BACK?

Will they not return to Egypt and will not
Assyria rule over them because they refuse to repent?
HOSEA 11:5 NIV

―――――――

We can hear God's sorrow as we read Hosea's prophecy. In Hosea 10, the prophet predicts Israel's destruction, but following on the heels of that, he zeroes in on the Father's love. "I led them with cords of human kindness, with ties of love. To them I was like one who lifts a little child to the cheek, and I bent down to feed them" (Hosea 11:4 NIV).

No matter how much love the Lord poured into His people, they ignored Him and were unfaithful. As slaves in Egypt, they cried for Him to rescue them. But when He did, they complained about everything, from the miraculous manna that sustained them for forty years to Moses' leadership. They wanted to go back to Egypt.

The Messiah rescues each of us when we surrender our lives to Him. Jesus leads us out of our own personal Egypt, where we were in bondage to sin, a cruel taskmaster. At first we're thrilled, like the children of Israel. But when life doesn't happen exactly as we expect, do we want to go back? Even though we were slaves, there was a degree of comfort in the familiar.

Jesus said, "I have come that they may have life, and have it to the full" (John 10:10 NIV). When we stay faithful to Him, our lives are filled with bountiful riches.

STAY TRUE

GOD said to me, "What do you see, Amos?"
AMOS 7:8 MSG

In a vision, Amos saw the Lord standing on a wall with a plumb line in His hand. Builders use plumb lines to make sure walls are perfect—precisely straight. God built Israel absolutely true to His standard. But when He measured her in Amos's day using the same standard, she had become defective and substandard.

So, when God asked Amos what he saw, he simply replied, "A plumb line."

Amos continued, "Then my Master said, 'Look what I've done. I've hung a plumb line in the midst of my people, Israel. I've spared them for the last time. This is it!'"

The people rebelled time and again, until God's patience came to an end. They could have repented at any point, and the Lord would have welcomed them back into His covenant of love. But in their arrogance, they refused to submit to Him or admit they might be wrong.

When God defeated the enemies of Israel and they settled the land, Joshua said, "Not one word failed from all the good words GOD spoke to the house of Israel. Everything came out right" (Joshua 21:45 MSG). But from this pinnacle of success, they slipped into gross immorality.

We can be blind to the truth and convince ourselves we're right. But the Lord will reach out to draw us back where we belong. Nothing is more perfect than to take His hand and step into His loving embrace.

FOLLOW THE LEADER

*Should I not pity Nineveh, that great city, in which are more than
one hundred and twenty thousand persons who cannot discern
between their right hand and their left—and much livestock?*
JONAH 4:11 NKJV

Some of the Bible heroes are amazing, including Jonah.

God told Jonah, "Arise, go to Nineveh, that great city, and
cry out against it; for their wickedness has come up before Me"
(Jonah 1:2 NKJV). So what did Jonah do? He tried to hide from
God by sailing to a distant city. That's when the famous "great
fish" swallowed Jonah and he experienced an epiphany that God's
reach is all-inclusive—unlimited. The realization forced him into
submission.

Jonah warned the people of Nineveh, and they turned from
their evil ways; even the king repented. Heaven rejoiced! God's
warnings are always intended to bring repentance, and His mercy
is available to every humble heart.

But Jonah had his own private pity party. He was angry because God had been merciful to Nineveh. So the Lord continued
to reveal His immeasurable love to Jonah.

Each of us is called to do whatever the Lord has planned. "For
we are His workmanship, created in Christ Jesus for good works,
which God prepared beforehand that we should walk in them"
(Ephesians 2:10 NKJV). We are each a necessary part of God's
eternal design. Whatever the Master calls us to do, whether His
plans are grand or simple, our lives will make a difference when
we obey Him.

GIVE GOD YOUR BROKEN HEART

What good is an idol carved by man, or a cast image that deceives you?
How foolish to trust in your own creation—a god that can't even talk!
HABAKKUK 2:18 NLT

Habakkuk lived during a critical period of Judah's history and was charged with a difficult task. He needed to warn the people of impending doom if they wouldn't give up their meaningless gods and return to the true God. The world around them was at war; they struggled with fear of invasion. But instead of trusting the Creator, they surrounded themselves with worthless idols.

Even in our high-tech world, there are people who worship man-made idols. Buddha statues clutter some countries. People in Hindu cultures bow before multiple grotesque gods, offering sacrifices the icons can't even see. Some who claim to be Christians kneel before stone carvings of angels or saints, or they kiss images of Christ.

"The LORD is in his holy Temple. Let all the earth be silent before him" (Habakkuk 2:20 NLT). In contrast to lifeless idols, the living God is powerful, ever ready to reveal Himself to those who come to Him with humble hearts.

"The sacrifice you desire is a broken spirit. You will not reject a broken and repentant heart, O God" (Psalm 51:17 NLT). The Lord yearns for our love—the only thing He has chosen not to control. Why would anyone choose a piece of stone when we're invited into an intimate relationship with the Master of the universe?

GODLY LOVE

"I have loved you," says the LORD. "But you ask,
'How have you loved us?' Was not Esau Jacob's brother?"
declares the LORD. "Yet I have loved Jacob."
MALACHI 1:2 NIV

Esau was an impetuous outdoorsman who seemed to enjoy life, until things got twisted. Although we're told he was his father's favorite, Esau didn't honor Isaac as a loving son would. He married two women his parents didn't approve of, sold his birthright for a bowl of stew, and was outfoxed by his twin brother when their father passed out blessings.

God's covenant relationship with Israel came through Jacob, Esau's twin. The Lord loved Jacob and his descendants beyond measure, but later, like Esau, they, too, ignored their birthright. Like Esau, they failed to value and treasure what was most precious.

We know "God does not show favoritism" (Romans 2:11 NIV), so the thought of Him loving Jacob more than Esau can be troubling. But He knows from the beginning who will follow Him and who won't. He offers unselfish agape love—the kind that expects nothing in return—even to those who ignore Him. But we have to respond to that love.

If the children of Israel had actually compared their condition with that of Edom, Esau's descendants, they might have seen God's tender care in spite of their adulterous behavior.

Sometimes we feel like He hasn't shown us any love. We hurt and want Him to make things right. But when we truly worship Him in the midst of our pain or sadness, we will be overwhelmed with love beyond measure.

WHEN GOD ISN'T PLEASED

Offer it then to your governor! Would he be pleased with you?
MALACHI 1:8 NKJV

People were offering defiled food on God's altar, the refuse and the spoiled. He had commanded them to offer animals without defect, but they had been sacrificing blind sheep, lame goats, and sick bulls—the worst of their flocks and herds, animals they themselves didn't want. They were treating the Lord with contempt, acting as if He were blind and wouldn't notice. God asked them to think for a moment what the reaction would be if they offered such things to their earthly rulers.

Too often today Christians treat God the same, thinking that He won't notice if they drop mere scraps from their paycheck in the offering basket, after their own needs and desires have been fully met. Or they profess that they love and worship the Lord but treat their fellow human beings—God's own children—roughly and unfairly. What parent would be pleased if you praised them, but slapped their child in front of them?

God is pleased, however, when you show love and mercy to your fellow man, and give generously to the needy and to His cause. If you bear in mind how another human would react to your attitude and behavior, you get an idea of how God feels. Remember, Jesus said, "Inasmuch as you did it to one of the least of these My brethren, you did it to Me" (Matthew 25:40 NKJV).

JESUS STRIPS DEATH'S POWER

Who got the last word, oh, Death?
Oh, Death, who's afraid of you now?
1 CORINTHIANS 15:55 MSG

The Message is a paraphrased version of the Bible, but in the two verses following this question we find significant insight to the above question. "It was sin that made death so frightening and law-code guilt that gave sin its leverage, its destructive power. But now in a single victorious stroke of Life, all three—sin, guilt, death—are gone, the gift of our Master, Jesus Christ" (1 Corinthians 15:56–57 MSG).

For those who have never trusted Jesus to forgive their sins, death can be terrifying. Even if they won't admit it, there is an instinctive, deep knowing that eternity is real and that God actually exists. Without faith in Jesus, they have no hope after they die.

Nearly everyone realizes they are sinners. Some flaunt their wrongdoing to the end. Others claim there is no God, no heaven, no hell. Death is just an end. But what if those friends who talk about spiritual things are right? What if. . . ?

When we put our hope in Jesus—believe He died on the cross to sanctify us—and have faith that God raised Him from the dead, fear of death disappears. When our physical bodies die, we begin real life. In John 11:25 (NKJV) Jesus gives His promise: "I am the resurrection and the life. He who believes in Me, though he may die, he shall live."

DOING WHAT'S RIGHT

If you do what is right, will you not be accepted?
GENESIS 4:7 NIV

When humans were still new on the earth, God gave them knowledge of agriculture and animal husbandry. He also taught them that they were to sacrifice lambs to Him as thank offerings and sin offerings. Now, Abel kept sheep, so when it came time to make an offering to God, he sacrificed a lamb from the flock. However, Cain tilled the soil, so he offered some of his produce. God was pleased with Abel's offering but not with Cain's, and this angered Cain. But God asked him, "If you do what is right, will you not be accepted?"

Ever since that day, people have been trying to please God by presenting to Him the fruit of their own efforts, thinking that their righteous works will please Him. On the other hand, those who look to God to make them righteous trust in the blood of Jesus, the Lamb of God. And God accepts them.

Do you want to do what's right and be sure that God accepts you? When the Jews asked Jesus, "What must we do to do the works God requires?" He answered, "The work of God is this: to believe in the one he has sent" (John 6:28–29 NIV). You must not only trust in Jesus to save you, but also trust Him to give you the grace, mercy, and power to live for Him each day.

GOD KNOWS YOU WELL

Have not I the LORD?
EXODUS 4:11 KJV

When God told Moses that He was sending him to Pharaoh to tell him to let His people go free from bondage in Egypt, Moses objected. He argued that he wasn't capable; after all, he stumbled in his speech and stuttered when he spoke. So God asked him who had made his mouth. God then answered with a question: "Have not I the LORD?" He let Moses know that He was fully aware of his speaking limitations since He had *made* his mouth, but that Moses' inabilities presented no problem to Him.

It doesn't do a lot of good to object when God asks you to do something. He knows everything about you, and He takes all of your strengths and weaknesses into consideration before He plans what you will do for Him. If He asks you to do something that you feel is beyond your abilities, He will give you supernatural help to get the job done. Either that, or He will send someone to help you. This is what He did for Moses. He sent his brother, Aaron, to be his spokesman.

Often, however, God knows that with His help you actually have it in you to do things that you never thought you could—and you just need to be stretched a bit and grow. So trust God that He knows what He's doing. He's well aware of what He has to work with.

CULTIVATE A BELIEVING ATTITUDE

*How long shall I bear with this evil
congregation who complain against Me?*
NUMBERS 14:27 NKJV

When the Israelites arrived at an oasis south of Canaan, they sent spies into the land. Forty days later, the spies returned, and most of them insisted that they couldn't conquer the Promised Land. The Israelites then complained that God had brought them all this distance only to let the Canaanites kill them. This deeply grieved the Lord, and He spoke to Moses about "all these men who have seen My glory and the signs which I did in Egypt and in the wilderness, and have put Me to the test now these ten times, and have not heeded My voice" (verse 22).

Like the Israelites, modern believers are frequently guilty of doubting that the Lord is able to fulfill His promises and give them victory in different areas of their life. Even though they've seen God do miracles many times in the past, they refuse to believe that He will help them *now*, and instead complain that the Lord has abandoned or failed them.

It's vital to keep God's faithfulness in mind and not forget His miracle-working power. Look to Him in trust, even when the test rages hot and you're tempted to doubt. Instead of complaining that He's about to fail you, cultivate a thankful attitude. Thank Him for all the victories He's gained in the past, and it will encourage you to believe for the future.

GOD SAYS NO, THEN BLESSES

Are you the one to build a house for me to live in?
2 SAMUEL 7:5 NLT

———————

David didn't think it was right that he lived in a new, beautiful cedar-paneled palace, but the ark of the covenant representing God's presence was housed in a cloth tent. So he told the prophet Nathan that he wished to build God a temple, an impressive edifice of marble, gold, and cedar. However, God had Nathan tell David that he wouldn't be the one to build a temple, but his son would. After saying this, however, God gave a powerful promise: *He* would build *David's* house—his descendants would sit upon the throne of Israel forever.

Often Christians have well-meaning ideas of how to serve God, but they haven't thought the details through carefully, or they aren't in possession of all the facts like God is. Or the idea might be a good one, but the timing simply isn't right. There are many reasons why even very good proposals and seemingly inspired plans won't work.

But God knows your heart, and even though He might not give you a green light to do what you envision right here and now, He blesses you accordingly—just as He did David in this situation. And David blessed God in return. He happily made many preparations—including drawing up blueprints—for the temple so that when his son *did* build it, he would have everything he needed (1 Chronicles 22).

ENOUGH OF YOUR NONSENSE!

Why do you confuse the issue? Why do you talk
without knowing what you're talking about?
Job 38:2 msg

Throughout the book named after him, Job repeatedly protested that he was innocent and had done nothing wrong to deserve the troubles God had allowed to enter his life. He demanded an audience with the Almighty so that he could present his case before Him. Job had started out wisely, refusing to accuse God of wrongdoing, but as time had gone on, he had eventually made it plain that he thought the Lord was being unfair. So in the end God showed up and asked him, "Why do you talk without knowing what you're talking about?"

When experiencing a prolonged period of confused suffering, modern believers tend to react the same way Job did—except that they're usually quite a bit *more* vocal in laying blame at God's feet. For example, you may wonder why Job protested so much, only to find yourself passionately pouring out your grievances to God in prayer when you yourself suffer.

In addition, you may reason back and forth, trying to figure out why you're experiencing trouble, but instead of achieving any clarity on the issue, you end up only confusing matters. It's not wrong to ask questions, but you must keep a trusting attitude and remain thankful. And you must be willing to let the jury remain out, and be content, even though you don't have all the answers you seek.

SNOW, HAIL, AND RAIN

Have you entered the storehouses of the snow or
seen the storehouses of the hail, which I reserve
for times of trouble, for days of war and battle?
JOB 38:22–23 NIV

In ancient days, kings had armories, storehouses of weapons that they kept for times of trouble such as sieges and days of war. God, too, has storehouses of weapons. He uses snow—and particularly hail—to batter His enemies. He demolished the Amorite armies at Gibeah with hailstones (Joshua 10:11; Isaiah 28:2). He also sent heavy rain to judge His people (1 Samuel 12:16–18).

Just before God questioned Job, a man named Elihu had stated, "The breath of God produces ice. . . . He brings the clouds to punish people, or to water his earth and show his love" (Job 37:10, 13 NIV). What a beautiful thought! While hail or heavy rain are sometimes used to punish, God also sends much-needed rain to demonstrate His love.

God promises, "There will be showers of blessing" (Ezekiel 34:26 NIV). We like that part of the verse, but there's a catch: In the *first* half of the verse, God specifies, "I will send down showers in season." That's often the reason that He doesn't answer your prayers right away. You have to wait until it's time. "Therefore be patient, brethren. . . . See how the farmer waits for the precious fruit of the earth, waiting patiently for it until it receives the early and latter rain" (James 5:7 NKJV).

DESIGNER OF AMAZING BRAINS

Who has put wisdom in the mind?
Or who has given understanding to the heart?
JOB 38:36 NKJV

God asked these questions of Job to drive home the point that He, God, was all-knowing and knew what He was doing, even though His workings looked like a hopelessly unjust mess to Job. In response to God's questions, Job had *no idea* how the human brain worked. We today have a far better understanding of how its incredibly complex neurotransmitters function and how it processes information—yet we're still just dipping our intellectual toe, so to speak, into the shallow end of the pool. We only grasp a tiny bit of all there is to know.

Some Hebrew scholars say that these questions should be translated, "Who has put wisdom in the ibis? Or who has given understanding to the rooster?" That would explain this verse being in the midst of passages about the weather, since the ancient peoples observed the behavior of the ibis and rooster to learn about looming weather changes. If this is the correct translation, then God's questions focus on the mysterious wisdom of His creatures—what we call instincts.

But whether we're talking about how *human* minds got wisdom or how the *ibis* got wisdom, the issue boils down to who designed brains with such amazing intelligence in the first place. And the logical answer is that there has to be a supreme being behind it all.

INSTINCT AND DIVINE WISDOM

*Does the hawk fly by your wisdom, and spread its
wings toward the south? Does the eagle mount up
at your command, and make its nest on high?*
JOB 39:26–27 NKJV

The Eurasian sparrow hawk is not native to Israel but is a migrating bird from the cold regions of northern Europe that briefly stops in Israel during its annual migration to Africa. Hence the statement that it flies "toward the south." And eagles instinctively make their nests "on high," in inaccessible locations where their young are safe from predators.

The instincts of the hawk and the eagle are based on God's wisdom; His commands are written into their DNA. When you see an intricate code that operates computer programs, you know that an intelligent human mind has designed it. Just so, nature is filled with intricate programming that displays God's handiwork. Mankind's genius at creating computer codes only serves to underscore the fact that an intelligent Creator must have been responsible for designing the incredibly complex world around us.

The Bible proclaims, "Great is our Lord, and mighty in power; His understanding is infinite" (Psalm 147:5 NKJV). And precisely because God's understanding is *infinite*, you can trust your life to Him. Your heavenly Father, who guides every sparrow hawk, also watches over every sparrow (Matthew 10:29). And this same God cares for you and is watching over you. "Do not fear therefore; you are of more value than many sparrows" (Matthew 10:31 NKJV).

DON'T MESS WITH DRAGONS

Could you shoot him full of arrows like a pin cushion,
or drive harpoons into his huge head?
JOB 41:7 MSG

In Job 41:1 (MSG), God describes "the sea beast, Leviathan." Many Christians are convinced that since it breathed fire (verses 19–21), Leviathan was a dragon-like plesiosaur. Others speculate that this is simply a poetic description of a Nile crocodile. However, though it was a dangerous endeavor, the ancient Egyptians *did* hunt crocodiles, so it seems Leviathan was more than a river reptile.

While its exact identity makes for interesting conjecture, God's main point was that if Job couldn't overcome Leviathan, how could he prevail against the Supreme Being who had *created* this monster? God warned, "If you so much as lay a hand on him, you won't live to tell the story. . . . If you can't hold your own against his glowering visage, how, then, do you expect to stand up to me?" (Job 41:8–10 MSG).

So often, like Job, Christians think God has made a mistake and wish they could gain control of the reins of power for a while—merely long enough to set Him straight. But just as giving it your best shot would be useless against Leviathan, so you're utterly unable to correct God and get Him to do your will. He is Lord and Master, and although you can sometimes understand what He's doing in your life, most of the time you'll have to be content just to trust Him.

GOD'S VINEYARD

What could have been done more to my vineyard,
that I have not done in it?
ISAIAH 5:4 KJV

Isaiah told a parable, saying, "My Well-beloved has a vineyard on a very fruitful hill. He dug it up and cleared out its stones, and planted it with the choicest vine. He built a tower in its midst, and also made a winepress in it; so He expected it to bring forth good grapes, but it brought forth wild grapes" (Isaiah 5:1–2 NKJV). God then explained in verse 7: "The vineyard of the LORD of hosts is the house of Israel. . . . He looked for justice, but behold, oppression; for righteousness, but behold, a cry for help."

God went to a great deal of trouble to cultivate godliness in His people, and He made extensive preparations for extracting the juice when they bore the fruit of righteousness. But they bore bitter, useless fruit instead. Likewise today, God puts forth great effort to cultivate godliness in His children. If people fail as Christians, it's not for lack of God's love and care. He asks, "What could have been done more to my vineyard, that I have not done in it?"

God is hard at work in many levels of your life. He leaves no stones unturned. But if you continually graft wild tendrils to your branch—sin and hatred and selfishness—instead of bearing fruit of "the choicest vine," you'll bear bitter fruit, useless for God's kingdom. So bear the good fruit of God's vine!

BASIC PUBLIC INFORMATION

Have you not known?
ISAIAH 40:28 NKJV

===

The Jews were succumbing to discouragement and complaining, "My way is hidden from the LORD, and my just claim is passed over by my God" (Isaiah 40:27 NKJV). So He asked them, "Have you not known? . . . The everlasting God, the LORD, the Creator of the ends of the earth, neither faints nor is weary. His understanding is unsearchable" (verse 28). Not only was God fully aware of their troubles, but He had limitless strength, so He was able to resolve their problems. In the meantime, He promised to breathe life into them.

On a purely intellectual level, you assent to these things. After all, God, to *be* God, has to have limitless wisdom and understanding. And you're aware that His Word says that He loves you. But on an emotional level, it's easy to come to the same conclusion as the ancient Jews did—that the reason God isn't acting on your behalf is because He has a blind spot when it comes to your problems. He doesn't know about them. But God questions how much *you* know when you assume such things.

The Lord had made it clear in the law of Moses that He was the eternal, omniscient, omnipotent God who had a deep, unchanging love for His children. This information is on public record. Whenever you start doubting these basic things, God returns your focus to them. Today, as in Isaiah's day, He asks, "Have you not known?"

GOD WILL TAKE ACTION

Will you not admit them?
ISAIAH 48:6 NIV

Most Jews in Isaiah's day worshipped idols, all the while mouthing faith in God. So He informed them, "I foretold the former things long ago. . .then suddenly I acted, and they came to pass. . . . Before they happened I announced them to you so that you could not say, 'My. . .metal god ordained them'" (verses 3, 5). Then God challenged His people: "You have heard these things; look at them all. Will you not admit them?" (verse 6). The proof of His power and love and care was now before their eyes, but knowing how stubborn and in denial His people were, God challenged them to own up to the facts.

Apart from prophesying about future events, God often makes personal promises. But His people often become impatient waiting for them. After all, the Lord says, "I foretold the former things *long ago*." As time drags on and the promised events don't come to pass, you can lose faith that they *ever* will. But take heart! God goes on to say, "Then *suddenly* I acted." That's so often the way He works.

God told Habakkuk, "The revelation awaits an appointed time; it. . .will not prove false. Though it linger, wait for it; it will certainly come and will not delay" (Habakkuk 2:3 NIV). God may require you to wait patiently for His promises to come to fruition, but be assured that He has an appointed time for their fulfillment.

DON'T FEAR GRASS

*Who are you that you fear mere mortals, human beings who
are but grass, that you forget the LORD your Maker. . .?*
ISAIAH 51:12–13 NIV

God's people were terrified of the Assyrians—with good reason,
it seemed. The Assyrians were merciless killers. When they
conquered a city, they beheaded thousands and piled the heads in
heaps. They frequently skinned people alive. God told His people,
"You live in constant terror every day because of the wrath of the
oppressor, who is bent on destruction" (verse 13). We today face
enemies who employ similar tactics, and like the ancient Assyrians, their goal is to strike terror into the hearts of the nations.

But God warns you, like He warned the Israelites, not to
fear. He reminds you that your enemies are mere men. They are
"but grass," and Psalms declares, "The life of mortals is like grass,
they flourish like a flower of the field; the wind blows over it and
it is gone" (Psalm 103:15–16 NIV). God understands that you'll
be tempted to fear, but He reminds you that He's infinitely more
powerful than your enemies and that giving in to fear means you
have taken your eyes off of Him.

He declares, "I am the LORD your God. . . . I have put my
words in your mouth and covered you with the shadow of my
hand" (Isaiah 51:15–16 NIV). When you're tempted to fear, quote
God's powerful promises. And remember, He will protect you. He
has you covered.

TRUE FASTING

Do you call that fasting, a fast day that I, GOD, would like?
ISAIAH 58:5 MSG

The idea of fasting is to turn from mundane preoccupations and to focus on God and His will. The Israelites started out right by refraining from food, but they failed to turn to God and change their sinful habits. As a result, they were merely going through the motions. Then they complained to God that He didn't bless them for fasting. So He asked them, "Do you think this is the kind of fast day I'm after: a day to show off humility? To put on a pious long face and parade around solemnly in black?" (verse 5).

Now, as then, there are times when God calls His people to a fast—not merely to skip a few meals, but to fast from selfish, unloving habits and actions. You are to fast from taking advantage of others and from exploiting your workers. You are to do true justice. God adds, "Share your food with the hungry, and give shelter to the homeless. Give clothes to those who need them, and do not hide from relatives who need your help" (verse 7 NLT).

Do these things and God's blessing will be upon your life. You won't have to ask God why He's not blessing you, because "blessings shall come upon you and overtake you" (Deuteronomy 28:2 NKJV). "Then when you call, the LORD will answer. 'Yes, I am here,' he will quickly reply" (Isaiah 58:9 NLT).

SATISFIED WITH GOD

What did your ancestors find wrong with
me that led them to stray so far from me?
JEREMIAH 2:5 NLT

The younger generation of Israelites was different from their un-believing parents, and they had the faith to follow God through desolate regions and into the Promised Land. So He said, "I remember how eager you were to please me as a young bride long ago, how you loved me and followed me even through the barren wilderness" (verse 2). But after the Israelites settled in Canaan, they abandoned God to worship idols. So He asked, "What did your ancestors find wrong with me that led them to stray so far from me?"

If you were to ask this question of many people today, you'd likely hear several answers: God, they insist, doesn't love them because He doesn't answer their prayers and give them what their hearts desire. Or, God is cruel because He allows wars and fam-ines in which innocent people die. Or, God isn't fair because He lets wicked oppressors become wealthy while the righteous barely earn enough to live on.

As a result, people's hearts grow cold to God and they drift away from Him. But these objections only reveal a lack of spiritual depth and betray a misunderstanding of God and His ways. "God is love" (1 John 4:8 NLT). And David declared, "You *are* good, and *do* good" (Psalm 119:68 NKJV, emphasis added). There's nothing wrong with God to cause you to leave Him.

ACCUSING GOD

Why do you bring charges against me?
JEREMIAH 2:29 NIV

Judah had abandoned the Lord and bowed down to idols that they had formed themselves. When trouble came, they prayed to these false gods, but when no help came, they halfheartedly decided to give God another try. But He replied, "Where then are the gods you made for yourselves? Let them come if they can save you when you are in trouble!" (verse 28). Because God didn't help them, the Jews accused Him of failing them. But He replied, "Why do you bring charges against me? You have all rebelled against me" (verse 29).

If you find yourself blaming God for not coming through for you, you're already in a losing game. Invariably, the fault lies not with God but with you. God has promised to help, but He has also made it clear that you must be obedient to Him if you expect Him to answer your prayers. Often, however, "your sins have hidden his face from you, so that he will not hear" (Isaiah 59:2 NIV).

But never lose sight of this fact: As a Christian, you're guaranteed forgiveness in Jesus Christ. "If we confess our sins, he is faithful and just and will forgive us our sins and purify us from all unrighteousness" (1 John 1:9 NIV). Pray sincerely to God today, and be restored to full fellowship with Him. You can richly enjoy His blessing on your life again.

ABANDONED TO YOUR DEVICES

Why should I even bother with you any longer?
JEREMIAH 5:7 MSG

God's words through Jeremiah may seem harsh to our ears and seem to be offering little hope, but you must understand that God had been patient—*very* patient—with His people for many decades, repeatedly pleading with them to get their hearts right with Him. During that entire time, He "supplied all their needs," but how did they thank Him? He told the Jews, "Your children have forsaken me. . .their rebellion is great and their backslidings many" (Jeremiah 5:6–7 NIV). And they were even now refusing to listen to His prophet Jeremiah.

In the days before the flood, "the LORD said, My spirit shall not always strive with man" (Genesis 6:3 KJV). There comes a time when God ceases striving with people's hearts and gives up trying to change them. He warns that those who stubbornly refuse to listen to repeated correction will finally be destroyed, and there will no longer be any remedy offered (Proverbs 29:1). But it takes a very long time to get to that point.

Even though God now told the Jews that their time had nearly run out and that judgment was looming, He continued to give warnings to them, urging them to repent. God has such amazing compassion and patience that we can't understand it. The Bible tells us that "he is patient with you, not wanting anyone to perish, but everyone to come to repentance" (2 Peter 3:9 NIV).

CAUSING YOURSELF TROUBLE

But is it me they're hurting? . . . Aren't they just hurting themselves?
Exposing themselves shamefully? Making themselves ridiculous?
JEREMIAH 7:19 MSG

The people of Judah oppressed widows, orphans, and the poor, committed adultery, murdered the innocent, and worshipped pagan gods. The children gathered wood, the men made fires, and the women baked cakes on them for the evil goddess Ashtoreth, the so-called Queen of Heaven. Then they would troop faithfully into God's temple. Yet all the while, as God said, "they go around pouring out libations to any other gods they come across, just to hurt me" (verse 18). But they were only really hurting themselves.

Some people actually attempt to snub God to get back at Him because they think that He's treated them unfairly. This attitude is immature and self-defeating. When they're angry with God and flaunt their disobedience before Him, they only make fools of themselves. This is a game that mortals can't win, so it's a good idea to come to God in humility and love.

God longs for fellowship with you, and the truth is, you *can* sometimes grieve His Spirit (Ephesians 4:30). But the one you're really hurting by your disobedience is yourself. You can't really hurt God. He will still be complete and utterly perfect no matter what you do. However, His heart will go out to you in pity and grief, knowing that you're losing out on the fullness of life and the joy you could have known.

MERCY EVEN IN JUDGMENT

Can their vows and sacrifices prevent their destruction?
JEREMIAH 11:15 NLT

Jeremiah had given his people warnings for decades, but they refused to repent. Finally, the *only* thing left that could wake them up and turn them back to God was to suffer judgment. So God said, "I am going to bring calamity upon them. . . . Though they beg for mercy, I will not listen to their cries" (verse 11). Apparently some of the Jews had been vowing to do better, because God asked, "Can their vows and sacrifices prevent their destruction?"

A modern example sheds light on this: Men and women committed to the Alcoholics Anonymous program have heard every excuse, promise, and vow imaginable from fellow alcoholics—but they're not buying any of it. They've been down that same road, and experience has taught them that people usually have to hit rock-bottom before they're willing to commit their lives to God and ask for His help.

When God finally determines to judge an individual or nation, it's usually the last resort, necessary because nothing else has worked. It took the destruction of their nation and a seventy-year exile in Babylon for the Jews to finally turn back to God. So God has a plan for mercy even in the midst of drastic actions.

But it's better to repent *before* that point. In Revelation 3:19 (NIV), Jesus says, "Those whom I love I rebuke and discipline. So be earnest and repent."

WHO CARES?

Who will stop to ask how you are?
JEREMIAH 15:5 NIV

God loved His people more than they could imagine, and He watched over them, protected them, and blessed them. His eyes were continually on their land, and He cared for it all year long (Deuteronomy 11:12). Thus, they did themselves a huge disservice when they abandoned Him and trusted rain and fertility gods to provide for them. When God was shut out, He asked, whom did they expect to care for them now? Who would be concerned enough to stop and ask how they were doing? The answer was "No one."

Many modern people have done something similar. They grow tired of their husband or wife, grow bored of their marriage routine, and take their love and care for granted. So they dump them and hitch their wagon to a more satisfying, "fulfilling" relationship. They find it exciting for a while, but eventually it comes crashing down. Only after further disappointments do they realize how good they had it with their former spouse.

If you're becoming bored with either the Lord or your mate and are thinking of going your own way, it would be good to count your blessings and learn to be satisfied with what you have. Probably no one will care for you like your present mate does—or be as willing to put up with your annoying habits. And certainly no one will love you like God does!

YOU CAN'T HIDE

Who can hide in secret places so that I cannot see them?
JEREMIAH 23:24 NIV

In Jeremiah and Ezekiel's day, the Jews said, "The LORD does not see us" (Ezekiel 8:12 NIV). But God replied, "Who can hide in secret places so that I cannot see them?" He then asked, "Do not I fill heaven and earth?" God was saying that since He existed everywhere, no matter *where* they chose to hide, He was already there, occupying that space.

David described this, saying, "If I go up to the heavens, you are there; if I make my bed in the depths, you are there. . . . If I say, 'Surely the darkness will hide me and the light become night around me,' even the darkness will not be dark to you; the night will shine like the day, for darkness is as light to you" (Psalm 139:8, 11–12 NIV).

You can't hide from God, so you might as well not even attempt it. But you may reason that even though God *can* see you, He's not paying attention and won't require you to give an account for your actions and words. So you can get away with things as if you *were* hiding. Don't be fooled. God sees and knows everything and will definitely call you before His judgment seat one day.

"Nothing in all creation is hidden from God's sight. Everything is uncovered and laid bare before the eyes of him to whom we must give account" (Hebrews 4:13 NIV).

BY INVITATION ONLY

I will invite him to approach me. . .
for who would dare to come unless invited?
JEREMIAH 30:21 NLT

———————

The almighty God is surpassingly beautiful and magnificent, yet He is also dangerous. When Moses asked to see His face, God told him, "You cannot see My face; for no man shall see Me, and live" (Exodus 33:20 NKJV). Likewise, when the high priest entered the holy of holies once a year, he had a rope tied to his ankle so that if he was overcome by God's holy presence and died, he could be dragged back out.

This gives context to God's statement that no one would dare approach Him unless he had been invited. It also underlines the wonderful promise in this question: God said that after His people had restored their relationship with Him and were once again living in their land, covered by His protection and blessing, He would invite the leader of His people to come near to Him. This shows that God looked upon His people with favor.

In the New Testament, the unknown author of Hebrews said, "Let us therefore come boldly to the throne of grace, that we may obtain mercy and find grace to help in time of need" (Hebrews 4:16 NKJV). What a wonderful privilege you have as a Christian— access to God's throne and presence. You should still be in awe of God, and not treat Him flippantly, but you need never doubt His love for you.

FLOOD-STOPPING POWER

Who is this like the Nile in flood?
like its streams torrential?
JEREMIAH 46:7 MSG

In Jeremiah's day, Egypt was considered the most powerful nation on earth. God described their armies sweeping forth like the Nile during flood season, when its waters surged over the broad Delta, unstoppable. Thus, in 605 BC, when Pharaoh Neco heard that the Babylonian army under Nebuchadnezzar was on the march, Neco's armies surged forth out of Egypt to engage them at Carchemish, a city far to the north. He confidently thought, "I'll take over the world. I'll wipe out cities and peoples" (verse 8). Instead, the Egyptians suffered a crushing defeat.

When your enemies seem to have no end of strength, like the Egyptian army did, and boast confidently that they're going to obliterate you, this can put you in great fear. And truly, without the Lord's intervention, your situation *can* be hopeless. But when God's on your side, the vaunted strength of your foes can be brought to nothing. In His Word, God has repeatedly promised to protect you. "When the enemy comes in like a flood, the Spirit of the LORD will lift up a standard against him" (Isaiah 59:19 NKJV).

When you're being attacked by your enemies and you fear that they're going to sweep you away, consistently quote God's promises of protection. (See Psalm 5:12; Isaiah 25:4; Zephaniah 3:17; Nahum 1:7.) He will come through for you!

NOBODY ESCAPES JUDGMENT

I tell you, if there are people who have to drink the cup of God's wrath even though they don't deserve it, why would you think you'd get off?
JEREMIAH 49:12 MSG

Jeremiah had prophesied chapter after chapter against the people of Judah, warning that disaster was coming. Most of his nation was deeply involved in sin, though there were a few innocent among them. But judgment couldn't be held back for the sake of the few. They would, unfortunately, suffer along with the guilty. And since the pagan Edomites were *truly* guilty and worthy of judgment, God assured them, "You will not go unpunished!" (Jeremiah 49:12 NLT).

Yet God had mercy even with the Edomites. Though He vowed that the calamity that swept over their land would be so severe that "Edom itself will be no more," He promised, "but I will protect the orphans who remain among you. Your widows, too, can depend on me for help" (verses 10–11 NLT). God is all-powerful and a God of justice, but He wraps a message of tender compassion inside even an announcement of wrath.

But remember, God is just and fair. He's aware that many people who suffer in our world don't deserve it but are simply caught up in the calamity along with the guilty. However, even though the innocent suffer, God will recompense them in the end. Meanwhile, He's determined to make sure that the guilty don't get away without a mark on them.

DELAYED PROPHECIES OF DOOM

*Son of man, what is this proverb you have in the land of Israel:
"The days go by and every vision comes to nothing"?*
EZEKIEL 12:22 NIV

Ezekiel lived in Babylon, and every now and then someone came from Judah, bringing news. They frequently mocked the Judean prophet Jeremiah who had been predicting doom for decades. They joked that many years had passed, but that his predictions hadn't come to pass yet. They accused him of being a failed prophet. They were slightly kinder to Ezekiel, saying, "The vision he sees is for many years from now, and he prophesies about the distant future" (verse 27). Basically, they were saying not to worry about Ezekiel's warnings.

A nation's proverbs sum up its mind-set at a particular point in history. The Jews weren't taking Jeremiah's prophecies seriously, just like people today who continue in their daily routines, untroubled by earthshaking changes, refusing to believe that the world economy will ever crash, or that the oceans are getting polluted, or that our globe will run out of resources. They have no sense of urgency about global events.

The Bible says, "A prudent man foresees evil and hides himself, but the simple pass on and are punished" (Proverbs 22:3 NKJV). If you keep your eyes open, you can see what's coming. After looking around the world today, it shouldn't be too difficult to believe that things have to come to an end soon. The prophets' visions will be fulfilled.

MYSTERIOUS MESSAGES

Will it not utterly wither when the east wind touches it?
EZEKIEL 17:10 NKJV

God gave Ezekiel an allegory: An eagle clipped the highest branch from a cedar and planted it in a distant city. This symbolized the king of Babylon taking Jehoiachin, king of Judah, to exile in Babylon. Then the eagle planted a seed from the cedar in a garden. This symbolized appointing Zedekiah as king in Jerusalem. But Zedekiah reached out his roots and branches to a second great eagle—the Pharaoh of Egypt—to help him rebel against Babylon. God then described the Babylonian army as a scorching desert wind that would wither the cedar.

This sounds straightforward, but when you read this allegory without a historical explanation, it's all very mysterious. So why did God use allegories? Well, after being repeatedly instructed and warned, people no longer listen. But a vivid story grabs their attention, and they don't quickly forget it. This is why Jesus told many parables. He didn't always explain them either, but He left people to mull over what He had said.

You may often wonder why God doesn't explain things plainly, or often doesn't seem to answer clearly when you pray for direction. You have to study, ponder, and consider alternatives to finally understand. It often takes real work to know His will. And that's the whole point. Second Timothy 2:15 (NIV) advises you to be "a worker who. . .correctly handles the word of truth." The learning process is an integral part of the answer.

WHO IS BEING UNFAIR?

Are my ways unjust, people of Israel?
Is it not your ways that are unjust?
EZEKIEL 18:29 NIV

The ancient Jews believed that they were suffering misfortune, not because of anything they had done, but because of their parents' mistakes. By saying this, they were refusing to take ownership of their sins. God explained, "Suppose there is a righteous man who does what is just and right. . . . He will surely live." But if he does evil, "Will such a man live? He will not!" (verses 5, 9, 13). When God explained that everyone was accountable for their own actions, they protested that this wasn't fair. God then asked who was *really* being unfair.

It's popular today for people to blame their parents for all their bad habits, hang-ups, and mental issues. While it's true that traumatic experiences from childhood can have a lasting effect on you, there comes a point when you must take responsibility for your problems. You must forgive those who've offended you and move on. You may argue that this isn't right, but God asks, "Whose ways are *really* not fair?"

It takes a great deal of love and grace to forgive others, and at times you won't feel like you're able to do it. You may have difficulty even believing that God requires this of you—but He does. He says, "Be ye kind one to another, tenderhearted, forgiving one another, even as God for Christ's sake hath forgiven you" (Ephesians 4:32 KJV).

READY TO CONFRONT

Are you ready to judge this city of murderers?
EZEKIEL 22:2 NLT

God laid out a litany of sins that His people were guilty of, and they were truly disgusting transgressions, the kind, unfortunately, that you frequently read about in headlines today. People were not only oppressing others and worshipping idols, but committing murder, adultery, and incest. As Paul said, "It is a shame even to speak of those things which are done of them in secret" (Ephesians 5:12 KJV). Up until that point, Ezekiel had avoided calling people out over specific sins, but God told him to get ready to begin confronting them.

Most people are not that confrontational. You may not readily get in people's faces and tell them what they're doing wrong. But there sometimes comes a time when you must be direct, even if you're ordinarily uncomfortable about it. God told the prophet Isaiah, "Shout with the voice of a trumpet blast. Shout aloud! Don't be timid. Tell my people Israel of their sins!" (Isaiah 58:1 NLT).

God loves people, even when they're sinning, and He wants to get through to them. He will often give you boldness when you're in extenuating circumstances, so that when you sense an overwhelming urge to speak out, and you know it's not just your temper, follow it. "For it is not you who will be speaking—it will be the Spirit of your Father speaking through you" (Matthew 10:20 NLT). Are you ready to speak out?

DON'T TRUST IN YOUR OWN WISDOM

Are you wiser than Daniel?
EZEKIEL 28:3 NIV

God questioned the proud king of Tyre, asking, "Are you wiser than Daniel?" At this time, Daniel was the greatest and wisest of King Nebuchadnezzar's counselors. A later queen mother said, "During Nebuchadnezzar's reign, this man was found to have insight, understanding, and wisdom like that of the gods. . . . This man Daniel. . .is filled with divine knowledge and understanding" (Daniel 5:11–12 NLT).

Alternately, God could have been asking, "Are you wiser than Danel?" Danel was a renowned wise man in ancient literature. "Daniel" seems to be the more likely choice, but whichever name was intended, God was challenging the king of Tyre's vaunted wisdom.

People often get the idea that they're so smart they can figure out everything on their own, and they don't need to listen to God. So they don't. But Jeremiah said, "The wise will be put to shame. . . . Since they have rejected the word of the LORD, what kind of wisdom do they have?" (Jeremiah 8:9 NIV). As it turns out, very little.

You may not take pride in being superwise, but you may still lean on your own understanding (Proverbs 3:5) when making important decisions, and this will work to your detriment. Like the king of Tyre, you may well arrive at the wrong conclusions, influenced by fears and wrong opinions. Remember how Daniel got his wisdom—by praying and trusting God, not himself.

EVIL OPPORTUNISTS

When my people Israel are established securely,
will you make your move?
EZEKIEL 38:14 MSG

═══════════════

This was God's question to Gog, chief ruler of Magog. Now, Magog was a son of Japheth (Genesis 10:2), and he founded a people group inside what is modern Turkey, though many believe that he established his nation in southern Russia. If it's the latter, this chapter may well refer to a Russian invasion of Israel in the end times. Whichever enemy it is, it will be an overwhelming military invasion that will seek to sweep God's people away.

Over the centuries, many nations have invaded Israel and sought to exterminate the Jews, and the fact that they're still around today and established securely in their land is testament to the miraculous protection of God. Most other ancient nations that inhabited the lands around Israel 2,000 to 2,500 years ago no longer exist. The Jews are still going strong, but their evil oppressors and greedy opportunists are no more.

God likewise promises to protect you who have faith in His Son, Jesus Christ. He warns that "everyone who wants to live a godly life in Christ Jesus will suffer persecution" (2 Timothy 3:12 NLT). But He will protect you through it all. You may have cause to exclaim, "If God hadn't been for us when everyone went against us, we would have been swallowed alive by their violent anger, swept away by the flood of rage, drowned in the torrent" (Psalm 124:2–4 MSG).

GOD'S AMAZING COMPASSION

Oh, how can I give you up, Israel?
HOSEA 11:8 NLT

God's people had rebelled against Him for long years, so He finally declared, "War will swirl through their cities; their enemies will crash through their gates. . . . For my people are determined to desert me" (verses 6–7). The enemy was prepared to totally wipe the Israelites out, and the only thing that spared them was that God declared, "My heart is torn within me, and my compassion overflows. No, I will not unleash my fierce anger. I will not completely destroy Israel" (verses 8–9).

God is still merciful today. He disciplines and chastises you when you're disobedient, but He doesn't execute judgment on you in anger. Though He says, "I cannot let you go unpunished," He states, "I will discipline you, but with justice" (Jeremiah 30:11 NLT). God still declares that He cannot, and will not, give up on His people. Although you may sometimes give Him good reason to be angry, His compassion overflows instead.

Many Christians go through life thinking that God is constantly angry at them because of their mistakes and failures, and they fail to realize the depth of His love and compassion. "For God chose to save us through our Lord Jesus Christ, not to pour out his anger on us" (1 Thessalonians 5:9 NLT). Think how much love God has for you! He simply won't give up on you, even when you give up on yourself.

OPEN YOUR EYES

Amos, what seest thou?
AMOS 8:2 KJV

God asked Amos what He saw in a vision, and Amos replied, "A basket of ripe fruit." Then the Lord said, "The time is ripe for my people Israel; I will spare them no longer" (Amos 8:2 NIV). The time of harvest had come, the time to judge their sins. This bears a striking resemblance to the following verse: "Then another angel. . . called in a loud voice to him who was sitting on the cloud, 'Take your sickle and reap, because the time to reap has come, for the harvest of the earth is ripe'" (Revelation 14:15 NIV).

In the past, the time was ripe to judge Israel. In the not-too-distant future, the time will be ripe to judge the entire world. It can be unsettling to think about the coming global troubles, wars, calamities, and disruption of basic services, but as one of God's redeemed children, He calls you to look beyond these things. "Keep your eyes on Jesus" (Hebrews 12:2 MSG). Keep your focus on heaven, on the other side of these troubles.

And remember, the end will not come before the Gospel has been preached to every people group in the entire world (Matthew 24:14). God deeply loves all human beings and longs to see them saved and receive new life in Christ. So, in this period of grace before God's judgment, be faithful to live the Gospel and share it with those around you.

LISTEN AND BE BLESSED

Do not my words do good to the one whose ways are upright?
Micah 2:7 niv

God warned Judah through the prophet Micah, "I am planning disaster against this people, from which you cannot save yourselves. You will no longer walk proudly, for it will be a time of calamity" (verse 3). However, they answered, "Do not prophesy about these things; disgrace will not overtake us" (verse 6). They rejected the thought that God would send calamity upon them. God replied that if they were righteous, they would have nothing to fear. They would be warned by His words, be convicted of their sins, turn, and be spared.

In the Bible, righteous rulers repented when they heard God's warnings, and spared themselves and their nation much trouble (2 Kings 22:10–20). Likewise today, you can spare yourself grief by hearing godly counsel, warnings, and admonitions. You do yourself a huge favor if you listen to older men and women who have lived lives of service to the Lord and have experienced all the pitfalls and temptations that you're now facing. Pay attention if they warn you that a certain course of action you're taking leads to ruin.

The Bible says, "Poverty and shame will come to him who disdains correction, but he who regards a rebuke will be honored" (Proverbs 13:18 nkjv). And God promises, "Come and listen to my counsel. I'll share my heart with you and make you wise" (Proverbs 1:23 nlt).

GOD SPEAKS TO YOU

Can an idol tell you what to do?
HABAKKUK 2:19 NLT

God said through the prophet Habakkuk, "How foolish to trust in your own creation—a god that can't even talk! Can an idol tell you what to do? They may be overlaid with gold and silver, but they are lifeless inside" (verses 18–19). Idols were typically carved from cheap blocks of wood but made to look impressive and valuable by being covered with a thin layer of silver or gold. But that didn't stop them from being dead. When you're in an emergency, an idol can't give you advice.

Throughout the scriptures, the Lord refers to Himself as "the living God" (Isaiah 37:4, 17). This was in stark contrast to lifeless idols. God can not only answer prayers, but He can speak to His people and tell them what to do. Some Christians don't think that God *can* still speak today—but He speaks into your life every time you read your Bible with a believing, expectant attitude. That's why you should pray, "Open my eyes to see the wonderful truths in your instructions" (Psalm 119:18 NLT).

In addition, God often speaks in your heart with the "still small voice" of His Spirit (1 Kings 19:12 KJV). The problem is, however, that you may think it's just a thought from your own mind and ignore it. And finally, God often inspires other Christians as they speak counsel and wisdom into your life. So listen to God today.

HONOR YOUR HEAVENLY FATHER

If then I am the Father, where is My honor?
MALACHI 1:6 NKJV

God frequently referred to Himself as a Father to His people. "I will be a Father to you, and you shall be My sons and daughters, says the LORD Almighty" (2 Corinthians 6:18 NKJV). Isaiah declared, "You, O LORD, are our Father; our Redeemer from Everlasting" (Isaiah 63:16 NKJV). God acted with great love and compassion toward His people, just like a father (Psalm 103:13). But the love wasn't always reciprocal. So He asked, "A son honors his father, and a servant his master. If then I am the Father, where is My honor?" (Malachi 1:6 NKJV).

Christians today are also sometimes in danger of not honoring God. They may give lip service to loving and honoring Him, but like the Jews of old, they may honor Him with their lips while their heart is far from Him (Matthew 15:8). So the question is, how do you honor God and bring honor to Him? By obeying Him.

It's wonderful that God is your Father in heaven who loves you, cares for you, and has compassion on you, but you must also be an obedient son or daughter. The first and greatest commandment is to love God with all your heart, mind, and strength, and make no mistake: If you love God that much, you will be sure to obey Him. God is not only "a" father, but "the" Father, so He is worthy of great honor.

THE STING IS GONE

O death, where is your sting?
1 CORINTHIANS 15:55 NLT

Paul wrote, "The dead will be raised incorruptible, and we shall be changed. . . . So when. . .this mortal has put on immortality, then shall be brought to pass the saying that is written: 'Death is swallowed up in victory'" (1 Corinthians 15:52, 54 NIV). Right now, death seems to have a terrible sting, killing loved ones and taking them from this life. But in the day when believers come back to life forever, death will be vanquished. Paul therefore asked, quoting the words of the Lord in Hosea 13:14, "O Death, where is your sting?" (verse 55 NKJV).

You may be extremely sorrowful when a loved one dies, and it might seem that death has lost none of its sting whatsoever. But if you think about it deeply, you realize that God will make all things right and wipe all tears from your eyes. This is why Paul said, "Dear brothers and sisters, we want you to know what will happen to the believers who have died so you will not grieve like people who have no hope" (1 Thessalonians 4:13 NLT).

One day in heaven, your immortal spirit will reunite with your resurrected physical body and live forever in the presence of the Lord with great power and glory. All sorrow will be gone, and there will be only joy and happiness for all eternity. Then the sting of death will be only a distant memory.

YOUR BROTHER'S KEEPER

Where is your brother Abel?
GENESIS 4:9 NIV

———

Cain was something special. He was the first son born to Adam and Eve after they were expelled from Eden. He must have been their first comfort after experiencing the pain of separation from the intimate presence and fellowship of God. The name *Cain* sounds like the Hebrew word *acquired*, and Cain soon had a brother.

In most cultures, the older brother has the responsibility of guiding and protecting the younger. But Cain let his pride and envy lead him to commit the first act of murder against his own sibling. Immediately God asked him to account for the whereabouts of Abel. Cain's reply was painful. He not only lied by saying he didn't know, but he then dared to ask God, "Am I my brother's keeper?" Yes, to a significant extent he was, just as Abel was Cain's keeper in return.

Perhaps, despite answering God's question so flippantly, Cain was struck by the fact that God was the One watching over them. God gave Cain a chance to realize the horror he had committed and to repent. Unfortunately, he neglected the heart-probing question. In the end, *God* was Abel's Keeper, as He is all of ours, and He brought justice.

How often does God send a similar call to your heart? Have you hurt a friend or neighbor, with whom you must seek reconciliation?

PROVISION FOR THE FEARFUL

What about your brother, Aaron the Levite?
EXODUS 4:14 NIV

When God appeared to Moses in the bush that wouldn't burn, He gave the eighty-year-old shepherd physical signs (a staff that turned into a snake and a leprous hand) to prove that He meant what He said. He was going to use Moses to speak to Pharaoh and bring the Israelites out of Egypt. God urged him on, saying, "Now go; I will help you speak and will teach you what to say." Moses' response, however, was, "Please send someone else" (verses 12–13).

This lack of faith, after so much evidence, angered God and led Him to ask Moses, "What about your brother, Aaron?" Aaron could speak well and would be the mouthpiece to Pharaoh that Moses was afraid to be. Moses would also not face Pharaoh's wrath alone.

When "we are faithless, [God] remains faithful" (2 Timothy 2:13) and draws us to see other ways by which He will bring about what He promised. Too often, like Moses, we come up with excuses, but in that marvelous Jewish way of providing an answer through the posing of a question, He makes us look at resources that He has been preparing for us all the while. What about your brother, sister, spouse, mother, or neighbor?

God may already be bringing them your way to accomplish what you're afraid to do but are nevertheless called to do.

ASSOCIATION AND INTENTION

Who are these men with you?
NUMBERS 22:9 NIV

The Israelites reached the plains of Moab on their journey through the wilderness to Canaan. Balak, the ruler of the land, was frightened out of his mind because he heard what had happened to the Amorites at the hands of this numerous people. His solution was to hire a local diviner to fight the strength of the Israelites with magic. Balak's men went to bring Balaam, a rather mysterious figure, to curse Israel.

This sorcerer told the messengers that he had to seek the counsel of Israel's God, and he invited them to spend the night until he had an answer for them. The Lord came to Balaam and asked him who these men were.

It wasn't as if God didn't recognize the officials of Balak. Rather, He wanted to bring into question Balaam's association with them and have him reflect on their intent. These were pagan officials asking him to curse God's chosen, and if Balaam had some knowledge of the Lord—enough it seems, to delay going with the officials in order to seek God's will—Balaam must have known the request wouldn't be accepted by God.

God may be drawing your attention not only to the company you keep, but also to the reasons you claim to seek God's counsel. Are you really willing to listen to God, and if so, why do you indulge in company that influences you to do things that are in direct opposition to Him?

FROM HEART TO HANDS

Wherever I have moved about with all the children of Israel,
have I ever spoken a word to anyone from the tribes of Israel. . .
saying, "Why have you not built Me a house of cedar?"

2 Samuel 7:7 nkjv

In the seventh chapter of 2 Samuel, readers are told that the Lord gave the king rest from his enemies. No longer having to worry about the issues of war gave King David time to think on other matters. He loved God, and he felt it was wrong that he, an earthly king, had a magnificent cedar palace while the King of creation had His symbolic dwelling place in a tent (regardless of how impressive a tent). David was keen to build God a temple.

However, God's holiness was adequately housed in the tent that held the ark of the covenant, and He hadn't asked for a temple. God's desire was always to be among His people, to tabernacle with them. In 2 Samuel 7:12–13, however, God revealed that a house would be built for His honor by a descendant of David.

God may lay something on your heart, not necessarily for you to accomplish but so that you may influence and prepare the way for others to carry out the task. You have to be careful that your desire is in line with God's desire and that you don't claim to do something for God that He doesn't call you to do.

Even if something is God's will, timing is often the key issue.

GOD SETS EVERYTHING IN PLACE

Where were you when I laid the foundations of the earth?
JOB 38:4 NKJV

When Job's friends finally stopped giving opinions as to why Job was suffering, God Himself responded to the cries of Job. All the reasoning and questioning of the previous chapters in the book of Job brought God to put this question to them: Where were they (and Job, specifically) at the start of His creation? The question brought to mind the eternality of God. He was—He existed—before the beginning, and being outside of space and time, He knew how to best order things into being.

Job was not there to see Him lay the earth's foundations and neither was anyone else, except the Spirit and the Word. Job had to, as we ourselves must, rely on their perfect testimony and guidance when things seemed uncertain.

Doubts inevitably come, and God's question may seem harsh. However, it was the disciplining answer of the Father who wanted to draw His children back to reality. His reality was hope-filled, and it contained the revelation that God is all-powerful and able to do anything He pleases. God set everything in place, and though creation was corrupted by the fall of man, He still has, and will always have, everything under His control.

We weren't there at the beginning, but God promises that we will be with Him beyond our mortal end.

SOURCE OF KNOWLEDGE

What is the way to the place where the lightning is dispersed,
or the place where the east winds are scattered over the earth?
JOB 38:24 NIV

Job had no way of answering these questions God posed to him. Even now most people can't say where lightning comes from or where exactly the wind starts. Scientists today tell us that water and ice particles are moved up by air currents and simultaneously moved down by gravity within clouds in the sky. When this happens, the particles of ice and water become electrically charged. So we have lightning. However, all the particulars of this process are still not understood in all their complexity.

And what of the east wind? Well, we claim that wind is caused by sun and air pressure—where air molecules move from regions of high air pressure to areas with low air pressure.

We may think we have come a long way since Job's day, but it's still God who revealed all of modern science to humans. If we read the question carefully, the answer is that God is the Source. He has arranged the processes of nature to function the way they do. In all their wisdom and discovery, humans must look to God as the Source.

Modern humans are in a more dangerous position than Job, because we're tempted to say we have the answers. However, if we trust Him who is the embodiment of truth, we will have authentic peace and wisdom.

GOD COUNT

Who has the wisdom to count the clouds?
JOB 38:37 NIV

Clouds have various symbolic meanings in the Bible. They are referred to a number of times in the book of Job alone, and almost always in regard to God's omnipotence and His wisdom. Here God again asks Job a seemingly impossible question: Who can count the clouds? He specifically asks who has the wisdom for such a task. But is it even wise to try counting them? Who has the stamina and the necessary speed, since clouds are constantly moving and changing?

One of the most important references to clouds is when God Himself took the form of a cloud to lead the Israelites through the wilderness by day. Just as we don't know the number of clouds in the sky, we also cannot understand God.

The question puts our ignorance into perspective. Our knowledge is limited and our wisdom often tainted by pride and selfishness. God wants to show this to us to be able to overcome it. Out of His love, He gives us of His wisdom to be able to understand, through the Spirit, some of the divine mysteries.

We come to understand more of these when we keep our eyes focused on the Divine Cloud, guiding us in prayer and Bible reading. "Who has the wisdom to count the clouds?" God showed us His wisdom by giving us peace through Jesus. We may not be able to count the clouds, but we can count on His love.

CORRECTING GOD

Shall the one who contends with the Almighty correct Him?
JOB 40:2 NKJV

Throughout the Bible, we read of faithful men and women who came before God contending with Him—struggling with situations and asserting their own arguments. Abraham and Sarah had a hard time believing they could have a son at their advanced age. Jacob physically struggled with God to bless him. The psalmists groaned over the apparent success of the wicked, and Peter tried to stop Jesus from going to the cross.

In the question above, God answered the cries of Job and the faulty answers of Job's friends. God doesn't condemn healthy questioning and heart-deep inquiries of His will. He does condemn prideful attempts by humans to offer their own answers to His plan or to think they have a better one.

Job didn't understand why he had to lose all his material possessions and all his children, or why he was forced to writhe in physical pain. But his answer to God's question above is filled with humility, and he continued to listen to and trust God. We may be angry at the way things are happening in this fallen world, and that's healthy, because the world's wrongs should disturb us—as they do God.

However, we can trust that His answers are better than ours. In His all-knowing and all-seeing power, He is going about the work of correcting hearts and minds.

UNDEFEATABLE

Who then is able to stand against me?
JOB 41:10 NIV

In chapter 41 of the book of Job, God presents the frightening creature called Leviathan. It is terrifying in size and power, yet God is still more powerful, because He created it. Put into context, this question was meant to bring at least two things to Job's mind and to your own: God is the most powerful, and earthly powers are temporary.

In your times of doubt, you may forget that the mighty things around you are God's handiwork. The mountains, oceans, and forests are sustained by systems that He initiated. He made the whales, bears, and lions, as well as the smallest microscopic organisms. If God created all these and many more, nothing can overpower Him. It is true that heartbreaking things happen as a result of humanity's rebellion against God, but He is still in control. He can use or turn all situations into something to strengthen and to build us up.

Since this is the case, then what seems to be our own power or wisdom, or the might of earthly powers, can only be temporary. What an encouragement! The strength of current oppressors will fail, and the justice of God will triumph. No one and nothing can stand against God and His angel armies.

We can trust in His promise that nothing devised by the evil one will prosper against Him or His children. Victory will be His, and through Him, ours, both now and in the end.

SONG OF THE VINEYARD

When I looked for good grapes,
why did it yield only bad?
ISAIAH 5:4 NIV

God was speaking to the people living in Jerusalem. At the start of the chapter, the vineyard owner is described as being diligent in his care for the vine. He fertilized it, cleared away the stones, grafted in the choicest vines, and built a watchtower from which to keep constant supervision. However, despite his diligent care, the harvest was bad.

In Isaiah 5:7 (NIV) the reader is told that "the vineyard of the LORD Almighty is the nation of Israel, and the people of Judah are the vines he delighted in. And he looked for justice, but saw bloodshed; for righteousness, but heard cries of distress."

Unfortunately, this applies today as well. God has worked continually to build up the body of Christ, but too often churches are not the places of justice and righteousness they should be. God gave Himself in the form of the Son to provide new life to the Church, but when He looked for a harvest of believers living like Jesus, He found too many bad grapes. People sought their own gain rather than humility and fellowship with God.

The result in the passage in Isaiah was that God promised to bring judgment and destroy the vineyard. But there is hope. If we listen to the Spirit's counsel as to why we produce bad fruit, then we can begin to repent and repair the condition of our hearts.

ON EAGLES' WINGS

Have you not heard?
ISAIAH 40:28 NIV

God spoke through the prophet Isaiah to tell the people of Judah, the Southern Kingdom, that they would go through horrible things because they had acted horribly. He wanted them to understand that their dishonest and oppressive systems could not go unjudged.

However, God mingled His judgment with hope throughout Isaiah's writings. In Isaiah 40 He called for His people to be comforted. This was not a reaction to what they did but an outpouring of His mercy. The sins of Jerusalem were paid for, as are ours, and God promised to gather the faithful as a shepherd protects his sheep.

As God asked the ancient Israelites, He asks people today: "Haven't you heard?" In the words that follow in Isaiah: The Lord is God, and He is everlasting. He will not grow tired or weary and His understanding no one can fathom. He gives strength to the weary and increases the power of the weak. Those who put their hope in Him will receive renewed strength—running and walking without fear of fainting.

Most of us have heard of the grace of God, but our hearts grow accustomed to it. Nevertheless, God draws His wandering sheep back into His arms and shows us His plans to rescue us through Jesus. Just as God calls us to listen, we must then go to others and ask the same: "Haven't you heard what God has done and what He will yet do?"

FEAR NOT

Is there any God besides me?
ISAIAH 44:8 NIV

God was in the midst of encouraging His people when He asked this question. In verses 9–20 of chapter 44, God described the foolishness of idol worship. He recounted how a man plants a tree then cuts it down to make an idol of his own fashion, and of the same tree he uses what is left for fuel for warmth and for cooking. As foreign as it may seem to Western readers, there are many cultures that continue to worship physical idols. Such a passage and description is not irrelevant in our time.

However, it's good to ask ourselves: Do I think and act as though there was another God? For those who struggle with fear of any kind, God raises this poignant question. The Lord surrounds it with plenty of evidence to show that there is no other God.

He tells Israel—and us—not to fear, because there is no other power as great as His. The Lord who formed us in the womb will be with us throughout our lives. He will give water to those who thirst and heal the parched land. He will pour His Spirit on the children of the faithful. He is the first and the last, who brings redemption for His people (Isaiah 44:6).

We must give our worries to Him, because no other god sacrificed His Son to reclaim us as God did.

TO GLORIFY AND ENJOY

How can I let myself be defamed?
ISAIAH 48:11 NIV

This is a question we often wish God would answer, as we hear skeptics ridicule Him or watch religious extremists commit unbiblical acts in His name. It is a question that many believers and nonbelievers alike ask. God posed this question to Israel to explain why He allowed them to experience affliction and yet how He didn't punish them as their actions deserved.

The people of Israel were always meant to be witnesses to the nations of God's glory and goodness. Christopher Wright's *The Mission of God* provides an excellent study of this grand narrative of God using Israel to reach and redeem all of humanity. However, Israel rebelled, just like the others.

God said that for His name's sake, He deferred His anger and didn't abandon His people. What would the nations say of Israel's God if they saw His people cut off? Who would remain to praise the one true God?

Nevertheless, He couldn't let the unjust and wicked actions of His chosen people be identified with Him. So He refined them in the furnace of affliction. He guided them through trials, as He does His followers today. He ultimately gives us beauty for ashes, once He has broken our hearts of stone and filled them with love. In the beauty and difficulties of truth, He is glorified and we are redeemed.

WHAT GOD SEES

And now what do I have here?
Isaiah 52:5 niv

God looked on Jerusalem and saw the oppression of His people, the desecration of His name by pagan leaders, and the sad physical and spiritual state of exiled Israel. God is looking at us today and asking the same thing. What does He see? Rampant brokenness, even in the Church, wars and hatred, abuse and oppression. What does He see in *your* heart?

The hope this question gives is that God *does* see. Not only is He aware of both the good and the bad, but He is moved to action. He promises to bring change and desires for His people to really know His name—the name at which every knee will bow, because it is the only name that brings peace.

God saves us from evil without and within and promises joy for the waste places of this world and of our hearts. He has showed us the strength of His arm in days of old and will call us to again witness His saving power in the eyes of all nations.

If we accept God's rescue plan and the guidance of the Comforter, the Holy Spirit, we will know His comfort and experience the rejuvenation of reconciliation that only God can bring. Therefore, when God asks the above question—"And now what do I have here?"—we will know the answer: redemption through Jesus and forever-fellowship with our Maker.

FASTING THROUGH CHANGE

Is this not the fast that I have chosen: to loose the bonds
of wickedness, to undo the heavy burdens, to let the
oppressed go free, and that you break every yoke?
ISAIAH 58:6 NKJV

This question is part of God's answer when the people of Israel asked, "Why have we fasted. . .and You have not seen? Why have we afflicted our souls, and You take no notice?" (verse 3). They thought they were following the laws given by God regarding dietary regulations and ways of showing repentance for sin. Through the above question, God chastised them for their hypocrisy.

The point of fasting is to draw a person into a renewed relationship with God and with the people around him or her, but the Israelites had turned fasting into a kind of pretense for demanding things of God because of their "holy" and "reverent" attitude.

Refraining from certain types of food is biblical and helpful, and Jesus Himself often fasted. Today, unfortunately, the spiritual discipline of fasting has been neglected by many Christians. The liturgical calendars of the Catholic and Orthodox Churches are a rare exception in providing a time of fasting for believers.

We must move beyond tradition, however. God points us to what He really wants of His followers: to be agents of change. We are called in our fasting to fight against the thoughts, attitudes, and actions that cause injustice in society. We get the power to do this from Jesus, the ultimate Yoke Breaker.

EXCHANGING IDOLS FOR LIVING WATER

Has a nation ever changed its gods?
JEREMIAH 2:11 NIV

Cultures are usually not in the habit of forsaking their traditional deities. The stories of Hindu gods and goddesses are millennia old; their temples and shrines are still in use, and their names are invoked by Hindus the world over. These, like many others, are false gods, and yet people still hold on to them.

In the days of the prophet Jeremiah, the people from the Southern Kingdom of Judah were about to be taken into captivity by the Babylonians because they had rejected the Lord. The God of Israel proved Himself to be the one true God, but the people of Judah sought the friendship of the surrounding nations and were drawn toward their religions. How was it that they who knew the true God were the only ones to consistently reject Him and His law?

Too often we also try to change our gods in hopes of finding something to placate our desires or idea of what is right. But God calls these attempts broken water jars that are formed broken from the start. What is amazing is that despite the fickle hearts of God's people, He never completely abandons them. Instead, He finds ways to fix our brokenness and draw people from all nations to Himself.

As Christians, we have Him who is Living Water, and like the Samaritan woman at the well, may we trust Him and thirst no more.

THE LIFE THAT GIVES LIGHT

Have I been a desert to Israel or a land of great darkness?
JEREMIAH 2:31 NIV

The short answer is "no." God has always been a source of light to His people, Israel. From the time of their captivity in Egypt, He made the land of Goshen, where they were living, continue to see the sun while Egypt lay in darkness for three days. In the forty years of desert wanderings, God was a pillar of fire for them by night. At the end of their wilderness wanderings, He was the One who brought them out of the desert into the bountiful land of Canaan.

So why was Israel so bent on leaving God? Probably the same reason that people today continue to walk away from Him. They become impatient with God, discouraged by His silences, and they give up serving Him.

God used the imagery in this question to draw the straying hearts of His people to remember how He had provided in the past. For people today, the question remains just as pertinent—even more so. In the darkest situations, God provided, and still provides, a way out. He gives us manna and quail and water from the rock when we think we're done for.

Those who come in earnest to God can look upon His rich history of faithfulness, even when His people were unfaithful. Let us remember that His ways are not like a desert and darkness, but as life and light.

PUNISHMENT BY GOD

Shall I not punish them for these things?
JEREMIAH 5:9 NKJV

God again spoke to Israel about their sin through the prophet Jeremiah. The things God was referring to in this question, for which He could not hold back punishment, were expounded in the previous verses of the chapter. People had forsaken God; they worshipped the idols of surrounding nations, coveted their neighbors' wives and their neighbors' things, and committed adultery. These were just *some* of the things they did.

Ultimately, the gravest transgression was that they were breaking their fellowship with the Creator. They, like many of us do today, dishonored Him through their selfish actions, thinking they could go on in their brokenness and perpetuating sin without suffering any consequences.

However, in this chapter of Jeremiah God called for the destruction of Israel and announced their impending captivity. They and we must pay because we have a just God who, because He is perfect, can't accept the injustices committed by humans. We have hope, nonetheless, because our God is merciful. In Jeremiah 5:10 He calls for Israel to be punished but not brought to a complete end. His goal is reconciliation and redemption.

Though He does punish like the wisest of fathers, He took the greatest punishment on our behalf. We have the promise that though He must punish sin, He will also do the healing and the binding up. Nowhere do we see this better than in the life of Jesus.

GET UP

When people fall down, do they not get up?
JEREMIAH 8:4 NIV

———————

When Adam and Eve sinned and all of humanity followed in the same path and pattern, God and creation always held the hope of getting back to the way things were before the fall. In this question, God lamented to Jeremiah the depths to which His people had sunk. It is natural for people to get up after they fall. However, God's people had fallen away from Him and refused to return. They clung to deceit and infected themselves and all of society with it. The leaders and teachers wrongly interpreted the law and misappropriated it for their own use.

This is the same situation the world is in today. God calls us to see that we have fallen—to realize just how *deeply* we have fallen—and to come back to Him.

In some circumstances people really can't get up, no matter how hard they try. We may find ourselves wanting to get up, but we are physically hindered from doing so. The aspiration to rise is still there, and when there's an earnest desire to leave sin behind, God is there to lift us up. He is telling us today through His question to Jeremiah that we can't remain in our sins.

If we listen to the urging of the Teacher, we will identify our faults and abandon our hurtful thoughts and actions. By His grace and through faith in His resurrection power, we *can* get up.

LAND OF PLENTY

How long will the land lie parched
and the grass in every field be withered?
JEREMIAH 12:4 NIV

This question reveals the weariness of living in a land devastated by drought and the heart-thirst of a people seeking spiritual renewal. Jeremiah cried out to God as believers cry out today across the world. *The Message* version of this verse states it more bluntly: "How long do we have to put up with this—the country depressed, the farms in ruin—and all because of wickedness, these wicked lives?"

Though the cry is made to God, later in the chapter the feeling of the oppressed is that God doesn't see what happens to them. Yet the fact that they cry out to Him for justice and healing means they still have hope in His promises.

The wicked people caused the land (and the people) to be parched and withered. The answer to the question would then seem to be until the wicked and guilty are punished. But how much longer? Perhaps until we no longer thirst for water or hunger for bread but are instead famished and thirst for God and His goodness. In Jeremiah 12:14–16 God promises to uproot His people from their land, but He promises to ultimately have compassion and bring them all back as one people to Himself.

We have damaged both the earth and the soil of our hearts, but God works through our brokenness to bring us to fulfillment in Him.

FORGED FOR HIS PURPOSE

Can a man break iron—iron from the north—or bronze?
JEREMIAH 15:12 NIV

The context of the question is again the impending judgment God will bring on the kingdom of Judah, but the question is specifically in reply to Jeremiah's cry that everyone is against him. He wasn't exaggerating. He was left to die in a pit, ostracized, and ridiculed for speaking the Lord's Word. God came to the weary prophet and promised deliverance and protection.

The northern iron he mentions was most likely brass or copper mixed with iron that the Chalybes to the far north of Palestine made into the hardest metal, similar to steel today.

God would also bring the Babylonians from the north, a force that the Israelites would be unable to break. In a similar way God built up Jeremiah, and for his faithfulness he wouldn't be broken by those who fought and cursed him. God has a hard but special call for His faithful ones today.

People cannot go against God and evade the consequences He predicted. However, part of His promise is to use believers in His work of reconciling fallen humanity to Himself. He will build His faithful witnesses like a "fortified wall of bronze" that cannot be overcome (Jeremiah 15:20 NIV).

No one will break the men and women God has forged. Just as He promised Jeremiah, He is with you to rescue and to save.

ALL-SEEING HEART

Do not I fill heaven and earth?
JEREMIAH 23:24 NIV

In Jeremiah 23 God chastised the wayward leaders and the false prophets who had led His people astray. They sinned with impunity as though God could not see, but God told Jeremiah that He filled the whole of heaven and earth. He is a God who is near. We can't hide from Him. Through the prophet Isaiah, God spoke against those who "go to great depths to hide their plans from the LORD, who do their work in darkness" (Isaiah 29:15 NIV). God is Light, and their evil will be exposed.

In Hebrews 4:13 (NIV) the writer says, "Nothing in all creation is hidden from God's sight." Everything is laid bare. Those who think they are free to do whatever they please, saying, "Who sees us? Who will know?" are deceiving themselves.

The Lord sees, He knows, and He will bring all to light. Apart from being a warning for those who think they can hoodwink God, the question is a comfort for the faithful. God is at work everywhere, in and around us through His Spirit. He does indeed fill heaven and earth, and because of this, we can trust that He sees not only our shortcomings, but also our attitudes of faith.

His presence is not only felt all around us, but in us. He fills us with Himself. Out of His lavish love, He will correct and encourage us.

AKIN TO EPHRAIM

Is not Ephraim my dear son, the child in whom I delight?
JEREMIAH 31:20 NIV

In this question Ephraim, the name of one of Joseph's sons whom Jacob adopted as his own, represents the wayward tribes of Israel. In the previous verses of Jeremiah 31, God said that He had heard Ephraim's moaning of repentance in which he recognized and accepted God's discipline. Ephraim said, "Restore me, and I will return. . . . After I strayed, I repented; after I came to understand, I beat my breast. I was ashamed and humiliated" (Jeremiah 31:18–19 NIV).

God replied with the question above. Wasn't Ephraim dear to Him? Didn't He delight in him? He asked this question of Israel to remind them that even in His discipline, He still loved them. God replied to His own question: "Though I often speak against him, I still remember him. . .my heart yearns for him; I have great compassion for him" (Jeremiah 31:20 NIV).

How beautifully Ephraim turned to God for forgiveness, an example for believers today. When we return to Him, we'll experience restoration. When believers understand their situation, they're ashamed, but in understanding God's love, they come to experience the Father's grace. He delights in His children and He yearns for them.

In Hosea 11:8 (NIV) God also asked, "How can I give you up, Ephraim?" God's heart is so deeply and intricately intertwined with the hearts of His children that He can't give you up.

THE LORD BROUGHT THEM DOWN

Why will your warriors be laid low?
JEREMIAH 46:15 NIV

In addition to warning Israel of their coming judgment, God also spoke through Jeremiah to warn other nations. Here God was speaking to Egypt. As Nebuchadnezzar would come against the kingdom of Judah, he would also come against Egypt—one of Israel's oppressors. All the false beliefs and unjust actions perpetuated by Egypt would also result in judgment. Though Egypt was known for its military might and cultural influence, God was sending a new, rising power to bring down her warriors.

There is a great comfort in knowing that although God's people suffer, either because of God's discipline in love or because of cruel earthly powers, He will make everything work together for good. The sustainers of oppressive governments, corrupt organizations, and dishonest individuals will be laid low through God's justice. They may be the most powerful institutions in our societies, but God is still the One in control. He will bring them and their sinful systems down in His perfect timing.

He already proved His strength against Egypt during the days of Moses, and the Israelites were yearly reminded of this during the Passover celebrations. Believers today have the Bible, which is full of evidence on how God brought down the powerful.

The beauty is that in His mercy, He can redeem even Egypt (and all she represents here) to win creation back (Isaiah 19:21–22).

FUNNY CHOICE

Who is the chosen one I will appoint for this?
JEREMIAH 49:19 NIV

God told Jeremiah how He would punish not just Judah but also the surrounding nations for dishonoring God. The above verse is in the section dealing with the judgment against Edom—the descendants of Esau. God was asking Jeremiah whom he supposed God had chosen to carry out justice against the people of Edom. They worshipped false gods, and their leaders drew the people further from the way God created humans to live and work together.

Just as with the kingdom of Judah, the Philistines, Ammon, Moab, Damascus, Elam, and others, God was going to use a specific man to carry out the punishment of Edom. Who was this man? It was the Babylonian king, Nebuchadnezzar.

God's mysterious ways are most evident in the people He chooses to work through. This pagan king was not a believing Gentile. Rather, in the story of Daniel's three friends, we see how Nebuchadnezzar made everyone in the kingdom bow down to an idol. But in that moment he was the one, bent on conquering the region, through whom God worked to bring justice and to make them reconsider their relationship with the Creator. Eventually Nebuchadnezzar would also come to call on Yahweh as the one true God, but it would take a large dose of humbling.

We may not understand why God chooses those whom He does, but His choices transcend human limitations. In the end they're perfect.

FALSE TEACHERS

Have you not seen false visions and uttered lying divinations
when you say, "The LORD declares," though I have not spoken?
EZEKIEL 13:7 NIV

During the time of the prophet Ezekiel, a contemporary of Jeremiah, God continued to call His people out on their wickedness. He specifically condemned those who falsely claimed to speak in God's name. With the fear of impending captivity in Babylon, the Jewish leaders were saying different things. Many said that God would not allow Babylon to defeat Israel. Some prophesied peace, while a few, like Ezekiel and Jeremiah, prophesied captivity. The latter were indeed speaking the words of God, but the false prophets knew what to say to tickle the ears of the people.

Just as there were during Ezekiel's day, there are teachers, ministers, and ordinary people today who claim to speak in God's name, but He didn't speak to them. Rather, they're spreading false ideas and interpretations of what God has revealed. Their motivation may vary (ignorance, greed, or other power plays), but it's important that believers remain rooted in God's Word.

If you diligently study the Bible, spend time with Him in prayer, and attend a church that takes learning about God seriously, then it will be easier to avoid the "false visions" and "lying divinations" of those who falsely call themselves Christians.

If we follow in the footsteps of Jesus, the Good Teacher and the embodiment of God's Word, we will know God's voice and not be easily led astray.

TRUE AND FRUITFUL VINE

Can its wood be used for making things,
like pegs to hang up pots and pans?
EZEKIEL 15:3 NLT

Jerusalem is compared in this passage to the useless wood of a vine branch. God told Ezekiel that just as the wood of grapevines couldn't even be used as pegs to hang up pots and pans, so the people of Israel had proven themselves weak. They were unfaithful to God, who had continually showed His faithfulness to them.

A vine is also useless if it fails to produce good fruit. It is then only good as fuel for a fire. God calls His people to produce good fruit. Their words and actions are the fruit that should flow out of their love for Jesus. He is the strong vine that believers are to emulate (John 15:5). Without His example for guidance and His presence in us for strength, we can't do anything right. The task required of us is to be careful of what our life produces, but not to be so fearful that we fail to do anything.

The puritan Richard Baxter wrote that he wanted to be a pen in God's hand. When we are completely at His disposal, we become useful in the most beautiful ways, furthering His redemption and reconciliation work among creation. If we remain faithful in our pursuit and obedience of God, the outcome will be healthy and delicious fruit—nourishment for our soul and the souls of those around us.

FAILURE TO INTERPRET

Do you not know what these things mean?
Ezekiel 17:12 NIV

In the verses leading up to verse 12, God relates the parable of an eagle and a vine to describe the relationship between Zedekiah, the king of Judah, and Nebuchadnezzar. Zedekiah had given his oath of loyalty to Nebuchadnezzar, but he then allied with Egypt in rebellion (2 Chronicles 36:13). The king trusted more in the power of Egypt than in God's Word; by breaking his oath, Zedekiah misrepresented and dishonored God.

God spoke to the rebellious Jews, asking incredulously how they could *not* interpret the events going on around them. Although Babylon would receive punishment in the future for their oppression of God's people, for the time being Judah was called to repent through being exiled to a foreign land.

God's message through Isaiah, Jeremiah, Ezekiel, and other prophets was clear, and yet the people refused to acknowledge their guilt and to reform. Christians today have the Bible and faithful witnesses throughout history to testify to God's plan. There are events and circumstances whose purposes remain hidden from us, but don't we really know that God is at work? God asks believers to be truthful in their words and actions to those around them but also to themselves. There may be clear reasons for why something happens.

Believers must be ready to suffer the consequences of their sin, and trust that if they live by love and faith in Christ, He will lead them.

WE, THE UNJUST

Is it not your ways that are unjust?
EZEKIEL 18:29 NIV

Christians and non-Christians alike are quick to pass judgment on how God chooses to act in different situations. Atheists and agnostics use the existence of evil and its perpetuation as their main argument against the existence of God; or if they concede there is a God, then they claim He must be cruel.

God confronted the Israelites with the above question, and He challenges us with it still. People claim that God is not just if He allows the troubles that plague society. However, who are the ones creating such atrocities? People. All are in rebellion against a love that demands dying to self and living for others. Comfortable, middle-class folk, Christian or otherwise, may not be the direct culprits of the horrors that occur in our world, but they often benefit from corrupt systems that have injustice as their foundation.

Before we start blaming God for the world's atrocities, we must critically and thoroughly examine our life choices, everything from where we buy our food and clothes, to what we do for a living, to where we go to church.

We have a God who from the beginning sought to bring justice to the downtrodden because, in the freedom of choice He gives, people choose to oppress. Then He gave us Jesus. God is merciful to forgive us when we live in the light of His sacrifice, and then He uses us to stand against injustice.

STRENGTH TO RECKON

*How strong and courageous will
you be in my day of reckoning?*
EZEKIEL 22:14 NLT

Just like the false prophets and their proud rulers, the people of Judah continued to sin. The NIV phrases God's question: "Will your courage endure or your hands be strong in the day I deal with you?" The people put on a good face and relied on their strength to obtain what they wanted, asserting their power over their neighbors.

People do the same today. Parents are treated with contempt; the unsuspecting are extorted; the orphans and widows are wronged; God—and all that is holy and good—is profaned (Ezekiel 22:7–8). The implication is that no matter how strong or prosperous sinful people seem to be, all will fade when they are called to give account of their actions before God.

However troubling God's question may be, there is always hope, even in the severest of His dealings. In the day that God deals with His people, it is to take "the uncleanness out of them" (Ezekiel 22:15 NLT), to thoroughly wash them.

The faithful will be humbled, knowing they failed to live in active love and that they deserve chastisement. But they will also trust that in the day of reckoning, their strength and their courage will be found in Christ. His love and grace in them will provide the humility they need to ask God for forgiveness and then to follow in the steps of Jesus.

GOD'S SANCTIFICATION CREATIVITY

Art thou he of whom I have spoken in old time by my
servants the prophets of Israel, which prophesied in those
days many years that I would bring thee against them?
EZEKIEL 38:17 KJV

The foreign nation of Gog, to whom this question is addressed, is the earthly power that God sends to judge His people. Gog doesn't appear specifically in older prophecies, but it is identified with the enemies of God's people mentioned by Isaiah, Jeremiah, and others. God used Gog's thirst for power in the same way He used the Babylonians: to reform and reconcile the Israelites to Himself. This shows God's love and mercy toward His children in using even the tragic things around them to bring new life.

However, God has a warning for Gog. He reminded His enemies that He knew they were coming. Didn't God speak through His prophets long ago to warn that these powers would come? God's omniscience is not something His enemies should take lightly. Though He may be allowing them temporary victory over His rebellious children, God won't let the guilty go unpunished.

If those who oppress God's people recant, then God will welcome them with open arms into His family of sanctified sinners. God can use anything in this process of being made holy, but it's the job of the offender to ask forgiveness and to live a life worthy of that forgiveness.

EXTRAVAGANT GRACE

How can I hand you over, Israel?
Hosea 11:8 niv

The holiness of God demands that He punish the guilty, which in the book of Hosea included His chosen people, Israel. However, His love for them was, and is, just as strong as His holiness. In chapter 11 God spoke of His people as a child whom He brought from afar, whom He taught to walk, and whom He fed and healed.

He had to administer discipline and justice, but God loved His children too much to let them go. After all, He had made a covenant that He would be their God and they His people. We are reminded throughout the Bible that God is gracious, compassionate, slow to anger, of great kindness, and One who relents from doing harm (Joel 2:13).

It may seem that everything around may be going wrong and that God doesn't care—or that He is vengeful. Yet, in the books of the prophets, where there are warnings upon warnings of calamity for sin, there are also the most beautiful expressions of God's love for the broken and the lost. He loves us too much to give up on us.

From a human point of view, it would be very easy for God to simply punish us, since we're constantly running from Him to the things of this world. But His extravagant grace gives us hope that no matter how bad our state, there is a way back to the beginning.

FROM JUDGMENT TO JOY

Will not the land tremble for this,
and all who live in it mourn?
Amos 8:8 niv

The "trembling of the land" refers to God's judgment on the people. Yahweh tells the prophet Amos that the people trampled on the needy, disobeyed His Sabbath laws, used deceitful weights in business transactions, and considered human life to have little value. They would have to face the consequences of these injustices, and they would tremble and mourn when they realized that God was serious about justice.

God continually calls people to stop their harmful actions. If His warnings of judgment don't move us, then His love and care should be what brings us to our knees to seek forgiveness and change. Unfortunately, humans, as part of our fallen nature, seem to respond more to fear. So God promises to humble His people, to start over, and to heal their hearts and minds.

In stubborn rebellion, believers sometimes forget that they were made to live in friendship with God. Their hearts continually seek to fill the void of this perfect relationship. But God told Amos that He would send a famine on the land, not of bread or of water, but of a deep longing to hear the words of the Lord (verse 11).

The longing will be filled, as promised. Those who love Him and feed on His Word look forward to the day when they can be joyfully united forever with the Father.

CRY IN FAITH

Why do you now cry aloud. . .that pain
seizes you like that of a woman in labor?
MICAH 4:9 NIV

The whole of Micah 4 is the encouragement of God to His people, who were overcome with fear by the coming exile. He proclaimed that one day the nations would come to Israel to learn about the Lord. War would no longer exist—swords would be turned into plowshares and spears into pruning hooks. God promised the future reestablishment of His people and the rescue of Zion. That's why He asked them why they were crying with such pain.

The pain when a woman gives birth is sometimes excruciating, and God compares the cries of His people to that of a mother in labor. But the Israelites were crying out in a spirit of hopelessness, forgetting that their King was the King of heaven and their Counselor was the God of all the earth.

Just as with a mother's cries during labor, the pain of God's faithful will be worth it when they see the new life that's produced.

We may get carried away in our pain and think there's no way out. There is a time for mourning, a season for sadness and grief, but believers should live with victory in mind. We may cry out in our deepest pain, but we should trust all the time that this is not the end. The Lord will rescue us, because His nature is redemptive love.

THE NEW TEMPLE—OUR BODIES

*Is it a time for you yourselves to be living in your
paneled houses, while this house remains a ruin?*
HAGGAI 1:4 NIV

During the days of the prophet Haggai, a remnant of the Jewish
people lived in Judah, but the majority of them were still in
Babylon. The people of Judah had rebuilt their homes, and though
they were still a conquered people, they had a measure of freedom.
God spoke through Haggai to convict them for not completing
the temple. It had been destroyed during the Babylonian invasion
and was only partially rebuilt, even though the Persians had given
them permission to rebuild it.

God was concerned about the physical state of the temple
because it reflected the spiritual state of His people. They built
up their houses, decorated, fortified, and paneled them, but they
neglected to finish building the temple. Christians often do the
same today, especially in the West, where houses, cars, and clothes
take precedence over kingdom-building investments.

However, we have to be careful not to invest so much in
church buildings that we neglect to help the poor and oppressed.
Though taking care of physical buildings is important, our houses
of prayer are not to be extravagant temples, and their aesthetics should not overshadow the needs of people. After all, God
dwells in people and not in buildings. Remember, God provided
everything we have, and we are called to give generously, both
physically and spiritually.

BEING A MIGHTY MASTER

If I am a master, where is the respect due me?
MALACHI 1:6 NIV

The context of this verse is God's condemnation of the priests of Israel. They charged God with being unjust when *they* were the unjust ones, bringing Him dishonor. The priests offered blind and lame animals—things they could easily do without—as their sacrifices. This revealed the lack of respect they gave to God. Apart from the quality of such sacrifices, the law specifically forbade giving such animals. The priests acknowledged Yahweh as God, but their actions revealed a weak faith.

Religious services are often still filled with people who profess a faith in God but who live as believers only as far as their comfort allows. They cut corners and put on a facade of holiness.

If believers have to show respect to their employers (even when they don't like them), how much more respect should they give to the Master of all creation? Reading of His past, present, and future provision in the Bible gives more than ample reason for giving Him the greatest respect.

He is a Master whom we can love and serve wholeheartedly, because He came down and took on flesh to serve us. Jesus' earthly life was one of complete service to God and to the redemption of humankind. With sincere hearts the Holy Spirit will guide us to give Him the respect He is due through our words and actions.

A CASE OF FIRSTS

The LORD said, "What have you done?"
GENESIS 4:10 NLT

Cain had the distinction of being first in so many categories. He was the first child, the first son, and the first older brother. Cain had a lot going for him, but it wasn't enough. He soon became associated with other firsts. He was the first to offer an inappropriate offering to God—which the Lord didn't accept. Cain's anger led to the murder of his brother Abel, whose offering God *had* accepted. And God's question shocked Cain into accepting responsibility for the world's first murder.

People like being in first place. It might start in school with sports or fine arts and continue on into a career. Being first has meaning for those who hold the title. As with Cain, however, these might not seem like enough.

Cain was older than Abel. Maybe he felt he should, therefore, have been God's favorite when it came to offerings. However, an offering had nothing to do with how likable the person was who brought it. The offering had everything to do with following directions. Cain was supposed to bring an *animal* sacrifice, but he brought remnants from a farmers' market.

God doesn't ask us to be first at any cost. He wants us to follow what He says, do what pleases Him, and respond in a way that mirrors His character. When we insist on our own way, we should be prepared to answer God's probing question: "What have you done?"

PERSONALLY ESTIMATED WORTH

How long will you refuse to humble yourself before me?
EXODUS 10:3 NIV

God was set to bring the eighth of ten plagues on Egypt. Pharaoh had seen seven other plagues devastate the land, but his response had followed a predictable pattern. Moses would warn Pharaoh about the next plague, Pharaoh would refuse to let God's people go, and then the plague would come, just as threatened. With each plague Pharaoh admitted his error and pleaded for relief. Once the plague was lifted, however, Pharaoh forgot all about his promise to let God's people leave. Pharaoh's selective amnesia was the reason for God's question above.

We, too, can forget how big God is. We forget all the promises He's kept. We forget how much He loves us. We. . .just. . . forget.

When we remember, however, God can bring us to a place of praise. Remembering can bring us closer to those we've forgotten. Recalling all we've learned and how we've grown places us in a position where we can help others.

When we refuse to remember, we adopt a wrong attitude toward God, a wrong response toward others, and a wrong motive for our actions. Forgetting God's power is an easy way to begin thinking more highly of ourselves than we should. Romans 12:3 (MSG) reminds us: "The only accurate way to understand ourselves is by what God is and by what he does for us, not by what we are and what we do for him."

ENEMY IDENTIFICATION

Are trees soldiers who come against you with weapons?
DEUTERONOMY 20:19 MSG

The Israelites were about to head out to war against the Canaan-ites, and God knew they'd need to cut down many trees to build siege-works to conquer the enemy cities, but the Israelites had to think of the resources they'd need once the war was over. So God asked a rhetorical question that included a word picture. If they cut down the fruit trees, they'd have no fruit to eat once they took over the land. It seemed the Israelites were in jeopardy of mis-identifying their enemy, so God was trying to tell them, "The fruit trees are your *friends*. Leave them alone."

We often make the same mistake today. We chop people down, or we keep them at a distance because they don't think the way we think. We verbally wrestle with other Christians because they have a differing opinion of what God's Word calls a disput-able matter (Romans 14:1).

One of the ways we attack others today is by withholding the love God asks us to share, spreading discontent among peacemak-ers and adopting the stance of a spiritual bully around those who have no idea there's a war. We should be careful to identify our real spiritual adversary and allow God to lead us. When we fail to understand who our enemy is, we risk chopping others down, leading to destroyed relationships and damaged reputations.

Be guided by love and wisdom. You'll be doing yourself a favor.

WHEN FACED WITH ADVERSITY

The LORD said to him, "What are you doing here, Elijah?"
1 KINGS 19:9 NLT

Elijah prayed it wouldn't rain, and the rivers dried up. He prayed for fire from heaven, and a sacrifice was incinerated. He prayed for the rain to fall again, and the king almost didn't make it back to his capital in the deluge. Elijah had the backing of almighty God. However, when the queen threatened his life, Elijah forgot about the answered prayers, the miracles, and the faith God had given him. He ran, he hid, and his reactions seemed confused. Elijah was hiding in a cave as if the Lord wasn't strong enough to save him. No wonder God asked, "What are you doing here?"

We all experience answered prayer. We see God work in our lives, we agree that He is powerful. . .and then we hide when unexpected confrontation arrives.

Have you ever wondered why we're so quick to run away when there's opposition? Maybe it's because faith is based on trust, and trust is easier to accept when it seems reasonable. We doubt God's trustworthiness and conclude that somehow a new confrontation is more challenging than God's abilities, and we begin searching for our spiritual running shoes.

When God is ready to present a solution, we're often in hiding. God's assurance is just what we need to stand strong in the face of adversity. God's always been with us—and He's not leaving now.

FAITH BLUEPRINTS

*Who decided on its size? . . . Who came up
with the blueprints and measurements?*
JOB 38:5 MSG

From the earth's core to the highest mountain peak, God simply *spoke* and everything He had in His mind came into being. Waterfalls danced and bubbled, bringing water to the sea. Dirt and sand were scattered in a variety of textures and colors. He set the planets in motion and tossed the stars in all directions for the enjoyment of humanity. Every square inch of this big blue marble bore the marks of its Maker. Job may have built a piece of furniture for his home, but God alone was capable of designing vast, complex galaxies.

Question after question was thrown at Job. To Job it may have seemed like the Lord was picking on him. It may have seemed as if God was saying, "I'm big and you're nothing." It may have appeared that God thought Job's questions were insignificant.

However, the real lesson in this line of questioning was that if God could create the entire world, then He could be trusted with everything we don't understand. This reminder to Job was just one more bit of evidence proving that no matter how much Job misunderstood what was happening, faith in God was the one thing he could always count on.

Bad days are just a good reminder to fix our eyes on the One who made us and who knows our life plan (Hebrews 12:2).

REMINDERS EVERYWHERE

Who created a channel for the torrents of rain? Who laid out
the path for the lightning? Who makes the rain fall on barren land,
in a desert where no one lives? Who sends rain to satisfy the
parched ground and make the tender grass spring up?
JOB 38:25–27 NLT

Job was an upright man. He didn't deny God or curse His name. As a target of oppression, Job learned there was much he took for granted. There's nothing that exists in this world that doesn't draw its source from God's creation. Job thought of his loss and forgot the One who created riverbeds, lightning strikes, cloudbursts, and green grass. Life doesn't take place by accident. Job would come to respond the way the psalmist had in Psalm 119:116 (NLT), saying: "LORD, sustain me as you promised, that I may live! Do not let my hope be crushed."

When we stand in awe of Niagara Falls, gaze out at the ocean, or cast a fishing line in a stream, we have a choice. We can view the scenery as mere therapeutic rest or as a means to recall that the God who "existed before anything else. . .holds all creation together" (Colossians 1:17 NLT).

Because God doesn't want our hope to be crushed, He provided extravagant reminders of His ability to sustain His creation. God has always given more than we deserve, more than we understand, and more than we will ever be able to give back.

THE WISDOM GIFT

Does anyone know enough to number all the clouds
or tip over the rain barrels of heaven when the earth
is cracked and dry, the ground baked hard as a brick?
Job 38:37–38 MSG

God challenged Job's wisdom. The patriarch's defense was flawed because it was based on what *he* understood, not on what *God* knew. One lesson in these rhetorical questions is that the answer most often is "God." Who knew the number of clouds? God. Who tips over the rain barrels of heaven? God. This same pattern is found throughout God's questioning of Job. God's message seemed to be, "Just because you can't understand what's happening doesn't mean it's without purpose."

The wisest-man-in-the-room award always goes to God. He challenges our thinking, and we do well to pay attention. Proverbs 12:15 (MSG) puts it this way: "Fools are headstrong and do what they like; wise people take advice."

God's questions offered Job a gift. It might not have felt that way at the time, but the gift was a greater understanding of God. He learned that when bad things happen to good people, then good people need to return to the great God who sometimes answers questions with questions.

So where does that leave us? Colossians 3:16 (NLT) says, "Let the message about Christ, in all its richness, fill your lives. Teach and counsel each other with *all the wisdom he gives*. Sing psalms and hymns and spiritual songs to God with *thankful hearts*" (emphasis added).

NOT HEARTLESS—NOT CRUEL

Would you discredit my justice?
JOB 40:8 NIV

─────────

God didn't ask Job if he could identify someone *else* who thought He was unjust. God wasn't interested in secondhand information. He made it personal. God wanted to know whether *Job* really wanted to spend time belittling the justice of God. Did Job really believe that God was untrustworthy, unjust, and uncaring? God wanted Job to think about whether he really believed the Lord was heartless and cruel.

Job was overwhelmed with what he was learning about God, and this led him to say, "I spoke once, but I have no answer—twice, but I will say no more" (Job 40:5 NIV).

We are wise to be quiet *before* God is finished teaching. That's how Job responded. When he decided to be quiet, God's lessons could finally get through the defensive wall Job had erected. In Psalm 46:10 (NLT) God reminds us: "Be still, and know that I am God! I will be honored by every nation. I will be honored throughout the world." There will come a time when God will be honored in every nation of the world, but those who follow Him *now* should honor Him *now*. Why? When we trust Him, we honor Him by waiting on Him.

When God questioned Job, He demonstrated that His reputation was not in question, His power is beyond understanding, His wisdom exceeds human knowledge, and His justice is just as important as His grace.

A DIVINE OBLIGATION?

Who has given me anything that I need to pay back?
JOB 41:11 NLT

God made everything. He ensures the world operates the way it needs to. He offers life, love, and understanding. God's question was posed to an experienced businessman. Job had frequently bought and sold. He had earned wealth. He had customers who owed him money, goods, or services. Was it possible that this man who loved God had come to the place where he believed God owed him something for his good behavior? In this case God answered His own question, "Everything under heaven is mine" (Job 41:11 NLT).

God expanded this idea in Psalm 50:9–11 (NLT): "I do not need the bulls from your barns or the goats from your pens. For all the animals of the forest are mine, and I own the cattle on a thousand hills. I know every bird on the mountains, and all the animals of the field are mine."

The God who has unlimited resources also asks us to give to those who do His work. If we do, God Himself will see to it that we don't lack. Luke 6:38 (NLT) says, "Give, and you will receive. Your gift will return to you in full."

This can sound like God owes us something when we put money in an offering plate. If we think that by giving one hundred dollars we will receive at least one hundred dollars in return, we misunderstand God's economy. God will bless us as He sees fit, not always in the way we might wish.

THE FORGIVENESS FACTOR

Whom shall I send? Who will go for us?
ISAIAH 6:8 MSG

———————

Isaiah was in the presence of God. Angels arrived with a message. Isaiah listened as doom was pronounced for the people of Israel. Isaiah was quick to admit his own guilt and inadequacies. He was just as quickly granted forgiveness. Once Isaiah's guilt was removed and God asked whom He should send with His message, Isaiah's bold reply was "Here I am. Send me" (Isaiah 6:8 NLT). Thus began the career of the willing and forgiven prophet.

Is it too simplistic to say that God called and Isaiah answered? Yes. Isaiah found absolute freedom to follow because of something we might easily miss. When Isaiah was in the presence of God, he might have refused to answer God's call because of his sin. It was God's *forgiveness* that moved him to show a willingness to do what God asked.

It wasn't Isaiah's skill set, persuasive speech, or notoriety that made him a great prophet. It was God's forgiveness paired with Isaiah's willingness.

Being forgiven makes us useful to God. If we continually believe God keeps His distance because we don't measure up to His standards, then we're less willing to follow His adventure for our lives. Forgiveness offers a close relationship with the Lord and an opportunity to be used by Him. Forgiveness is a key element in relationship and productivity. Ephesians 4:32 (MSG) says, "Forgive one another as quickly and thoroughly as God in Christ forgave you."

BE CONTENT—RESIST COMPLACENCY

Who recruited him for this job, then rounded up and corralled
the nations so he could run roughshod over kings?
ISAIAH 41:2 MSG

King Cyrus would liberate the Israelites from Babylonian captivity. If you envision a job fair with God reviewing the résumés of potential deliverers, you may have forgotten that God is all-knowing. He knew Cyrus would end the exile of His people, and He enlisted his help in planning a homecoming. Cyrus's plan? No. God's plan? Yes.

Have you ever been surprised by a friendship? You encountered someone with whom you had few common interests, backgrounds, or family dynamics. You might not have picked them using compatibility comparisons, but they were just the friend you needed. Someone may come into your life who will help move you to a new and better place. The above question suggests that God will sometimes use unexpected people to help dislodge us from complacency.

Here's some perspective: Proverbs 1:32 (NLT) says, "Fools are destroyed by their own complacency." God never wants us to settle for less than His best. He often uses relationships to inspire us to move.

However, the apostle Paul wrote in Philippians 4:11 (MSG), "I've learned by now to be quite content whatever my circumstances. I'm just as happy with little as with much, with much as with little." You can be content without being complacent, and you can be complacent without being content. In fact, you can't be both. Be content and thank God for relationships that help you grow.

THE ONE, THE ONLY

Who but a fool would make his own god—
an idol that cannot help him one bit?
ISAIAH 44:10 NLT

Before this question was asked, God said something that helped the hearer understand there was no identification loophole for the one true God. In Isaiah 44:6 (NLT) God said, "I am the First and the Last; there is no other God." The question above, therefore, suggests there were those who made gods from their own imagination. God was clear: *These idols can't help you.* The Israelites had a long history of adopting the gods of the people they were around. These gods were in vogue, enticing, and entertaining. They were part of the death culture of the wayward nations.

Today's culture seems more than willing to embrace a buffet of spiritual ideas. We can embrace *God culture* but reject things in God's Word we don't agree with. We borrow an idea from other faiths and create something we intend to be a positive religious hybrid. However, this leads to confusion and denies the Lord His rightful place as the one and only God worthy of our worship.

We can make personal pursuits a god. It could be work, hobbies, children, cars, sports, video games, or food. When we worship at the altar of modern culture, we minimize the depth and clarity of our relationship with God. Understanding, accepting, and believing there is only one true God helps us make the most of our limited time on earth.

READ ALL ABOUT IT

Who among the gods has delivered the news?
ISAIAH 48:14 MSG

God sent Isaiah out like an ancient newspaperman. If this had happened in another era, it might have sounded like: "Extra, extra, read all about it! God enlists foreigner to set His people free!" There was only one source reporting this news. This same news source had said the exile would last seventy years. Now it was providing the name of the man responsible for setting the Israelites free: "I, GOD, love this man Cyrus, and I'm using him to do what I want with Babylon. I, yes I, have spoken. I've called him. I've brought him here. He'll be successful" (Isaiah 48:15 MSG).

All other news sources (gods) were unreliable, unable to respond to questions, and unavailable. Any god of our own making will leave us uninformed and misguided.

If we put our trust in the god of money, we find no satisfaction, because enough is never enough. If our god is sports, it will fail us, because we're worshipping a game. There's only one God who knew us before we were born, who supplies the way to Him, the truth we need, and life that is real life (John 14:6).

God's news is true and accurate 100 percent of the time. Any other god's news will be little more than a gossip column. You have access to the best news. Share it.

AN INVITATION TO DINE

Why spend your money on food that does not give you strength?
Why pay for food that does you no good?
ISAIAH 55:2 NLT

The nation of Israel was on the verge of celebration. They were being set free, but some continued to act like slaves. They were dining on religious junk food when God had provided a relational banquet. Maybe they just couldn't believe freedom was really for them. God had a message to share with the people, and it would impact their future: "Come to me with your ears wide open. Listen, and you will find life" (Isaiah 55:3 NLT). The news was amazing; God's future for His people was far better than their present.

Are we ever guilty of dining at a spiritual snack bar when we have an invitation to a banquet? Do we enjoy just enough junk food to reduce our hunger when we could be dining with God? Have we settled for less? Why? There's much we can learn from God. He offers more answers than many of us will ask. He offers solutions we've never tried. He wants to hear from us, but we're not sure what to say.

This doesn't have to be our response. We need to believe God is willing to provide something more substantial than trail mix. Dine on His words, believe what He says, be changed. Second Corinthians 5:17 (NLT) says that "anyone who belongs to Christ has become a new person. The old life is gone; a new life has begun!"

ACTORS NEED NOT APPLY

Is it not to share your food with the hungry and to provide the poor
wanderer with shelter—when you see the naked, to clothe them,
and not to turn away from your own flesh and blood?
ISAIAH 58:7 NIV

God wanted His people to be transformed; they offered Oscar-worthy performances. God wanted His people to fast and humble themselves; they were too busy trying to get God to notice them. God wanted the people to be kind; they exploited others. God wanted compassion; they participated in boxing matches. So God asked the above question as a way to help the people understand clearly how they should treat others. The curtain needed to come down on their self-righteous stage play.

God wants transparency and transformation to be a part of how others see us. We don't have it all together, but God is working in us. We don't have all the answers, but we know who does. We can't claim responsibility for the change in our lives, but we can humbly acknowledge God's ability to change lives.

Jesus said there were two great commandments—love God and love everyone else (Luke 10:27). How often do we look at our decisions in terms of whether it's showing love to other people? Do we really love God, or do we only try to stay on His good side?

Don't act the part of a Christian. Be one. Don't just hear what God wants. Do something about it.

EMBRACE FREEDOM

*Why has Israel become a slave? Why has he
been carried away as plunder?*
JEREMIAH 2:14 NLT

───────

The way Israel was responding made no sense to God. They were the children of His promise. He accepted them as family, but the people related to God as if they were servants. A child should have a close relationship with his parents. A servant may be loved or unloved, but relate to the master as a detached worker with no rights to family connection. The master is only a boss—not a father. The self-imposed demotion caused a separation that disappointed God and kept the people from accepting Him as their Father.

Jesus told a similar story. The prodigal son was loved by his father but made some mistakes that led him away from his family. By the time this son realized he'd done wrong, he felt so much shame he was willing to become a servant. His father wouldn't hear of it. "This son of mine was dead and has now returned to life. He was lost, but now he is found" (Luke 15:24 NLT).

God's Word provides a perfect position statement for Christians. Galatians 5:1 (MSG) declares, "Christ has set us free to live a free life. So take your stand! Never again let anyone put a harness of slavery on you."

Being ashamed of your actions should lead you to return to the Father, to embrace His forgiveness, love, and freedom.

CLOSE TO GOD

Why do my people say, "Good riddance!
From now on we're on our own"?
JEREMIAH 2:31 MSG

Israel had run from God. They weren't seeing many "yes" answers
to their halfhearted prayers. It seemed as if God had abandoned
them. Prophets like Jeremiah told them it was their indifference
and poor choices that separated them from God. James 4:8 (NKJV)
provides the antidote: "Draw near to God and He will draw near
to you. Cleanse your hands, you sinners; and purify your hearts,
you double-minded." You're only on your own when you refuse
God's help and insist on doing things your way.

Think back to what it was like when you were in high school.
You might remember a tension that resulted in a strained relationship with your parents. In most cases the parents don't move away
from their children—their children move away from them. The
net result is a strained relationship until the child rediscovers value
in their parents.

If you ever doubt God's willingness to stay close, consider the
psalmist's words: "The LORD is close to all who call on him, yes, to
all who call on him in truth" (Psalm 145:18 NLT).

God doesn't force Himself on anyone, but if you ever wonder
why God may seem far away, the most likely answer is the distance *you* create between your life and the life God has in mind
for you. You can't pursue your own interests and God's interests
without defining who's really in charge.

SERIOUS DISCIPLINE

Don't you think I'll take serious measures against a people like this?
JEREMIAH 9:9 MSG

God's people found themselves in a breach of contract. They'd been given God's law book, and they'd invented loopholes, disregarded statutes, and minimized the severity of every infraction. In their minds the rules weren't really commands as much as they were antiquated guidelines. As time passed the people thought less of God's law and more of their personal interests. The evidence of their sin was without dispute, and God was ready to take action and deliver justice.

Jesus talked about this when He said, "If you love me, show it by doing what I've told you" (John 14:15 MSG). Jesus put a spotlight on why we follow God's commands: love. God gave His rule book as a means of helping humanity see how their actions affect relationships. If we love God and follow His commands, then it will positively impact the quality of our friendships, marriage, and parenting.

When God indicated that He planned to take serious measures against lawbreakers, He was demonstrating an interest in doing what needed to be done to reestablish relationship. How loving would it be if God either didn't care about sin or destroyed His people when they sinned without offering an alternative?

Hebrews 12:11 (MSG) reminds us, "At the time, discipline isn't much fun. It always feels like it's going against the grain. Later, of course, it pays off handsomely, for it's the well-trained who find themselves mature in their relationship with God."

TURN AROUND

Then why do these people stay on their self-destructive path?
Why do the people of Jerusalem refuse to turn back?
JEREMIAH 8:5 NLT

It's been said, "The definition of insanity is doing the same thing over and over again but expecting different results." God's people had pursued a self-destructive path—and they stayed on that path. Instead of returning to truth, they kept taking a run at a lie. The result was always the same. Poor decisions never lead to God.

The idea of repentance means turning around, heading back the way you came, and remembering to follow the God who leads in perfect directions. Luke understood this when he wrote in Acts 3:19 (NLT), "Now repent of your sins and turn to God, so that your sins may be wiped away." Luke wrote that sin in the first century was not unique: "You are heathen at heart and deaf to the truth. Must you forever resist the Holy Spirit? That's what your ancestors did, and so do you!" (Acts 7:51 NLT).

Following God should be a daily decision because people get off track so easily. Jeremiah 17:9–10 (MSG) says, "The heart is hopelessly dark and deceitful, a puzzle that no one can figure out. But I, GOD, search the heart and examine the mind. I get to the heart of the human. I get to the root of things. I treat them as they really are, not as they pretend to be."

Turn around and avoid the insanity.

DESIRING JUSTICE?

*If you stumble in safe country, how will
you manage in the thickets by the Jordan?*
JEREMIAH 12:5 NIV

Jeremiah needed a tender heart and calloused skin. An idealistic Jeremiah asked God to bring justice to people who were breaking His laws. God said He *would* bring justice but that there would be nothing for the prophet to enjoy. If Jeremiah struggled with the response of his own people, he would struggle even more with those who would bring God's justice to Israel.

Not every prophet's message was accepted. Many were imprisoned, were ridiculed, and endured physical violence. Their willingness to share only what God told them to say put them in conflict with family and friends.

God said in Joel 2:12–13 (NLT), "Turn to me now, while there is time. Give me your hearts. Come with fasting, weeping, and mourning. Don't tear your clothing in your grief, but tear your hearts instead." God will show mercy, but He has to deal with injustice.

Jeremiah would suffer for his prophetic message. He would speak God's words, and the people would fault the messenger. His was not an enviable job, but it would invite repentance. It must have been disappointing for Jeremiah, however, to witness a lack of shame for national sin.

We're never promised an easy life, but God can and will use us to move His plan forward. It may be the most difficult but fulfilling thing we'll ever be a part of.

HEART OF DECEIT

Who really knows how bad it is?
JEREMIAH 17:9 NLT

Jeremiah was learning much about God's plan for justice in Israel. Sometimes God's message brought him to tears. He would discover that God searches the heart and examines the mind. He came to understand that riches fail us and when we trust in money we're made to look foolish. He saw that God paid attention to conduct.

More importantly, Jeremiah learned, "The heart is deceitful above all things and beyond cure" (Jeremiah 17:9 NIV). The question God posed can be answered easily. *God* knows how bad our hearts are. And He holds us accountable for our choice to sin.

The apostle Paul was a prolific writer of New Testament books. His story is impressive, his zeal unrivaled, his work ethic without equal. Yet this writer demonstrated how his personal efforts at right living failed miserably.

"I know that all God's commands are spiritual, but I'm not. Isn't this also your experience? Yes. I'm full of myself—after all, I've spent a long time in sin's prison. What I don't understand about myself is that I decide one way, but then I act another, doing things I absolutely despise. So if I can't be trusted to figure out what is best for myself and then do it, it becomes obvious that God's command is necessary" (Romans 7:15–16 MSG).

Because we have no ability to redeem ourselves, God sent His Son to alter the future of those with deceitful hearts in need of forgiveness.

RESIST THE CHARLATAN

Has even one of them cared enough to listen?
JEREMIAH 23:18 NLT

Jeremiah heard from God and shared a difficult message, but he wasn't alone in sharing messages. There were those who claimed to be prophets, were accepted as prophets, but had no real connection to the Lord. These false prophets made a living from helping people *feel* safe. They gained listeners from excusing the sin of a nation, and people accepted their assessment. They didn't pronounce God's actual message. These false prophets weren't listening to Him. Jeremiah had an uphill fight to convince the nation that God's judgment was on the way.

A charlatan is someone who falsely claims to know something important. Every generation has faced men and women who make claims they say come from God but which can't be backed by scripture.

God addressed this issue in 2 Timothy 4:3–5 (MSG): "You're going to find that there will be times when people will have no stomach for solid teaching, but will fill up on spiritual junk food—catchy opinions that tickle their fancy. They'll turn their backs on truth and chase mirages. But you—keep your eye on what you're doing; accept the hard times along with the good; keep the Message alive; do a thorough job as God's servant."

Jeremiah was one of God's servants. He accepted both good and bad. He kept the message alive. He was a worthy example for all who seek God's truth above catchy opinions.

GRANDIOSE ILLUSIONS

Do these prophets give two cents about me as they
preach their lies and spew out their grandiose delusions?
JEREMIAH 23:26 MSG

If you were to read Jeremiah 23, you might envision a group of false prophets gathered to share their next story. In order to be successful, the story would need to connect with the audience on an emotional level. It would need to inspire a positive outlook on the future. It would need to be sold as passionately as a true prophecy. These *storybook prophecies* were finding an audience. They were making a living for those who spun their tales. The people preferred these lies to Jeremiah's truth.

Sometimes we can be well intentioned, but we fit the descriptions of those in Jeremiah's day who bought into these appealing illusions. We hear so-called biblical principles and superpositive promises and gladly accept them as solid biblical teaching. We can take in doctrines that aren't true, but because they're worded so persuasively we accept them as biblical concepts.

God has given us a way to avoid the spread of teachings that don't reflect His Word. Second Timothy 2:15 (NLT) says, "Work hard so you can present yourself to God and receive his approval. Be a good worker, one who does not need to be ashamed and who correctly explains the word of truth."

To explain God's Word, we must know God's Word.

THE WANDERER

How long will you wander, unfaithful Daughter Israel?
JEREMIAH 31:22 NIV

God's question was filled with a sense of weariness. The history of God's people was riddled with unfaithful leadership, heartbreaking decisions, and a blatant disregard for God. The people wanted the shiny, the new, the fashionable. They routinely expressed a willingness to trade in the true God for a lesser god with a clever mythology, fewer laws, and unique benefits. In times past, this type of attitude caused the writer of the book of Judges to say, "People did whatever they felt like doing" (Judges 17:6 MSG).

God gave the Law, established servants in the temple, and secured kings at the people's request. Many of the priests and kings were unfaithful, and the people felt no obligation to follow God. Even so, we routinely disappoint God. Our decisions often deny our allegiance. Our words suggest His teachings have no life influence.

God may well ask us, "How long will you wander?" Many things fight for our attention, but the most radical and life transforming are regarding the identity of Jesus Christ. The apostle Peter said to Jesus in John 6:68 (MSG), "You have the words of real life, eternal life."

Proverbs 4:20–22 (NLT) says, "Listen carefully to my words. Don't lose sight of them. Let them penetrate deep into your heart, for they bring life to those who find them." We can stop our wandering today if we agree we've been wrong, consult God's Word, and make Him our greatest priority.

THE TROUBLE WITH SELF-SUFFICIENCY

How can you say, "We are warriors, men valiant in battle"?
JEREMIAH 48:14 NIV

God is pleased to hear people say, "Some nations boast of their chariots and horses, but we boast in the name of the LORD our God" (Psalm 20:7 NLT). However, God wasn't hearing those words from Israel. He wasn't hearing them from Moab. It's true, Moab wasn't God's covenant nation, but still, that didn't excuse their self-confident pride. God said, "You trust in your deeds and riches" (Jeremiah 48:7 NIV). The self-reliance of Moab had become a de-structive national vice. So God was compelled to punish them. All their wealth and self-proclaimed warrior status couldn't change the judgment that was coming.

We sometimes hear of "culture wars" (a conflict between opposing belief systems), and in some ways this is what was happening when God pronounced judgment on Moab. Their lack of respect for the Lord was setting a negative example for Israel. Israel's culture of honoring and worshipping God had shifted to a Moabite attitude of stubborn self-reliance. First Corinthians 15:33 (NLT) warns us, "Bad company corrupts good character."

It can be hard to remove yourself from negative influences. People may think you believe you feel superior. When you take a stand for God, even family members may seem like adversaries. But God can help you deal with the pain when others won't sup-port your decision to "love the LORD your God with all your heart, all your soul, and all your strength" (Deuteronomy 6:5 NLT).

WALKING AWAY

I'll take my pick of the flock—and who's to stop me?
JEREMIAH 49:19 MSG

God describes Himself as a lion in His justice plan for Edom. The nation's founder was Esau, the twin brother of Jacob. Edom originally had faith in the same God as Abraham and Isaac, yet God considered this nation among the worst offenders. God said, "I'm bringing doom to Esau. It's time to settle accounts" (Jeremiah 49:10 MSG). They'd originally had the right credentials, but Edom had walked away from God.

A set of parents who believe in the Lord, love Him, and seek to raise their children to do the same can be disappointed when a child grows up to disengage, turn their back, or walk away from God. Parents can be heartbroken, but this happens for one very specific reason: each person on earth is responsible to personally accept or reject the Lord.

The people of Edom were no different. At some point there was a turning away from the God of their fathers. Was it Abraham's fault? Perhaps Isaac had done something wrong? Maybe it was the fault of Esau's twin brother, Jacob? No, while none of these patriarchs was perfect, each member of Esau's family had the responsibility to either follow or reject God.

Our children's choices about God may not be a slight against us (Luke 10:16). The Lord may need to take them through some difficult circumstances to get them to change course and come home. Pray for that day.

PROPHECY IMPROV

*Do you think you can trap others without
bringing destruction on yourselves?*
EZEKIEL 13:18 NLT

Surrounding nations were leading God's people in new directions.
False prophets were creating a vibrant industry, saying what
people wanted to hear. God's question was directed at women
who joined their male counterparts in lying. It was a profitable
game of prophecy improv. By believing the false prophet's lies, the
people were in peril. Ezekiel 13:19 (NLT) says, "By lying to my
people who love to listen to lies, you kill those who should not die,
and you promise life to those who should not live."

Jesus had the same view when it came to truth in instruction.
In Matthew 18:6–7 (MSG), He said, "If you give them a hard time,
bullying or taking advantage of their simple trust, you'll soon wish
you hadn't. You'd be better off dropped in the middle of the lake
with a millstone around your neck. Doom to the world for giving
these God-believing children a hard time!"

Humanity has always looked for magic pills that make life
easy, that make excess weight vanish, and that provide instant
riches or fame. Because we'll buy almost anything that makes our
lives easier, we purchase ideas that can't deliver on their promise.
The result can be a decreased faith in mankind, a jaded view of the
world, and a belief that maybe even God isn't worth following.

Is it any wonder that God deals so strongly with those who
intentionally introduce fiction into His absolute truth?

FIGHTING AGAINST GOD

Will he succeed?
EZEKIEL 17:15 NIV

God announced His justice initiative. This plan would be carried out. In time, the people would return to the God who'd given them life. The prophecy was sure. . .certain. . .irrevocable. God chose Babylon as the invading force. Babylon demanded that a member of Israel's royal family assist them in bringing the best and the brightest captives to Babylon. This was God's plan. However, the king went off script and tried to get Egypt to fight against Babylon. The king's plan failed.

Many centuries later, a Pharisee named Gamaliel was asked advice about how they should treat the growth of Christianity. This leader of the Pharisees may have remembered the king's decision in the Babylonian exile when he said, "Let them alone. If this program or this work is merely human, it will fall apart, but if it is of God, there is nothing you can do about it—and you better not be found fighting against God!" (Acts 5:38–39 MSG).

Today, we can also find ourselves opposing God. We have a tendency to chase new ideas, we invite new religious ideas to entertain our brains, and we can even decide to oppose those who believe God's Word is the source of absolute truth. We may believe we know what we're doing, but when we stand opposed to God's plans, we will *never* succeed. Success comes from being on God's side. It's where we've always belonged.

CHOOSE LIFE

Why would you choose to die, Israel?
Ezekiel 18:31 msg

In Sodom and Gomorrah, sin was embraced like a best friend at a class reunion. So God was on His way to destroy the twin sin cities. Abraham argued that God wouldn't destroy an entire city if there were fifty righteous people who lived there. God agreed: "If I find fifty decent people in the city of Sodom, I'll spare the place" (Genesis 18:26 msg). Eventually God consented to spare the city if there were *ten* righteous people. There weren't.

The people of Israel remembered this story, knew God's loathing for sin, but in the midst of sin, facing judgment, they said, "That's not fair! God's not fair!" (Ezekiel 18:25 msg).

The deplorable decision-making skills of His people led God to ask why they chose death. Obedience was the remedy for their predicament, but the hearts of the people were stone-cold committed to rebellion against God.

God had given a choice, centuries earlier in Moses' day: "Today I have given you the choice between life and death, between blessings and curses. . . . Oh, that you would choose life, so that you and your descendants might live!" (Deuteronomy 30:19 nlt).

God's desire for His followers has always been obedience. We obey those we trust. We trust those with whom we have a relationship. When there's no relationship with God, there's no interest in obeying Him. May we be careful to trust, obey, and accept the friendship of God. It brings life, love, and liberty.

SO CONFRONTATIONAL

Son of man, will you confront Oholah and
Oholibah with what they've done?
EZEKIEL 23:36 MSG

This question might not make much sense at first, but it would
help to know that Oholah represents Samaria, the ancient
capital of Israel, while Oholibah represents Jerusalem, the capital
of Judah. Both kingdoms represented God's people of promise.
But these kingdoms seemed to view the accumulation of sin as a
contest they were committed to winning. The one-upmanship of
self-destruction was impossible for God to watch without proclaiming they were both winners in a contest of losers.

If we must confront someone, we have to believe that what
that person is doing is wrong. The best confrontations are those
balanced between truth, which leads to correction, and love, which
shows that you really care about the person.

God isn't shy about confrontation. Perhaps this can be
explained by His desire for us to return to Him as soon as possible. He doesn't want us to misuse or waste time by separating ourselves from His plan, purpose, and protection. The confrontation
God initiates is almost always about restoring relationship. When
confrontation comes, it's either to remind us of expectations
already established or to define new expectations. Parents often
have to confront children, and business leaders confront employ-
ees for these exact same reasons.

Confrontation isn't wrong, but we can't guarantee our concerns will be well received. God's example shows that appropriate
confrontation defines expectations and opportunities. Then someone else has to make a choice.

A RIVER DEFINED

He asked me, "Son of man, do you see this?"
EZEKIEL 47:6 NIV

God had given Ezekiel a visual parable. What he saw represented a brave new future. You almost get the sense that God was excited to show Ezekiel something he would probably never understand. A key part of the vision was "Swarms of living creatures will live wherever the river flows" (Ezekiel 47:9 NIV). This picture represents the coming new covenant, with Jesus as a river that would bring life. Ezekiel saw water flowing from God's temple, covering the world with its influence. This was a prophecy of God's ultimate restoration. It was on its way. Ezekiel could only faithfully write what he didn't understand.

God gave humanity all the time needed to prove or disprove the possibility of living a sin-free life. However, the most perfect human alive was still imperfect. The person who'd done the most good was still a lawbreaker.

Pour a cup of water on dry ground and the water saturates everything it touches. This is the picture of the greatest news God could possibly share in the midst of judgment: A time was coming when grace would come from God's Living Water. Jesus would restore what our sins had crushed. Life would come from death. Forgiveness would be offered to sinners. Hope would be a gift to those all too familiar with despair.

Jesus was coming. Ezekiel had witnessed a picture of God's ultimate plan.

THE TRUSTY KING

Where is your trusty king you thought would save you?
HOSEA 13:10 MSG

———————

The question was a challenge in a time of judgment. If a human spoke these words, it might sound sarcastic, but since God spoke them we're left to genuinely consider who could possibly rival the power of God. There's no appropriate entry in our *perfect person* ledger. No one who's ever lived can compare with God. Or can they? There *was* a trusty King who came to save us. He's the Son of God. What was not accomplished before Jesus came was completed for eternity, because He offered Himself as payment for our sin.

One payment for all time and all people. That's the gift made available when Jesus was crucified and God accepted the sacrifice. Where is that trusty King? Nailed to a cross. Did He really come to save? He did, and He rose from the dead. Did we expect this gift? No, but we can see now how it was the only way we could be right with God.

Before Jesus, God's judgment couldn't be controlled by kings. After Jesus came, kings and queens, rich and poor, men and women, old and young, and people of all shapes, sizes, and colors could receive forgiveness. Justice was no longer the universal tool for dealing with sin.

Justice would soon meet grace. Punishment would be introduced to mercy. The penalty for sin would be marked, "Paid in Full." Trusty King Jesus changed history.

OF EQUAL IMPORTANCE

Are you Israelites more important to me than the Ethiopians?
AMOS 9:7 NLT

It was a time of clarification for Israel. The people thought they might have been exempt from punishment because their forefathers had been told, "GOD, your God, chose you out of all the people on Earth for himself as a cherished, personal treasure" (Deuteronomy 7:6 MSG).

Being God's cherished, personal treasure meant many things. It meant that God cared about the people, but it also meant He couldn't allow their bad behavior to go unpunished. Israel wasn't exempt from God's judgment, and they weren't the only people He cared about. God would speak of non-Jews who experienced their own "exodus" from nations that held them captive. God had intervened for them, too.

It can be easy to think that somehow God might be *for* some people and *against* others. But even in the Old Testament God made it clear that His love was for *every* human being. There was no one left out. There was no one overlooked.

The apostle Paul challenged the thinking of people who believed God only loved the nation of Israel. In Galatians 3:28 (MSG) we read, "In Christ's family there can be no division into Jew and non-Jew, slave and free, male and female. Among us you are all equal. That is, we are all in a common relationship with Jesus Christ."

It doesn't matter who we are or where we came from. We're family when we have a common relationship with Jesus.

INFORMED RESPONSE

Have you no king to lead you?
MICAH 4:9 NLT

Very likely the answer to this question was *not* that the nation was without a king, but that the people had rejected God as their King. This was no more evident than the exile of God's people and the national disgrace brought about by their sin. Micah wasn't looking forward to a homecoming of exiles but the era of New Jerusalem. This describes a future time when the people of God would be on the same page as Jesus, the King they would reject.

Prophecy in the Old Testament often referenced corrective judgment. On occasion, the prophecies were related to the end of time. The question God posed was nestled in the middle of one of these Last Days' prophecies—a time when the Lord will be King, the people will be willing followers, and God's plans are everyone's highest priority. What a difference this will be from the course corrections common in prophecy books of the Old Testament.

It would be wonderful to have a national movement directed toward God, but none of us needs to wait for some future occasion. Each of us can make a personal decision to allow God's plans to direct our response—today.

Future prophecy should inspire hope among Christians. What God says, He will do. He said He would return for those who follow Him. He is our King, and He's willing to lead now and forever.

A DELAYED RETURN

Why?

Haggai 1:9 niv

A one-word question challenged the thinking of a nation. God's people were returning from Babylon. They were rebuilding their homes. They were working to bring life back to the land. They were glad to be home. Maybe they hadn't exactly forgotten God, but they had determined that repairs to His temple could wait until they were finished improving everything else. They would get around to the repairs. . .someday.

Enter God's question: "Why?" Hadn't the people noticed things weren't going well? Hadn't they learned the lesson of exile? The people had returned home, but God wasn't a priority yet.

Are we guilty of the same thing? God wants disciples, and we present a long-range strategy that keeps our schedule full for the foreseeable future. Oh, we plan to get around to following Him because we're pretty certain it's important, but maybe we'll follow next month, next year, or when we reach a certain age. We become comfortable talking about becoming passionate followers of God—as long as we can keep the start date fixed in the future.

The "why" question may be just as valid today as it was when God asked it of His people. If God is really the key to life, why do we act as if He's just a great idea whose time hasn't quite arrived yet? Maybe we should heed the reminder of Hosea 12:6 (msg): "What are you waiting for? Return to your God!"

SEEKING TRUE WORSHIP

When you give blind animals as sacrifices, isn't that wrong?
Malachi 1:8 nlt

The laws for sacrifice were set by God, but the temple leaders let things slide. Instead of offering healthy animals, the people brought defective animals they'd be embarrassed to sell. Some of these animals were possibly near death when they were brought to be sacrificed at the temple. God wanted their best. . .they brought the used-up and broken. God wanted their hearts. . .He received a quick glance of recognition. God wanted their obedience. . .they offered what they thought they needed to get by.

King David once wanted to offer a sacrifice. He was offered the free use of anything he would need, but the king set an example, saying, "I will not sacrifice to the Lord my God burnt offerings that cost me nothing" (2 Samuel 24:24 niv).

Giving something away you no longer need might be called a gift. Giving something away you find it hard to do without transforms a gift into a sacrifice.

We might be guilty of treating worship as if it's all about *us* and the expectations *we* have for how worship should make *us* feel. So we enter worship wanting something from God without ever believing we have something to offer God. Worshipping wrongly becomes more about our needs than His honor.

Sacrifices are not really sacrifices when there's no sense of loss for the giver.

GOD HEARS YOUR CRY

Where have you come from, and where are you going?
GENESIS 16:8 NIV

After Sarai concluded she wouldn't have any children, she offered her slave, Hagar, to her husband, Abram, hoping to build a family through her. After learning Hagar was pregnant, though, Sarai was filled with jealousy and mistreated her, causing her to flee. Alone, and maybe even ashamed, Hagar made her way to a spring in the desert, where an angel of the Lord found her and inquired about her plans.

Many believe Hagar encountered a Christophany—that is, a pre-incarnate appearance of Christ. He heard her cry of affliction and went in search of Hagar to gently lead her back onto the right path, back to Sarai. There she would deliver a child named Ishmael, who, the angel promised, would go on to father many. In spite of being trapped in a less-than-ideal situation, Hagar learned how much God cared for her.

Throughout the ages, God's people have gone on the run for various reasons. Sometimes they run for their lives due to persecution. Other times, they run because they fear the outcome of a situation. And still other times, they run from their own sin.

No matter the reason, we should find great comfort in the fact that we can never outrun God. He hears our cry of affliction and asks us even this day, "Where have you come from, and where are you going?"

TIME FOR ACTION

Why are you crying out to me?
EXODUS 14:15 NIV

───────

Pharaoh had second thoughts about letting God's people go when he realized how much free labor he was losing. But even before Pharaoh and his army began pursuing them, God was preparing Moses. God told him to turn the Israelites back to encamp near Pi Hahiroth, between Migdol and the sea, directly opposite Baal Zephon. God wanted Pharaoh to believe Israel was lost, but He was setting the stage to show His power to the Egyptians—*and* the Israelites.

But when the Egyptian army closed in, Israel panicked, trusting in their eyes rather than in the Lord. "It would have been better for us to serve the Egyptians than to die in the desert!" they complained to Moses in verse 12. Many commentators agree that while Moses listened, he was either praying silently or uttering groans of displeasure over Israel's attitude. Either way, God heard his cry and openly questioned why Moses was crying out to Him.

This wasn't the time for questioning and/or depression. It was time to act by raising his staff and stretching it out over the sea so the Israelites could pass through it. This would set the stage for God to send judgment on Egypt, which He quickly did.

Have you been spending time praying or groaning about a situation that God has already clearly spoken to you about? Stop praying and groaning. Act in faith, and the Lord will respond.

GLASS HOUSES

Have I not commanded you?
JOSHUA 1:9 NIV

When Moses passed away, God was ready to lead Joshua and the Israelites into the Promised Land. This promised territory extended from "the desert to Lebanon, and from the great river, the Euphrates—all the Hittite country—to the Mediterranean Sea in the west" (Joshua 1:4 NIV). God promised to go forth with them in battle, but they were to obey Him. And He commanded them four times in Joshua 1 to be "strong and courageous."

Sadly, Israel never fully realized this full possession of the Promised Land. John Wesley, in his *Explanatory Notes on the Whole Bible*, didn't mince words when writing about their ability to only partially realize God's promises: "That was from their own sloth and cowardice, and disobedience to God, and breach of those conditions upon which this promise was suspended: Though their possessions extended not to Euphrates, yet their dominion did, and all those lands were tributary to them in David's and Solomon's time."

When we read about this in the scriptures, we find it easy to criticize Israel. All they had to do was obey and be strong and courageous, and the land was theirs for the taking. Instead, they were weak and cowardly. Fair enough. But how often do we read God's commands not to covet, or not to lust, or not to think too highly of ourselves, and then we do it anyway? Has God not commanded *us*? Yes, He has.

TEARING YOUR CLOTHES

Have you noticed how Ahab has humbled himself before me?
1 Kings 21:29 niv

When King Ahab wanted the vineyard of a farmer named Naboth, but Naboth refused to give it up, Ahab's wife, Jezebel, took things into her own hands. She had Naboth killed, and Ahab was then only too happy to step in and take over the vineyard. But the Lord was watching, and He sent Elijah to confront the king about his sin, pronouncing a curse of death on him, his wife, and every male descendant.

To his credit, Ahab didn't defend himself or try to justify his sin. He was guilty and he knew it. In response, he tore his clothes, put on sackcloth, and fasted, putting on a meek countenance. Today, we wear black and express grief or sadness with solemn faces. But why did Jews tear their clothing to express mourning? One theory, put forth by Sam O'Neal—managing editor of the *Quest Study Bible*—is that they lived an agrarian lifestyle in which producing clothing was very time consuming, making them valuable commodities. Tearing them showed true remorse.

God took notice of Ahab's gesture and subsequent repentance and asked Elijah if he saw it. As a result, God showed mercy toward Ahab and promised not to bring disaster on him or his family immediately. You may not have blood on your hands like Ahab, but God has lovingly sent correction your way for one sin or another at some point. What was *your* response?

THE CORNERSTONE

What supports its [the earth] foundations, and who laid its cornerstone as the morning stars sang together and all the angels shouted for joy?
JOB 38:6–7 NLT

As God questioned Job, He asked him who had laid the earth's cornerstone as all the angels celebrated. Cornerstones are foundation stones in a corner on the outside wall of a building. Often a construction crew will lay the cornerstone of an important building during a formal ceremony, and the date the building was constructed is written on it. So the cornerstone is the starting point—the base for the entire building—and the date gives those of us who weren't at the original ceremony a context. Sometimes we get a little more.

In January 2015, a time capsule that had been buried inside the cornerstone of the Massachusetts State House was opened. According to CNN.com, the capsule had been placed there by Paul Revere and Samuel Adams in 1795, when George Washington was still president. The contents included five folded newspapers, a title page from Massachusetts colony records, a Massachusetts commonwealth seal, and twenty-four coins—one of which dated back to 1652. The original construction crew is long gone now, but their handiwork gives us a context for the time period and a deep appreciation and respect for what they did.

In a much bigger sense, God laid the cornerstone of the earth and set His creation in motion. How can we not revere what He has done?

THE FATHER OF RAIN

Has the rain a father? Or who has begotten the drops of dew?
From whose womb comes the ice?
JOB 38:28–29 NKJV

Weather conditions are not random, even though we like to complain about them as if they were.

For rain to occur, many factors come into play. The air we breathe contains water vapor. As warm air rises for any number of reasons (the presence of mountains, low pressures, cold fronts, jet streams), it begins to cool, and that causes condensation, which leads to droplets. As droplets merge and become heavier, the air is no longer able to support them, and they fall to the ground.

Dew is formed on objects when radiational cooling occurs at night and the layer of overlying air comes into contact with ground objects.

Ice forms when the ambient temperature of air is lower than water temperature.

Who but God could father such a system? Without precipitation, our ecosystem couldn't survive. Crops wouldn't grow. Electricity wouldn't exist. We wouldn't have any way to wash our clothing or bathe, and we and our livestock wouldn't have anything to drink.

Mankind is incapable of creating such a system on a scale large enough to support our planet. When you jump into the shower this morning, when you twist the cap off of your bottled spring water at lunch, and when you enjoy three healthy meals today, know that none of those things would be possible if God hadn't caused rain to fall from the sky.

THE INSTINCTS OF A LION

Can you hunt the prey for the lion, or satisfy the
appetite of the young lions, when they crouch in
their dens, or lurk in their lairs to lie in wait?
JOB 38:39–40 NKJV

Instinctively, lions know to hunt at night. They prefer fresh meat from a variety of animals, including antelope, buffalo, and giraffe. As magnificent and intimidating as their presence can be, they are in the habit of crouching and lurking, patiently waiting to pounce on unsuspecting animals as they pass. Death usually comes quickly as the lions go for the throat or the back of the neck.

Even if Job had studied lions and knew their natural hunting tendencies, he certainly didn't fathom their killer instinct or understand precisely how to attack and kill for food the way they do. But God did. He designed the food chain, knowing exactly how to keep it all in balance. If lions kill more animals than necessary, their food source ceases to exist. If they kill fewer than they need, *they* cease to exist.

Meanwhile, as humans, we have finite understanding about such things. We eat one meal at a time with little regard for where the food came from or how it got onto our plate. And that's okay, but when we contemplate the complexities of the food chain and the way God designed it to function, it should cause us to pause and worship Him.

FOR APPEARANCES' SAKE

Would you condemn me to justify yourself?
JOB 40:8 NIV

While God allows His children to ask Him questions, it's possible to go too far based on faulty, underlying assumptions. Job's line of questioning implied that God had been too harsh with him, causing him to suffer too much.

In Job 7:20–21 (NIV), he asked God the following questions: "If I have sinned, what have I done to you, you who sees everything we do? Why have you made me your target? Have I become a burden to you? Why do you not pardon my offenses and forgive my sins? For I will soon lie down in the dust; you will search for me, but I will be no more." Later, Job said accusingly, "You turn on me ruthlessly; with the might of your hand you attack me" (Job 30:21 NIV).

When God addressed Job's questions, He wanted to know whether Job was willing to condemn Him for the sake of appearances, in order to justify himself. We cringe when we read such words from Job and God's subsequent response, but don't we do the same thing every time we tell God that He isn't treating us fairly?

We work hard, try to do right by our family and friends, and serve at church, but yet, at times the Lord still allows our finances and/or health to falter, and we complain about His "injustice." And so He asks us, "Will you condemn me to justify yourself?"

WHO DARES PLAY OFFENSE?

Who can strip off its outer coat?
Job 41:13 NIV

While we aren't certain whether Leviathan was a whale, a crocodile, a giant serpent, or some other unknown monstrosity, we know from Job 41:1 (NIV) that it probably couldn't be caught by natural means: "Can you pull in Leviathan with a fishhook or tie down its tongue with a rope?" If it couldn't be *caught* by natural means, how could anybody remove its outer coat (its hide)? Why would God even ask Job such a question?

No matter what the beast, God seemed to be asking Job if he was brave enough to approach and remove its skin. If he had been, would he have the first inkling about how to do so? If you've ever gone swimming in the ocean or gone for a stroll at night near a marsh, then you know that you're always on the defensive, wondering what might lie under the surface or in the brush. Your senses are heightened and you're on full alert. You don't consider going on the offensive. And even if you do, what chance would you have at success?

If such a ferocious beast can garner such awe and respect, how much more ought God? He struck Nadab and Abihu dead when they offered unauthorized fire (Leviticus 10:1–2), and He struck down Uzzah for touching the ark of the covenant (2 Samuel 6:1–7). Never go on the offense against God.

GOD'S PERSONAL TOUCH

Who has done such mighty deeds, summoning each
new generation from the beginning of time?
ISAIAH 41:4 NLT

God, through Isaiah, called the "lands beyond the sea" (verse 1) to a summit and asked a question that only had one answer: Who summons each new generation from the beginning of time?

How many people lived in your home before you did, and what are their stories? How many people sat in your chair at the office before you took the job, and why did they leave? Flip through your grandmother's photo album and stop when you come to a generation of family members you've never met; ask yourself what they believed, where they worked, and what they enjoyed doing with their free time.

People have such finite understanding of what has come before them. Even if you know a few names and a few answers to some of the questions in the previous paragraph, you often know little more. In contrast, God summons each new generation from the beginning of time. He's the only One who can, because He is eternal. But more than that, He is personal.

He formed you in your mother's womb, and He called you by name (Isaiah 43:1). He even knows how many hairs you have on your head (Luke 12:7). He redeems you and prepares a place for you in heaven (John 14:3). Who but the one true, eternal God could do such things?

CHASING IDOLS

Shall I make a detestable thing from what is left?
Isaiah 44:19 niv

───────────

There is none like God. And yet, some of the most learned among us often worship idols. Earlier in this chapter, God pointed out the folly of the blacksmith and the carpenter who used their skills to fashion idols. They cooked a meal with some of the wood, yet they used what was left to make a "god." They lacked the understanding to ask themselves whether they should have been performing a task that the Lord hated.

No matter how intelligent a person might be, we shouldn't fear him, nor should we give his idol worshipping a second thought. He's on the road to destruction. His worship holds no power, and his gods are dead. His knowledge is futile and won't hold up in the final judgment. We seem to understand this when it comes to people who actually bow to inanimate objects, ascribing power to gods that don't actually exist. But we're less understanding about the need to avoid figurative idols.

On any given Sunday, more than half of the population in our country (including some Christians) ignore God and indulge in sleep, personal time, golf, fishing, shopping, and ultimately selfish pursuits, rather than gathering with God's people to worship Him. You might not consider any of this idolatry, but what else is it when practiced over a lifetime? Thankfully, it's not too late to begin anew now.

GOD REMEMBERS

Can a mother forget her nursing child?
Can she feel no love for the child she has borne?
ISAIAH 49:15 NLT

During times of affliction, self-induced or otherwise, God's people have often been quick to forget His tender mercy. Isaiah 49 describes such a situation. Their work often feels useless, so they feel purposeless (verse 4). "At just the right time" (verse 8), God responds to them with a promise of protection. They return (verse 12), only to claim that He has forgotten them (verse 14). And so the cycle continues.

Even so, God responds the way He always does, this time using the metaphor of a mother who will never forget her nursing child. Just as it isn't possible for a mother to forget her child, so He never forgets us. A nursing child has no capacity to understand her surroundings. Her well-being is totally dependent on her mother. And while she will fuss and cry when she doesn't get her way, it never dawns on her to pull away from her mother, believing her mother to be cruel or indifferent.

What is your current affliction? Is someone you love dying? Are you out of work? Are you still trying to have a child with your spouse, against all odds? Whatever your lot, God has not forgotten you. You may not understand what He's up to, but He is your heavenly Father, and He will never leave you nor forsake you. It's not in His nature.

GOD CANNOT BE MOCKED

Who are you mocking?
ISAIAH 57:4 NIV

———

Those who walk uprightly, Isaiah says, find rest as they lie in death (verse 2). If you've ever been at the bedside of a believer who is minutes from passing from this life into the next, then you know this to be true. But those who have embraced sorcery and sexual immorality (verse 3) tend to mock God and His followers, because to do otherwise would mean coming face-to-face with their sin.

This is just as true today as it has ever been. Christianity is mocked in pop culture at every turn. And with the continual passage of antidiscrimination laws, ironically, "Christians are frightened to reveal their religious beliefs to colleagues at work," according to a 2015 article titled "Christians ARE Too Scared to Admit Beliefs—Because They Fear Being Mocked or Treated Like Bigots, Say Equality Chiefs" in the *Daily Mail*.

"When they do declare their Christianity, whether in the office or on the shop floor, they are often mocked or treated like bigots—and their children are even ridiculed at school."

One day soon, though, those who mock God and His followers will have their worst fears realized. "Do not be deceived: God cannot be mocked. A man reaps what he sows. Whoever sows to please their flesh, from the flesh will reap destruction; whoever sows to please the Spirit, from the Spirit will reap eternal life" (Galatians 6:7–8 NIV).

WEEP NO MORE

Who are these who fly like a cloud, and like doves to their roosts?
ISAIAH 60:8 NKJV

An article on the University of Delaware website informed read-ers about a massive flock of black birds that makes its way to Churchman's Marsh in the winter, just before sunset: "This flock of several million birds forms a solid black carpet in the sky; if it was earlier in the day, when the sun is higher, the flock would blot it from view," the article says.

As fascinating as this phenomenon is, Isaiah foresaw some-thing even more spectacular—a time in which Gentile converts would flock to the Church in numbers so great that when God's people saw it, they would be in awe. The new converts would de-scend from the sky in multitudes, like doves to their roosts.

Do you often find yourself down in the dumps over the direc-tion our world or our country is headed? Do the statistics about the growing number of young people who are leaving the Church cause you to fret? Are you worried about the lack of member growth, or worse, maybe even decline, in your own church body?

If the answer to any of those questions is "yes," then you're in good company. Even Jesus wept when He entered Jerusalem and thought about its imminent destruction (Luke 19:41). But don't lose hope. A time is coming when converts will flock to the faith in unprecedented numbers.

GOD'S FOOTSTOOL

Could you build me a temple as good as that?
Could you build me such a resting place?
ISAIAH 66:1 NLT

———————

In Isaiah 65:17, God says He will create a "new heavens and a new earth" someday, "and no one will even think about the old ones anymore." Then He "will rejoice over Jerusalem and delight in [His] people" (Isaiah 65:19 NLT). Everything will be made right. Justice will be administered. The wolf and lamb will feed together. And all pain will disappear. "Heaven is [His] throne, and the earth is [His] footstool" (Isaiah 66:1 NLT). How could man build anything in comparison?

Throughout history, Christians have differed on the topic of aesthetics (the study of beauty and taste)—especially in relation to worship. Some want to set the mood for a reverential worship experience by creating a building that contains as much beauty as possible, while others say the best way to do so is not to provide any physical distractions or creature comforts. No matter where you fall in this spectrum, one thing is certain—mankind is incapable of creating anything that can resemble the perfection that will occur when Jesus returns to make all things right.

Undoubtedly, you've suffered one injustice or another in your lifetime. You've probably also seen or experienced your share of conflict. And you may have watched a loved one suffer and die with a terrible disease. But one day soon, all of this will end and we will rejoice.

SELF-INFLICTED WOUNDS

*Have you not brought this on yourselves by forsaking
the LORD your God when he led you in the way?*
JEREMIAH 2:17 NIV

In her youth, Israel loved the Lord (verse 2), but eventually she began to stray from the Lord in favor of worthless idols (verse 5). Her ancestors forgot God and His faithfulness to them (verse 6)—to the point that even her priests stopped seeking Him (verse 8). Israel suffered as a result; her land was laid waste and her towns were burned (verse 15).

God's question to her is the same one He asks all of us today after we've strayed: "Have you not brought this on yourselves by forsaking the Lord?" Bible commentator Matthew Henry adds this about verse 17: "Then when he was leading thee on to a happy peace and settlement, and thou wast within a step of it, then thou forsookest him, and so didst put a bar in thy own door."

Remember when you were young in the faith? The Word was sweet, your prayer life was vibrant, and you frequently sensed God's presence. You sought Him regularly and spoke about Him to all who would listen. But then hardship or the cares of this world came and you strayed from Him. He called you back time and time again, but you didn't listen, and now you find yourself far from Him. The good news is, it's never too late to return to Him.

A BRIDE DOESN'T FORGET

Does a young woman forget her jewelry,
a bride her wedding ornaments?
JEREMIAH 2:32 NIV

In her self-deception, Israel claimed to be clean (Jeremiah 2:23), but in reality, God equated her actions to a wild female donkey in heat that was easily found by any male at mating time (verse 24). In her infidelity, Israel lost her way and worshipped wood and stone gods (verse 27), probably because false gods required nothing from her.

A young woman who is preparing for marriage never loses her way. Usually she's been thinking about and planning for her wedding day since she was a young girl. An article in the *Daily Mail* recently confirmed this, saying: "Brides spend 36 days planning their wedding (and three-quarters of them make most of the big decisions for the big day before they've even MET the groom)." The chances that she would forget her wedding attire and accessories are nonexistent.

And yet we often forsake our first love (Christ)—the very thing Jesus held against the church in Ephesus in Revelation 2:4. It's not that we forget Him, as much as we get lost in our infidelities, honoring our possessions, our time, and ultimately ourselves more than our relationship with Christ. In a sense, we forget our wedding attire in favor of worthless rags.

If a young woman who is preparing for marriage stays on point, how much more ought we, as Spirit-filled Christians, do the same?

FEAR GOD

Have you no respect for me?
Why don't you tremble in my presence?
JEREMIAH 5:22 NLT

———————

We fear all sorts of things, don't we? We fear the possibility of getting cancer, or of dying from it if we do. We fear losing our jobs, knowing our savings will only sustain us for a limited time. We fear losing our spouse to death or someone else. We fear losing our children. We fear not having a large enough nest egg for retirement. And we fear persecution. The possibility of any of those scenarios coming to fruition makes us tremble—probably more so than we tremble in the presence of the Lord.

And yet He asked Israel, as He asks us today, "Have you no respect for me? Why don't you tremble in my presence?" The Bible says, "I, the LORD, define the ocean's sandy shoreline as an everlasting boundary that the waters cannot cross. The waves may toss and roar, but they can never pass the boundaries I set" (Jeremiah 5:22 NLT). Given God's power and ability to define even the shoreline, how much more should we fear Him than the other temporal, albeit painful, losses we might face someday?

The scriptures help us to reorient our fears and set them in the only place they belong. Luke 1:50 (NLT) says that God "shows mercy from generation to generation to all who fear Him." And Acts 10:35 (NLT) says that God "accepts those who fear him and do what is right."

PERPETUAL SIN

Why does Jerusalem always turn away?
JEREMIAH 8:5 NIV

At this stage in Israel's history, the nation had drifted far from God in worshipping the created (the sun, moon, and stars), rather than the Creator. They were so far removed that God told the prophet Jeremiah to stop praying for Israel to be spared judgment (Jeremiah 7:16). They had reached the point of no return, and God planned to give them over to their desires. The bones of the dead were to be removed from their graves and exposed to the sun, moon, and stars that they had worshipped (Jeremiah 8:2).

Typically, when a nation that follows God falls into a period of sin, it eventually turns back to Him (Jeremiah 8:4). But that was no longer the case with Israel: "Showing them to be the worst of all people: it is a common saying, 'it is a long lane that has no turning'; but these people, having departed from the Lord, return no more." So says John Gill in his *Exposition of the Entire Bible*.

This caused God to ask: "Why does Jerusalem always turn away?" In other words, "Why is the nation I have shown such mercy and grace to always in a perpetual state of sin?" Apparently, the nation loved its sin too much to turn back to God. It would pay a huge price for this. If you're in a long pattern of sin, learn from Israel's mistake and turn from it.

HOW LONG?

If you have raced with men on foot and they have
worn you out, how can you compete with horses?
JEREMIAH 12:5 NIV

As Jeremiah looked around, he saw evil prospering, and he couldn't understand why God had allowed such a thing. "How long will the land lie parched and the grass in every field be withered?" he asked in Jeremiah 12:4 (NIV). "Because those who live in it are wicked. . . ."

Do you ever feel the way Jeremiah did? Maybe regular church attendance and family devotions were the norm when you were young, but now your children's children have abandoned those practices in favor of self-indulgence. Maybe you look around and see self-entitled people at every turn who not only don't fear God, but who openly mock Him. And it wears on your soul.

Jeremiah, the weeping prophet, watched his country slowly slipping away, and he couldn't help but wonder why God wasn't intervening. When God answered Jeremiah's question, He did so in a curious fashion, asking if mere men were wearing him out, how would he feel when he came face-to-face with stronger enemies?

Herein lies the problem with focusing too much on circumstances and not enough on the task at hand. God called Jeremiah to be a faithful prophet, to repeatedly warn Israel to turn from her adulterous ways, but Jeremiah wasn't responsible for the results. In fact, God never guaranteed him any results. He only called him to be faithful.

STRAW OR GRAIN?

For what has straw to do with grain?
JEREMIAH 23:28 NIV

Many false prophets arose in Israel to lead God's people astray. Some were prophesying by Baal (Jeremiah 23:13), and others were involved in adultery (verse 14). Of course, God noticed and promised to bring disaster on them (Jeremiah 23:12). Their deception was intentional, as we see in verse 27 (NIV): "They think the dreams they tell one another will make my people forget my name, just as their ancestors forgot my name through Baal worship."

God warned His people to stop listening to these false prophets (verse 16), asking what straw had to do with grain. False doctrine and untruth are associated with chaff or straw, which we can be certain won't withstand the fires of judgment (1 Corinthians 3:12–13). On the other hand, truth and sound doctrine are associated with grain, which brings nourishment. Subsequently, straw and grain don't belong together.

Today, deceit is usually more subtle than it was at that point in Israel's history. Sadly, in Jeremiah's day, God's people had slipped so far from the truth that they no longer had any discernment. But long-believed orthodox Christian doctrine is being questioned by religious leaders in our own day, as well, usually done so in the name of love.

Can you tell the difference between the straw and grain being offered to you from the pulpit or the broadcast media? How do you typically respond?

FUTURE GRACE

Is anything too hard for me?
JEREMIAH 32:27 NIV

Jerusalem was on the verge of destruction, and it would end with God's people being carried into captivity. The Babylonian army was already besieging Jerusalem, and Jeremiah was confined to the courtyard of the guard of the royal palace of Judah (Jeremiah 32:2). But in the midst of such chaos, God spoke to Jeremiah and told him to buy a field in Anathoth, located just two or three miles outside Jerusalem (verse 7).

Why would God have Jeremiah concern himself with such matters, when his people were about to be carried off and their city razed? It was a promise of future grace. One day, God intended for them to return to their land, and their way of life would continue, for nothing is too hard for the Lord. Judgment was necessary, but mercy would follow—just as it has since the days of the Flood and the rainbow that followed.

Has one sin or another been costly to you? Are you in a period in which you're under judgment, causing you to despair about the future? Is anything too hard for the Lord? While He did bring judgment, He also brings mercy. In fact, He earnestly desires to reconcile you to Himself. Endure the hardship, turn from your sin, and look to the future. God will restore you there and return you to blessed patterns of life. He's already preparing the way.

TURN BACK

What has happened there?
JEREMIAH 48:19 NLT

Moab, once the home of Naomi and her family during a famine, was a proud nation. It trusted in its wealth and skill, and it bowed its knee to the god Chemosh (Jeremiah 48:7), but its bragging was about to come to an end (verse 2). As a result, God pronounced judgment on the towns. The people who lived in Aroer (a border city) were commanded to stand beside the road and watch, shouting one question at escapees: "What has happened there?" They'd had barely enough time to pack and flee.

Moab wasn't the first country to trust in its wealth and skill, and it certainly won't be the last—nor will it be the only one to bow to a false god. But it should serve as a warning for nations who have turned their backs on the one true God. He is merciful and His grace runs deep, but the clock will eventually strike midnight, and with the chimes will come judgment, causing those who remain to ask: "What has happened there?"

The West has been slowly drifting from God for decades, and it's hard for Christians to watch. We aren't privy to when God's mercy might run out concerning our own nation, but until it does, it's not too late to warn people. You might even start by asking them what they think might happen if we *don't* return to God.

FRET NOT

*If thieves came during the night, would they
not steal only as much as they wanted?*
JEREMIAH 49:9 NIV

The nation of Edom, which was located south of Judah, had a long history of feuding with God's people. According to Albert Barnes in his *Notes on the Bible*, the feud "caused the Edomites to cherish so bitter an enmity against Judah, that they exulted with cruel joy over the capture of Jerusalem by the Chaldeans, and showed great cruelty toward those who fled to them for refuge."

Moses forbade attacking Edom in his day (Deuteronomy 2:5), but by the time of the prophets, Edom's time for judgment was growing close. Obadiah 1:5 (NIV) used similar language to what Jeremiah used in pronouncing God's pending judgment: "If thieves came to you, if robbers in the night—oh, what a disaster awaits you!—would they not steal only as much as they wanted? If grape pickers came to you, would they not leave a few grapes?"

Both prophets were warning Edom that God would destroy their country, leaving no survivors—going so far as to say that He would be more thorough than a thief, who at least left gleanings. In fact, Jeremiah 49:17 says that Edom would become an object of horror and that everyone who passed by it would be appalled and would scoff because of its wounds.

Does it bother you to see wicked nations prospering, even though they oppose God's people? Fret not, for a day is coming when God will make all things right.

TEND YOUR SOUL

Why has the city of renown not been abandoned,
the town in which I delight?
JEREMIAH 49:25 NIV

Damascus, located about 130 miles northeast of Jerusalem in Syria, is believed to be one of the most ancient cities in the world. Known for its vibrant trade, affluence, and beautiful climate, it was the envy of the world—referred to as a city of renown. Some even believe the prophet Jeremiah enjoyed visiting it—and that the phrase "the town in which I delight" in Jeremiah 49:25 are *his* personal sentiments.

The city certainly had a resilient history. David conquered it once (2 Samuel 8:6), and King Ahab joined forces with the Assyrians to take it yet again (2 Kings 16:7–9). But by the time of Jeremiah, the city had gained her independence again and was thriving. Even so, the prophet foresaw yet another instance in which Damascus would be taken and abandoned because of its carnality. God can turn a city of renown into a city of terror at the snap of His fingers. He can do the same thing to a human heart when it trusts in the wrong things.

Damascus looks and sounds a lot like modern-day life, doesn't it? We live for comfort and carnality. Soccer games, Netflix, and the pursuit of pleasure crowds out any time we might otherwise spend tending to our souls. If we aren't intentional about our own spiritual growth, it won't happen.

IDOLS IN THEIR HEARTS

Should I let them inquire of me at all?
EZEKIEL 14:3 NIV

In Ezekiel 8:1, Ezekiel met with a group of elders from Judah in his own house. Later, in Ezekiel 14:1–3, he met with a group of elders from Israel. Some believe the terms "elders of Judah" and "elders of Israel" can be used interchangeably, while others make a distinction. Either way, Judah no longer had any moral high ground to stand on at this point in her history.

When this group of elders from Israel inquired of Ezekiel about a certain matter, God spoke to Ezekiel, revealing their true motives: "Son of man, these men have set up idols in their hearts and put wicked stumbling blocks before their faces" (Ezekiel 14:3 NIV). So why, then, should God listen to their requests?

These men, who ought to have been offering spiritual guidance and direction to their people, had long since abandoned the true faith—setting up physical idols and cherishing them in their hearts. They approached Ezekiel as others might approach a palm reader or a shaman—hoping for some sort of guidance but having no desire to be close to the one true God in the process.

Do you act in a similar manner sometimes? Are you far from God most days, engaged in activities that you know aren't pleasing to Him, only hoping for some direction from Him on occasion? If so, why should He listen to your request?

DO NOT RETURN TO EGYPT

Can Israel break her sworn treaties like that and get away with it?
Ezekiel 17:15 NLT

Nebuchadnezzar installed Zedekiah as king of Judah during the exile. Zedekiah swore allegiance to Nebuchadnezzar but then turned and violated his treaty by sending ambassadors into Egypt to secure a great army with many horses.

In doing so, he violated Deuteronomy 17:16 (NLT): "The king must not build up a large stable of horses for himself or send his people to Egypt to buy horses, for the Lord has told you, 'You must never return to Egypt.'" And he violated Isaiah 31:1 (NLT): "What sorrow awaits those who look to Egypt for help, trusting their horses, chariots, and charioteers and depending on the strength of human armies instead of looking to the Lord, the Holy One of Israel."

When circumstances become difficult to bear, mankind often breaks promises and allegiances in an effort to escape. Sadly, history has proven that God's people are not the exception. Here, His people had been exiled for disobedience and indifference toward their Creator, and rather than repenting, they returned to Egypt to try to build up their firepower so they could overthrow their captors—even though they had been warned repeatedly never to return there.

What is *your* Egypt? What former way of life are you tempted to return to when life presses in on you? Forsake it today and repent, for God's people can't break a sworn treaty and get away with it.

HOW DARE YOU?

Have you come to inquire of me?
EZEKIEL 20:3 NIV

———

For generations, the people of Israel had been profaning God's Sabbaths and offering sacrifices to idols out in the open, but He preserved them for the sake of His good name.

Showing that He is full of mercy, God renewed His message with each passing generation: "I said to their children in the wilderness, 'Do not follow the statutes of your parents or keep their laws or defile yourselves with their idols. I am the LORD your God; follow my decrees and be careful to keep my laws. Keep my Sabbaths holy, that they may be a sign between us. Then you will know that I am the LORD your God'" (Ezekiel 20:18–20 NIV). And yet, they rebelled anyway.

True to form, in the seventh year of their captivity, and two years after Ezekiel began to prophesy, Israel's elders came to inquire of the Lord, causing God to ask: "Have you come to inquire of me?" The NLT translates His question this way: "How dare you come to ask me for a message?" Israel had no concern for God and His ways prior to this, so why should God listen to them now?

The danger for any of us who say we know God, while continuing to walk in our own ways, is that there comes a time when God will give us over to the sinful desires of our hearts (Romans 1:24).

TREMBLING COASTLANDS

*Will not the coastlands tremble at the sound of your fall,
when the wounded groan and the slaughter takes place in you?*
EZEKIEL 26:15 NIV

By all accounts, Tyre—a city in Phoenicia on the coast of the Mediterranean—was a renowned city (Ezekiel 26:17). In Isaiah 23:8 (NIV) the prophet referred to the city as "the bestower of crowns, whose merchants are princes, whose traders are renowned in the earth."

"She was strong in the sea, easy of access to her friends, but to her enemies inaccessible, fortified by a wall of water, which made her impregnable," says Matthew Henry in his *Commentary on the Whole Bible*. "So that she with her pomp, and her inhabitants with their pride, caused their terror to be on all that haunted that city, and upon any account frequented it."

When Tyre saw that the gates of Jerusalem had been broken down, it saw an opportunity to prosper (Ezekiel 26:2)—to become even greater in the eyes of the world. What Tyre didn't realize was that it was setting itself against God, and its coastlands were no match for Him. In fact, He promised that even the coastlands would tremble at Tyre's impending doom.

We can draw multiple inferences from Tyre's pride. First, we should always be careful not to rejoice about an enemy's downfall. Second, pride truly does come before destruction. And third, mankind is never a match for God—no matter how strong our position might appear.

SPIRITUAL ROADBLOCKS

*Since you eat meat with the blood still in it and look to
your idols and shed blood, should you then possess the land?*
EZEKIEL 33:25 NIV

Going back to the days of Noah, God's people knew they weren't
supposed to eat meat with the blood still in it (Genesis 9:4).
Some believe this meant that they weren't supposed to eat raw
flesh. Commentators say such a prohibition exists primarily
because life is in the blood, and while the blood still flows, the animal belongs to God. A man who eats raw meat exhibits savagery,
much like Saul's men did in 1 Samuel 14:32.

So when an escaped fugitive from Jerusalem approached
Ezekiel to tell him the city had fallen, he shouldn't have been surprised to hear the Lord's response through the prophet (Ezekiel
33:21). The people had been mumbling, saying Abraham was only
one man, yet he possessed the land (Ezekiel 33:24). But they were
many in number and couldn't do so. What gives? God simply
reminded them that they would have no part in taking the land
because they had violated His law by eating meat with the blood
still in it and because they were still clinging to their idols.

Are you seeing spiritual roadblocks in your own life? If so,
examine yourself. Are you currently violating any clear biblical
teachings—ones you know to be true but are simply ignoring
for convenience or preference? If so, this may be hindering your
spiritual victory.

KNOWING GOD

So should the LORD feed her like a lamb in a lush pasture?
HOSEA 4:16 NLT

The message the Lord gave Hosea rings as true today for our modern society as it did for Israel when the prophet penned this book in 715 BC.

Israel lacked faithfulness to the Lord, kindness in general, and an overall knowledge of God (Hosea 4:1). They made vows and broke them, and theft, murder, and adultery were rampant (verse 2). Wine robbed God's people of their understanding (verse 11), and they consulted a piece of wood for advice (verse 12).

Given Israel's stubbornness, why shouldn't God feed these people in a lush pasture, preparing them as lambs for the slaughter? The situation was so dire that God instructed Hosea to abandon Israel to its own devices (verse 17). They weren't interested in knowing Him, anyway.

In 2014, Barna released a study revealing that "only 37% of Americans report reading the Bible once a week or more. Among those who have read Scripture in the previous week, not quite six in 10 (57%) say they gave a lot of thought to how it might apply to their life." It's not possible to know how to live a life that is pleasing to God without knowing His character or His statutes. Such ignorance is the downfall of every once-great nation.

How is your Bible reading going? How are you applying what you're learning? What can you change to make improvements?

A RHETORICAL QUESTION

Where are all the leaders of the land, the king
and the officials you demanded of me?
Hosea 13:10 nlt

After Israel split into the northern and southern kingdoms, King Jeroboam (who was of the tribe of Ephraim) became the first king under the newly organized kingdom of Israel. The Northern Kingdom apostatized, and they were led away from the faith, in part because Jeroboam set up golden calves for his people to worship, fearing they might otherwise return to the fold in Jerusalem (1 Kings 12:25–27).

In Hosea 13, God spoke through the prophet, saying that because of its actions, Ephraim would disappear like a morning mist (verse 3). When the Northern Kingdom demanded a king, it showed an unwillingness to depend solely on the Lord, and here in Hosea 13, He reminded them of that fact. While Ephraim was under judgment and in the midst of being devoured for its actions, God wanted to know whether the leaders they had cried out for could save them. Of course, the answer was "no." They were incapable.

God often allows us the desires of our hearts, even when those desires are bent away from Him, but when He does so, it comes with a curse, of sorts. We will never find fulfillment and satisfaction apart from Him, but He allows us to try. Is there something in your life that you desire but you know it isn't from God? Don't trust it, for it will only lead you astray.

GOD'S FAITHFULNESS

*Did I not bring up Israel from the land of Egypt,
the Philistines from Caphtor, and the Syrians from Kir?*
AMOS 9:7 NKJV

Is it possible to rest too much in God's faithfulness in the past? Will He always maintain His favor on a nation or people group if He provided it once? In case there was any doubt, He answered that question here in Amos 9:7 in the form of another question: "Did I not bring up Israel from the land of Egypt, the Philistines from Caphtor, and the Syrians from Kir?"

Orthodox believers know that God governs in the affairs of men. We don't always understand what He's up to—in fact, we rarely understand what He's actually doing, but He's always active. He's also always on the lookout for people who are faithful to Him, and He acts accordingly. In this case, Israel had rebelled yet again, and God was under no obligation to intervene. Instead, He promised judgment, just like He had brought on other nations that had rebelled against Him.

How has God been faithful to you and your family in the past? Did He bring you through some great tragedy or illness? Did He save you from a life of self-indulgence to set you on a new course? Have you become complacent, as we are wont to do? Don't rest your security on God's prior faithfulness. Yes, He is faithful, but He also commands obedience.

DESPAIR NOT

Has your counselor perished?
MICAH 4:9 NKJV

A s of this writing, a denomination in Canada is wrestling with whether it should allow a pastor in one of its Toronto churches to continue behind the pulpit, given that she is a confessed atheist. The fact that this denomination is even struggling to find an answer to this dilemma is telling.

Our great-grandparents wouldn't recognize what the modern world has become—not only because technology has changed so much, or because so many nations have come and gone since their day, but because the West is no longer the light bearer it once was for the Gospel of Christ. The moral order has been turned on its head as we've fled from truth. It's enough to make modern believers despair as we face affliction and even the possibility of becoming outcasts.

In Micah's day, counselors vanished after failing to heed the warnings of the prophets. But God didn't want His faithful to fall into a pit of despair, even though religious instruction was lacking. He doesn't want that for us either, even when instruction is lacking in our own churches.

Micah 4 speaks about a day in which the Lord will assemble the lame and gather the outcast to make a strong nation (Micah 4:6–7). People will flow to God's mountain, war will cease, and we will walk in His paths (verses 1–2). Everything will be made right, and we will no longer struggle to do what is right.

UNFINISHED BUSINESS

If one of you is carrying some meat from a holy sacrifice in his
robes and his robe happens to brush against some bread or stew,
wine or olive oil, or any other kind of food, will it also become holy?
HAGGAI 2:12 NLT

If one drop of poison can pollute an entire cup of water, you might think the opposite would also be true—that one drop of holiness can sanctify an entire cup of water—but that isn't how holiness works. An element, or a person, must be sanctified, or completely set apart for the work of the Lord, to be considered holy. Neither the element, nor the person, can have contact with the unholy and still be considered sanctified. The priests to whom Haggai was speaking understood this.

Haggai shared such a message at the Lord's prompting because he wanted them to get back to work on the rebuilding of the temple. Eighteen years prior, the Persian king had allowed many of the Jews to return to Jerusalem and they had begun the work, but when neighboring peoples objected, the Jews began to concentrate on their own homes and crops. God wanted them to understand that they were missing out on His covenantal blessings by not following through with the rebuilding. Simply being near the incomplete temple wasn't enough.

Do you have unfinished work in the Lord—a task or a mission He has clearly called you to but that you haven't followed through on? Today is the day to begin anew.

THE CONSEQUENCE OF FALSE BELIEF

And isn't it wrong to offer animals that are crippled and diseased?
MALACHI 1:8 NLT

Sometime after the temple had been rebuilt, God's people had returned to worshipping Him there, but they were indifferent toward Him. Apparently they didn't believe He really loved them (Malachi 1:2). As a result of such feelings, they approached Him haphazardly and in clear violation of Deuteronomy 15:21 (NLT): "If this firstborn animal has any defect, such as lameness or blindness, or if anything else is wrong with it, you must not sacrifice it to the LORD your God."

"A son honors his father, and a servant respects his master," God said to the priests in Malachi 1:6 (NLT). "If I am your father and master, where are the honor and respect I deserve? You have shown contempt for my name!"

False beliefs always have consequences. God's people didn't feel loved by Him, perhaps because they perceived God had withheld something from them or because He had allowed their captivity, so they grew complacent in their relationship with Him, bringing Psalm 78:11 (NLT) to life: "They forgot what he had done—the great wonders he had shown them."

When life doesn't go as planned, it's easy to fall into the trap of blaming God and then grow cold toward Him. But He never changes and He never moves. His love for us endures, and He patiently waits for our return.

GOD REVEALS HIS DOINGS

Shall I hide from Abraham what I am about to do?
GENESIS 18:17 NIV

One day, God and two angels visited Abraham's camp atop the hills of Hebron and ate a meal together under the shady oaks of Mamre. As they were leaving, Abraham walked a short way with them. Below them to their left, they could see the distant plains where Sodom and Gomorrah rose, and God said, "Shall I hide from Abraham what I am about to do?" He decided that He would not, so He told Abraham that He was about to destroy those two wicked cities. This moved Abraham to plead with God to spare their inhabitants.

In Genesis 20:7, God declared that Abraham was a prophet, and Amos stated, "Surely the Sovereign LORD does nothing without revealing his plan to his servants the prophets" (Amos 3:7 NIV). But chances are good that you're not a prophet, and you may feel that God hides *many* of His plans from you. In fact, most of your life may feel like you've been walking along blindfolded, praying for guidance and directions, and only getting vague hints of which way to turn.

Nevertheless, God has promised to *all* believers, "Call to me and I will answer you and tell you great and unsearchable things you do not know" (Jeremiah 33:3 NIV). So seek God with all your heart, continually pray to Him for guidance, and eventually He *will* "instruct you and teach you in the way you should go" (Psalm 32:8 NIV).

OBEYING GOD'S COMMANDS

How long do you refuse to keep My commandments and My laws?
EXODUS 16:28 NKJV

———————

God sent the Israelites fresh manna every morning and commanded, "Let no one leave any of it till morning" (verse 19). But some of them disobeyed, and the manna bred worms and stank. The Sabbaths were exceptions, however. God didn't want the people to work then, so He sent a double supply of manna every Friday and commanded the Israelites to keep the surplus for the next day. Nevertheless, some people headed out on the Sabbath to gather. . .but found nothing. Exasperated, God asked, "How long do you refuse to keep My commandments and My laws?"

The Lord's commands weren't complicated or hard to understand. But the people were willfully choosing to ignore them, thinking that they had a "better idea," or that God surely couldn't have meant what He said. How often do believers today do the same thing!

For example, Leviticus 19:18 (NKJV) says, "You shall not take vengeance, nor bear any grudge. . .but you shall love your neighbor as yourself." But you may conclude that this "advice" doesn't work well in the real world, and that God couldn't actually expect you to obey it, so you go on your way despising others, bearing grudges, and taking petty vengeance on those who cross you. And on and on the list goes. . .

God's commands are often simple and straightforward. Don't be like the stubborn Israelites in the desert. Obey God today.

PRAYING THE WRONG PRAYER

Get up! Why are you lying on your face like this?
Joshua 7:10 nlt

———————

God had promised to be with the Israelites, yet when they went out to battle the army of Ai, they were defeated. So they bowed facedown to the ground and prayed all day until evening. Joshua cried, "Oh, Sovereign LORD, why did you bring us across the Jordan River if you are going to let the Amorites kill us? . . . For when the Canaanites. . .hear about it, they will surround us and wipe our name off the face of the earth" (verses 7–9). But instead of pitying Joshua, the Lord commanded him to stop praying. The fault wasn't with God. Israel had sinned.

When hit with unexpected setbacks and defeats, many Christians cry out to God, asking why He failed them. Like Joshua, they accuse Him of making a mistake by leading them into a certain situation, job, or ministry, knowing full well that it would likely end in disaster. But God doesn't want to hear these prayers, and He commands such people to stop praying.

It's a good thing to pray sincerely and desperately, even from a heart overflowing with grief and pain, but *not* if it involves you accusing God. Instead of blaming God, first repent and get yourself right with God. Then you'll pray the kinds of prayers God wants to hear.

A DIFFICULT QUESTION

Who will entice Ahab into attacking
Ramoth Gilead and going to his death there?
1 Kings 22:20 niv

God had decreed judgment on evil King Ahab, so He asked an assembly in heaven who would persuade Ahab to attack Ramoth Gilead so that he'd die there. One spirit said he'd speak false prophecies through Ahab's prophets, assuring him of victory in battle. God gave permission for this proposal (1 Kings 22:19–23). This entity was probably an evil spirit who, like Satan, often appears before God's throne, requesting authorization to bring grief to individuals or to severely test them.

The Bible indicates that God is responsible for everything that happens in the world, including calamities and other evils. Amos 3:6 (niv) asks, "When disaster comes to a city, has not the Lord caused it?" (See also Exodus 4:11; Isaiah 45:7.) But some people think that the devil is always responsible, since Jesus said, "The thief comes only to steal and kill and destroy; I have come that they may have life" (John 10:10 niv).

We don't know for certain how all this works, but it appears that while Satan has free rein to act in the lives of the wicked (Ephesians 2:2), he can only bring grief to the saved with God's permission (Job 1:6–12; 2:1–7; Luke 22:31–32). But whatever calamity or test of faith God allows, He uses it to bring good in the end. "We know that in all things God works for the good of those who love him" (Romans 8:28 niv).

THE WAVES STOP HERE

*Who shut up the sea behind doors when it burst forth from
the womb. . .when I said, "This far you may come and
no farther; here is where your proud waves halt"?*
JOB 38:8, 11 NIV

———————

The Message paraphrase of the Bible presents a startling picture,
saying, "Who took charge of the ocean when it gushed forth
like a baby from the womb? . . . I made a playpen for it, a strong
playpen so it couldn't run loose, and said, 'Stay here, this is your
place. Your wild tantrums are confined to this place'" (verses 8, 10–
11). Surprisingly, this *is* the picture God had in mind. In the New
King James Version, God refers to darkness as the sea's "swaddling
band" (verse 9). To swaddle a baby meant to wrap it tightly in
blankets or cloths to restrict the movement of its limbs.

It may seem odd to picture the ocean's basins as a gigantic
playpen that the water sloshes around in, or of darkness as swaddling bands constricting its movements, but the point God wanted
to make here is that He's in control of the oceans, and He sets a
limit on them so that they can't rise up and sweep over the land.

God has similar control in your life. Troubles may seem
overwhelming at times, and you may fear that they're about to
sweep you away, but you only need pray, "Save me, O God! For the
waters have come up to my neck" (Psalm 69:1 NKJV), and God will
deliver you.

MARVELS OF ICE

Who is the mother of the ice?
Who gives birth to the frost from the heavens?
JOB 38:29 NLT

————

It doesn't often snow in the Middle East, but sometimes the temperature dips low enough that it does. And it wasn't often that the ancients woke to see dizzyingly beautiful patterns of frost covering the ground or ponds covered with ice. "For the water turns to ice as hard as rock, and the surface of the water freezes" (verse 30). Then as now, people were fascinated. So God asked Job who was responsible. The obvious answer was that the Lord was. He was the One who set up the amazing laws of nature in the first place.

Mankind continues to be astonished by the marvels of our universe. A little over a hundred years ago, explorers discovered that there was an entire continent covered with ice at the bottom of the world. And in 2015 the *New Horizons* spacecraft took the first photos of towering ice mountains on Pluto. Not only that, but it's home to ice volcanoes several miles high. Who is the mother of the cryovolcanoes on this distant dwarf planet? The same God who created the wonders of ice on Earth.

God creates breathtaking beauty across the universe with His marvelous creations. Humanity is only beginning to understand what He is capable of. "Oh, the depth of the riches both of the wisdom and knowledge of God! How unsearchable are His judgments and His ways past finding out!" (Romans 11:33 NKJV).

ON THE MOVE AND SEEKING

Who provideth for the raven his food?
JOB 38:41 KJV

———

God provides food for all the birds of the air, including ravens. In the Gospels, Jesus said, "Look at the birds of the air, for they neither sow nor reap nor gather into barns; yet your heavenly Father feeds them. Are you not of more value than they?" (Matthew 6:26 NKJV). But even though God provides food for the birds, they still have to be constantly on the move, looking for it. The vast majority of birds in the world can't depend on kind, elderly ladies with bird feeders.

"When his young ones cry unto God, they wander for lack of meat" (Job 38:41 KJV). When birds lack food, they must wander—often far afield. This is very much like believers. At times God sends a lack, and Christians are forced to search diligently for what they need. They must think outside the box and seek in new ways and new places. Such experiences can be painful, but they're often necessary to stretch your faith and help you grow. They help you to become independent of others and dependent on God alone.

And remember, the point of Jesus' statement is that if God provides for the birds—even while requiring them to keep on the move and search diligently to meet their needs—He is even more certain to provide for *your* needs. So "cry unto God" like the ravens, and He will lead you to what He has for you.

OUR INCOMPARABLE GOD

Do you have an arm like God's,
and can your voice thunder like his?
JOB 40:9 NIV

God challenged Job that if he claimed he had an arm like God's—that is, if he had great power like the Almighty—then he should prove it: "Adorn yourself with glory and splendor, and clothe yourself in honor and majesty. Unleash the fury of your wrath, look at all who are proud and bring them low, look at all who are proud and humble them, crush the wicked where they stand. Bury them all in the dust together" (verses 10–13). If Job couldn't do these things, then he needed to acknowledge that he couldn't compare to God, and therefore he shouldn't judge Him.

"The voice of the LORD is powerful; the voice of the LORD is majestic. The voice of the LORD. . .breaks in pieces the cedars of Lebanon. . . . The voice of the LORD strikes with flashes of lightning. The voice of the LORD shakes the desert" (Psalm 29:4–5, 7–8 NIV). With this in mind, consider God's question: "Can your voice thunder like his?"

You can sometimes get an exaggerated sense of your own power and abilities, and it does you good to realize how vast is the gulf between your strength and God's. The same thing applies when you're tempted to think, *If I were God, I wouldn't allow this or that to happen*, but you have no understanding of His wisdom and power, and you are in no position to judge Him.

DON'T OPEN THAT DOOR

Who dares open the doors of its mouth,
ringed about with fearsome teeth?
JOB 41:14 NIV

Leviathan was a fierce, legendary monster of the primordial oceans that had an enormous mouth ringed with fearsome teeth. God asked Job who dared to force open its mouth. Only a foolhardy person would. The next thing they knew, those teeth would be snapping shut around them, crushing them in its powerful bite. Likewise, to taunt such a monstrosity until it opened its jaws, roaring in rage, was to court death.

There are certain other doors you shouldn't open. Once you open them, the effects may be nearly irreversible. There are certain lines you shouldn't cross, certain temptations you shouldn't give in to. They can be like opening Pandora's box, unleashing evils into your life that can't be stuffed neatly back inside. This can be true for drug abuse, for sexual sin, for rash words, and for many other things. You will live to regret all of these. . .if you *live*.

God's warning about an adulterous woman applies here: "Do not go near the door of her house, lest you lose your honor to others and your dignity to one who is cruel, lest strangers feast on your wealth and your toil enrich the house of another. At the end of your life you will groan, when your flesh and body are spent" (Proverbs 5:8–11 NIV).

Avoid disastrous choices, and you'll be very grateful for your restraint years later.

PARTY'S OVER

What is happening? Why is everyone running to the rooftops?
The whole city is in a terrible uproar. What do I see in this reveling city?
ISAIAH 22:1–2 NLT

After asking the above questions, God declared, "Bodies are lying everywhere, killed not in battle but by famine and disease. . . . Chariots fill your beautiful valleys, and charioteers storm your gates. . . . You run to the armory for your weapons. You inspect the breaks in the walls of Jerusalem. You store up water in the lower pool. You survey the houses and tear some down for stone to strengthen the walls. . . . But you never ask for help from the One who did all this" (verses 2, 7–11). God was describing the Assyrian army sieging Jerusalem.

Like the Jews of old, modern Christians often fail to seek God for help. They're obsessed with all practical details and fixes, but they miss addressing the underlying spiritual problems that brought the trouble on them. They sometimes even continue in their revelry until the hour is very late. Finally, they have to face the seriousness of the crisis, but by that point their entire life is in an uproar.

Don't wait till the last minute to seek God. By then it may be too late, and you may be running to the rooftops to escape the enemy breaking through the gates. How much better to be in the habit of seeking the Lord daily, keeping your heart right with Him, and getting His solutions to your problems.

DON'T MOCK GOD

Who do you think you've been mocking and reviling all
these years? Who do you think you've been jeering and
treating with such utter contempt all these years?
Isaiah 37:23 msg

The entire ancient Near East was in the darkness of idolatry, and God's people in Judah were worshipping false gods as well, so He used the cruel Assyrian Empire to conquer them. He told the Assyrians, "This is a longstanding plan of mine. . .using you to devastate strong cities" (verse 26). Now, the Assyrians were right in mocking all the useless gods the pagans worshipped, but the mistake they made was also to mock the *true* God. So He finally said, "I'll show you who's boss" (verse 29).

It shouldn't surprise you to learn that God often uses even proud, worldly unbelievers to accomplish His purposes. He used the Assyrians for *years* even though they mocked those who had faith in Him. Of course, God can use unbelievers better if they're *not* in contempt of Him.

Even if your boss is an outspoken unbeliever, God is still using him to meet your need for gainful employment. If he stubbornly persists in his attitude, however, the Lord will finally show him who's in charge. God is loving and He has long patience, but don't "despise the riches of His goodness, forbearance, and longsuffering," since "the goodness of God leads you to repentance" (Romans 2:4 nkjv). Or as *The Message* paraphrase of this verse says, "God is kind, but he's not soft."

PREDICTING THE FUTURE

*Let me ask you, Did anyone guess that this might happen? Did anyone
tell us earlier so we might confirm it with "Yes, he's right!"?*
ISAIAH 41:26 MSG

In the verse above, God announced the coming of Cyrus, king of
Persia, conqueror of the ancient world: "I, God, started someone
out from the north and he's come. He was called out of the east
by name. He'll stomp the rulers into the mud" (verse 25). God
went on in Isaiah 44:28 and 45:1–4 to call Cyrus *by name*. Then
He challenged the pagans: "Did anyone guess that this might
happen?" No. The diviners had no idea that the Persians would
rule. After all, it was 680 BC, the Assyrian Empire still reigned
supreme, and Cyrus wouldn't begin to rule for another 120 years.

Many modern people put a great deal of stock in soothsayers,
mediums, and psychics, because they sometimes have a *limited*
amount of power to predict the future. Paul once encountered a
"female slave who had a spirit by which she predicted the future"
(Acts 16:16 NIV). But none of these spirits are able to tell the
distant future in detail, like God did.

Some people point to Nostradamus's prophecies, written centuries ago, but they were written in obscure rhymes open to many
different interpretations, and they have, in fact, been repeatedly
mistakenly applied to current events. Whatever success the world's
fortune-tellers have, none of them could ever match the Bible for
sheer accuracy.

GOD'S PURPOSES FOR YOU

Do not tremble; do not be afraid. Did I not
proclaim my purposes for you long ago?
ISAIAH 44:8 NLT

⸻

Centuries before Isaiah was born, God had declared that the Israelites were His special treasure, His chosen people, with whom He had an everlasting covenant. He prophesied that even if they sinned grievously against Him and He banished them to the ends of the earth, if they returned to Him and obeyed His commands with all their hearts, He would restore their fortunes, have mercy on them, and gather them back from all the nations where He had scattered them (Deuteronomy 30:2–4).

You may sometimes be uncertain of the way God feels toward you, and you may not be sure what He has in store for you, but He is well aware. God has great love for you. " 'For I know the plans I have for you,' says the LORD. 'They are plans for good and not for disaster, to give you a future and a hope'" (Jeremiah 29:11 NLT).

God's promises to the Israelites also apply to you today. "The LORD who made you and helps you says: Do not be afraid, O Jacob, my servant, O dear Israel, my chosen one. For I will. . . pour out my Spirit on your descendants, and my blessing on your children" (Isaiah 44:2–3 NLT). God repeatedly tells you not to be afraid but to trust that He has good in mind for you. God is love, and He loves you.

BLOCKHEADS

Pretty stupid, wouldn't you say? Don't they have eyes in their heads?
Are their brains working at all? Doesn't it occur to them to say,
"...Here I am praying to a stick of wood!"
ISAIAH 44:18–19 MSG

If God ever became exasperated, this would be one of those times. In Isaiah 44 He protested the utter folly of idol worship, and He asked why the people didn't think to ask themselves, "Shall I bow down to a block of wood?" (Isaiah 44:19 NIV). Here they had just used part of the wood for a fire. They warmed themselves in front of its flame and baked bread on the coals. Then, from the wood that remained, they carved a god, bowed down to it, and prayed, "Save me!" It was *so* ridiculous.

Most people in the West today wouldn't pray to a wooden carving. But they would trust in technology to save them, and trust the word of scientists to be absolute truth. But doesn't it occur to them to ask, "Man has made all these things. How can I then trust them to provide me with ultimate truth?"

Others put their trust in money, even though it's only a little green ink on paper, was produced by people on a printing press, and is only worth as much as the economists say that it's worth. And since paper money is made of wood, modern people are, in fact, still falling down on their knees today in front of a piece of wood. Pretty stupid, wouldn't you say?

GOD KNOCKS AT THE DOOR

*Wherefore, when I came, was there no man?
when I called, was there none to answer?*
ISAIAH 50:2 KJV

God frequently complained about His people, "I spoke to you, rising up early and speaking, but you did not hear, and I called you, but you did not answer" (Jeremiah 7:13 NKJV). God is often the ignored visitor whom people don't let in their homes. He's frequently left out in the street like an unwanted salesman, turned away, while we go on with our lives. True, He often comes at times when we're not expecting Him, and in forms we don't often recognize, but all too often we *know* who He is and still we choose to ignore Him.

Jesus said, "Behold, I stand at the door and knock. If anyone hears My voice and opens the door, I will come in to him and dine with him, and he with Me" (Revelation 3:20 NKJV). But you have to have your ears open and be listening for His knock—and you have to *want* God to visit, so that you actually *open* the door when you hear His gentle rapping.

God frequently sent prophets and wise men to Israel, warning them to turn back to Him, pleading with them to heed His words, but the Israelites had a long history of ignoring God. In fact, instead of responding in love, they often reacted in anger and persecuted those whom He had sent. Soften your heart today, open the door, and let God into your life.

RIDICULING AND MAKING FACES

Whom do you ridicule? Against whom do you
make a wide mouth and stick out the tongue?
Isaiah 57:4 nkjv

Many of the people of Jerusalem mocked Isaiah and scoffed at his simple message. " 'Who does the Lord think we are?' they ask. 'Why does he speak to us like this? Are we little children, just recently weaned? He tells us everything over and over'" (Isaiah 28:9–10 nlt). Isaiah therefore referred to them as "you scoffers" (Isaiah 28:14 niv). God asked them whom they were ridiculing, at whom they were sticking out their tongues. They thought they were merely mocking Isaiah, but in reality, they were ridiculing God, who had sent him.

You may be tempted to look down in disdain at some Christians who have what you consider to be a simplistic, naive understanding of spiritual matters, and while there's nothing wrong with disagreeing with mistaken views, be careful that you don't mock other believers for being simple. Jesus said, "Assuredly, I say to you, inasmuch as you did it to one of the least of these My brethren, you did it to Me" (Matthew 25:40 nkjv).

Sometimes you don't realize how "off" your attitude is until someone overhears your reaction and questions you about it. You may have thought it was all right to make fun of someone, until you understand how it came across to others. So endeavor to always treat people with respect and love, just as you yourself would want to be treated.

EVERYTHING BELONGS TO GOD

Has not my hand made all these things,
and so they came into being?
Isaiah 66:2 niv

———

After Solomon had built a temple for the Lord, he asked, "Will God really dwell on earth? The heavens, even the highest heaven, cannot contain you. How much less this temple I have built!" (1 Kings 8:27 niv). Centuries later, God asked the Israelites, "Heaven is my throne, and the earth is my footstool. Where is the house you will build for me? Where will my resting place be?" (Isaiah 66:1 niv). God then asked the question in Isaiah 66:2 above, pointing out that He had made everything, including the materials from which they had built the temple.

When gathering supplies and making preparations for building God's house, David asked God, "Who am I, and who are my people, that we should be able to give as generously as this? Everything comes from you, and we have given you only what comes from your hand" (1 Chronicles 29:14 niv). Knowing that everything you have comes from God should not only inspire you to give generously, but it should also put things in perspective. God created everything, so He doesn't actually *need* anything. Don't start feeling that you're so generous or that God is so dependent on you. Everything comes from Him.

Just be thankful that you're His child and that He has given you what you have. That keeps things very uncomplicated and prevents you from getting too high an opinion of yourself.

THE COOL, DEEP NILE

And now, what do you think you'll get by going off to Egypt?
Maybe a cool drink of Nile River water?
JEREMIAH 2:18 MSG

The arid lands of the Middle East had fluctuating rainfall amounts and often experienced drought, so patriarchs like Abraham and Jacob went down to Egypt in desperate times. The Nile always flowed, even when drought consumed the surrounding lands.

In later centuries, the Israelites also found Egypt's isolation and abundance appealing when armies from the north were overrunning their nation. The Egyptians had built a great stone wall along their border to keep invaders out. So Egypt came to represent security and safety to the ancient peoples. The problem was, the Jews began to look to Egypt as their safety net instead of looking to the Lord. Hence God's question in Jeremiah 2:18.

Another point: Egypt had a large, powerful army, so even if the Jews decided to stay in their own land, they often looked to Egypt's armies to protect them.

God therefore declared: "My people have committed two sins: They have forsaken me, the spring of living water, and have dug their own cisterns [large underground tanks], broken cisterns that cannot hold water" (Jeremiah 2:13 NIV). In the natural world the waters of the Nile were deep, cool, and abundant, yet compared to the Lord, Egypt was like a broken cistern that could hold no water.

What abundant source of supply or protection are you depending upon instead of the Lord?

FICKLE SOLUTIONS

Why do you go about so much, changing your ways?
JEREMIAH 2:36 NIV

The Jews had first looked to the northern power of Assyria to defend them from the aggressive kingdom of Aram (2 Kings 16:7–9). But they were disappointed when, after Aram's fall, Assyria began expressing a desire to conquer them. So the Jews began looking to Egypt to protect them from the Assyrians (2 Kings 18:19–21). But in all this, they failed to trust the Lord to protect them. God saw them flitting from one "protector" to another, and He asked, "Why do you go about so much, changing your ways?" He later asked, "How long will you wander, unfaithful Daughter Israel?" (Jeremiah 31:22 NIV).

Some people are very changeable, constantly running around like chickens with their heads cut off, seeking quick fixes to their problems. This attitude betrays a lack of confidence and security and often results in people becoming nervous wrecks. The Bible warns, "Do not associate with those given to change" (Proverbs 24:21 NKJV).

God *does* require you to think problems through and find solutions yourself, but there's a tremendous difference between a person who has a strong confidence in the Lord—who takes care of what he *can* take care of and trusts God to take care of what he *can't* take care of—and a person driven by fear and worry, constantly rushing from one faltering solution to another. Do your best, then trust God, whatever situation you're in.

A HOUSE OF CARDS

But what will you do in the end?
JEREMIAH 5:31 NKJV

Judah was spiritually and morally bankrupt. The Jews feigned loyalty to the Lord and went through the motions of worshipping God, but they also worshipped heathen idols. The priests used their positions of authority to make this unholy syncretism work. Judah was in a vise between Babylon and Egypt, and the tension was palpable at times. The prophets propped things up by giving false prophecies about peace and prosperity, and the rulers attempted to maintain the status quo. On the surface, the situation *seemed* to be holding together. . .but God asked, "What will you do in the end?"

Many people today manage to wire their messed-up lives together with a mixture of deception and false fronts, glossing over serious problems and pretending that everything is all right, when things are *not* all right. Eventually the strain gets to be too much, and the whole house of cards comes tumbling down.

You can make things work for a time, even if you're operating under false principles, but eventually gravity takes over and the situation collapses.

"Do not be deceived, God is not mocked; for whatever a man sows, that he will also reap. For he who sows to his flesh will of the flesh reap corruption, but he who sows to the Spirit will of the Spirit reap everlasting life" (Galatians 6:7–8 NKJV).

A BIRD-EAT-BIRD WORLD

Has this one I hold dear become a preening peacock?
But isn't she under attack by vultures?
JEREMIAH 12:9 MSG

God described His people like a beautiful peacock, vainly fanning out its resplendent tail feathers to attract attention to itself. But in the end, all it did was attract vultures. Because Judah was caught up with her own beauty, it destroyed her in the end. Another allegory gives more insight: God compared Judah to a lovely woman then described how she began using her great beauty to get what she wanted and to enjoy a life of idolatrous pleasure. God said, "You trusted in your beauty and used your fame to become a prostitute" (Ezekiel 16:15 NIV).

When you see an exceptionally beautiful woman or an especially attractive man, you may be tempted to envy them. Their good looks draw attractive members of the opposite sex to them. They are treated like royalty, and they often enjoy a rich lifestyle. They may seem to have no lack, and they may seem happy. But don't envy them. Their beauty brings many temptations and griefs. Often those who rise the highest on superficial beauty fall the farthest and crash the hardest in the end.

If you've become proud of your good looks, you would do well to remember Prince Absalom's demise: "In all Israel there was none to be so much praised as Absalom for his beauty" (2 Samuel 14:25 KJV), but his five pounds of lovely locks—of which he was so proud—ultimately led to his death (2 Samuel 14:26; 18:9–14). Trust in God, not your beauty.

WALKING IN THE MUD

Has anyone ever heard of such a thing,
even among the pagan nations?
JEREMIAH 18:13 NLT

The people of Judah had turned from God and His just laws, so He warned, "I am planning disaster for you instead of good. So turn from your evil ways. . . ." But the people replied, "Don't waste your breath. We will continue to live as we want to" (verses 11–12). Had they repented, God would have had mercy. But they didn't, so He said, "They have stumbled off the ancient highways and walk in muddy paths" (verse 15). Even the heathen were astonished. They followed the laws of *their* lands, but the Israelites seemed to relish abandoning righteousness and wallowing in the mire.

God has made "the Highway of Holiness" for His people to walk on (Isaiah 35:8 NKJV), and He explains, "The highway of the upright is to depart from evil" (Proverbs 16:17 NKJV). You can stay away from a great deal of trouble and avoid getting splattered with the mud of the gutters and drenched with the mire of the ditches if you stay on the path the Lord has prepared. "Holiness" doesn't mean strutting along feeling holier-than-thou; it simply means following God's commands—walking on His path.

David prayed, "Teach me your way, LORD; lead me in a straight path" (Psalm 27:11 NIV). And His commands are simple. You are "to love the LORD your God, to walk in all His ways, and to hold fast to Him" (Deuteronomy 11:22 NKJV).

WHEAT OR WORTHLESS CHAFF?

Is not my word like as a fire? saith the LORD;
and like a hammer that breaketh the rock in pieces?
JEREMIAH 23:29 KJV

There were many so-called prophets in biblical times but few actual prophets. Many men simply made up messages from God. Jeremiah declared that they were "prophets who prophesy lies," things that never came to pass, "prophets of the deceit of their own heart" (Jeremiah 23:26 NKJV). God asked, "What is the chaff to the wheat?" (verse 28). His words were like solid, good grains of wheat, whereas the words of mere men were lighter-than-air chaff blown away by the wind—or burned to nothingness by the fire of God's Word.

There are many religious figures in the world today who promote themselves as spiritual authorities but whose words are literally as worthless as chaff. Jesus said, "It is the Spirit who gives life; the flesh profits nothing. The words that I speak to you are spirit, and they are life" (John 6:63 NKJV). Only God's Word, inspired by His Holy Spirit, contains life and bestows life. The chaff is of no profit whatsoever.

This principle holds true even of believers who speak from their own imaginations and who make plans based upon their own surmising and impulses. It's destined to come to nothing.

Even if the words of the wannabe prophets seem as solid as stone, God's Word is like a huge iron hammer that shatters the rock to bits. There's simply no comparison.

SECOND-GUESSING GOD

Have you not noticed that these people are saying,
"The LORD has rejected the two kingdoms he chose"?
JEREMIAH 33:24 NIV

God was very upset with the Northern Kingdom of Israel and the Southern Kingdom of Judah. Taken as a whole, He was through with them. But just because He was done with the kingdoms, that didn't mean He was finished with every individual person in them. God said, "If I have not made my covenant with day and night. . .then I will reject the descendants of Jacob. . . . For I will restore their fortunes and have compassion on them" (Jeremiah 33:25–26 NIV).

When the surrounding nations saw God judging the Israelites, allowing the invaders to carry them into exile in distant Babylon, they came to the conclusion that God had rejected His people. People can get the same impression about Christians today. When they see you going through hardships and troubles, they often ask, "Where is your God?" But just as sure as the sun rises in the morning and sets in the evening, God won't abandon you. He promises, "Never will I leave you; never will I forsake you" (Hebrews 13:5 NIV).

By the same token, when you see a fellow Christian going through prolonged periods of low finances, poor health, or relational crises, don't automatically jump to the conclusion that God is judging them. He could simply be doing a profound work in their life, after which He will restore their fortunes.

THE BUTT OF JOKES

Wasn't it you, Moab, who made crude jokes over Israel?
JEREMIAH 48:27 MSG

When the Jews were suffering under the Babylonians, the Moabites looking on from the sidelines joked about their anguish. The Moabites gawked at the Jewish men and women stripped down naked and chained together, hands tied together above their heads, being marched off into exile (Isaiah 20:1–4; Jeremiah 2:37). They mocked their humiliation and made crude jokes about them.

But God had words for the Moabites as well. He said, "Turn Moab into a drunken sot, drunk on the wine of my wrath, a dung-faced drunk, filling the country with vomit—Moab a falling-down drunk, a joke in bad taste" (verse 26 MSG). Moab had made jokes in bad taste, but God declared that the Moabites *themselves* were a joke in bad taste. In fact, Moab's turn was coming to be judged. Then they who had made crude jokes about the misery of God's people would suffer in the same way.

The early Christians "were publicly exposed to insult and persecution; at other times [they] stood side by side with those who were so treated" (Hebrews 10:33 NIV). So don't be disturbed if the ungodly laugh at you and mock you in your troubles. God isn't about to forget what they did, or overlook their jokes. He will see to it that they are fully recompensed for what they have done. Although their comments may sting now, their turn is coming.

DRIVING GOD AWAY

Son of man, do you see what they are doing, the great
abominations that the house of Israel commits here,
to make Me go far away from My sanctuary?
EZEKIEL 8:6 NKJV

Ezekiel was in the land of Shinar when God lifted his spirit from his body and carried him to distant Jerusalem. First, God showed him an idol standing in the temple of God. Then God let him look in on seventy Israelite elders worshipping drawings of pagan deities. Then God showed him women crying in desire for Tammuz, the Babylonian fertility god. So God asked, "Do you see this, son of man?"

The elders justified worshipping other gods by saying, "The LORD has forsaken the land" (verse 12 NKJV). But God was still *there*—though He was greatly grieved. He asked Ezekiel if he saw the "utterly detestable things the Israelites are doing. . .that will drive me far from my sanctuary" (verse 6 NIV). God hadn't left *yet*, though He was about to, since the Israelites were persisting in their idolatry.

You may be discouraged about past sins and failures and feel like the Lord has abandoned you. This can make you think, *What's the use in trying to please God if He's going to be mad at me anyway? I might as well go whole-hog into my sins.* This is a deception of the devil. It takes persistent sinful behavior to cause God to lift His Spirit from your life.

Recognize that feeling for what it is: the condemnation of the devil, trying to discourage you so that you give up on serving God. Don't be fooled!

NOT QUALITY WOOD

Son of man, how does a grapevine compare to a tree?
Is a vine's wood as useful as the wood of a tree? Can its wood
be used for making things, like pegs to hang up pots and pans?
EZEKIEL 15:2–3 NLT

After asking these questions, God then proceeded to answer them, saying, "No, it can only be used for fuel, and even as fuel, it burns too quickly. Vines are useless both before and after being put into the fire! And this is what the Sovereign LORD says: The people of Jerusalem are like grapevines growing among the trees of the forest. Since they are useless, I have thrown them on the fire to be burned" (verses 4–6). The people of Judah were useless for anything good.

In the New Testament, Paul described individuals who said they were believers: "Such people claim they know God, but they deny him by the way they live. They are detestable and disobedient, worthless for doing anything good" (Titus 1:16 NLT). Like the vine, they try to pass themselves off as quality wood, but they are of inferior quality and useless for every purpose. They can't even serve small purposes like pegs.

This allegory may not describe your overall life, fortunately, but it can sometimes describe specific areas. In certain situations, you can fall short and be "clouds and wind that bring no rain" (Proverbs 25:14 NLT). If you promise refreshing, make sure that you actually deliver.

JUDGING PEOPLE

Will you judge them?
Ezekiel 20:4 niv

One day several elders of the Jews came to Ezekiel to inquire of the Lord, but God asked, "Am I to let you inquire of Me, you Israelites?" He wasn't interested in their questions and quibbles about hairsplitting theological issues, and He told the prophet Ezekiel to "confront them with the detestable practices of their ancestors" (verse 4). Why? Because it wasn't just ancient history, something only their forefathers had done long ago. God knew what they were up to and bluntly told them, "You continue to defile yourselves with all your idols to this day" (verse 31).

Christians are often uncomfortable with the thought of judging other people. They remember that Jesus admonished, "Judge not, that you be not judged" (Matthew 7:1 nkjv). Just the same, many believers *are* nevertheless quick to judge if someone offends or slights them personally. Then they readily forget Jesus' command and leap to angry, often ill-informed conclusions.

But though God commands you to refrain from judging others out of selfish motivations or anger, there are often times when He requires you to judge people's actions and motivations. You make many judgment calls every day as to whether someone is being honest, what their motivations are, etc. But the point is: You have to judge with the right motives. Jesus said, "Do not judge according to appearance, but judge with righteous judgment" (John 7:24 nkjv). God asked Ezekiel, "Will you judge them?" and He sometimes asks us the same question.

THE MIGHTY ARE FALLEN

Was there ever such a city as Tyre, now silent at the bottom of the sea?
EZEKIEL 27:32 NLT

W as there ever such a city as Tyre? Never. Tyre was the greatest city of Phoenicia, the bustling commercial and shipping center of the ancient world. They were fabulously wealthy and believed they'd last forever. God said, "The merchandise you traded satisfied the desires of many nations. Kings at the ends of the earth were enriched by your trade. Now you are a wrecked ship, broken at the bottom of the sea" (verses 33–34). Though they dominated the world for many long years, God said, "Everything is lost— your riches and wares, your sailors and pilots, your ship builders, merchants, and warriors" (verse 27).

Today, some people, movements, and organizations seem so powerful that you can't imagine them ever falling. A few decades ago, people thought the same about communism. But it collapsed in nation after nation around the world. So even though rulers may seem unstoppable and dominate the headlines today, God can dispose of them.

When you gaze upon the silent remains of some great power, the ruins of former splendor and wealth, it can be hard to grasp that they once ruled the waves and terrorized the nations. David wrote, "I have seen wicked and ruthless people flourishing like a tree. . . . But when I looked again, they were gone! Though I searched for them, I could not find them!" (Psalm 37:35–36 NLT).

WORTHY TO INHERIT

Should you then possess the land?
EZEKIEL 33:26 NIV

The Jews of Ezekiel's day reasoned, "Abraham was only one man, yet he possessed the land. But we are many; surely the land has been given to us as our possession" (verse 24). They figured that their sheer numbers entitled them to the fulfillment of the promises. They forgot that Abraham inherited the land because of his faith and obedience to God. The later Jews believed in God, but they didn't obey Him. God listed several of their most blatant sins then asked, "Should you then possess the land?"

Many Christians apply this principle to salvation then worry that they're not obedient enough to qualify for eternal life. Though the Bible declares plainly that you're saved by God's grace (Ephesians 2:8–9; Romans 10:9–10), people still get the idea stuck in their heads that He initially saves them, but from then on it's their responsibility to *keep* themselves saved. To this Paul asks, "Are you so foolish? Having begun in the Spirit, are you now being made perfect by the flesh?" (Galatians 3:3 NKJV).

God saves you, but for you to enjoy the fullness of His blessing, He says, "I urge you to live a life worthy of the calling you have received" (Ephesians 4:1 NIV). Yield to His Spirit and He will enable you to obey Him. After all, you were "created in Christ Jesus to do good works, which God prepared in advance for us to do" (Ephesians 2:10 NIV).

SPARED FROM WRATH

How can I make you like Admah?
How can I set you like Zeboiim?
HOSEA 11:8 NKJV

———————

When God wanted to remind people of how the wicked would be destroyed, He frequently referred to the destruction of Sodom and Gomorrah (Isaiah 13:19; Jeremiah 49:18; 2 Peter 2:6). But two smaller cities, Admah and Zeboiim, were destroyed at that same time, "which the LORD overthrew in His anger. . . ." He then declared, "The whole land is brimstone, salt, and burning. . .nor does any grass grow there" (Deuteronomy 29:23 NKJV). Though the Israelites often angered Him, His sympathy was stirred, and He couldn't bring Himself to destroy them completely like Admah and Zeboiim.

God has great compassion on believers today as well. He still says, as He said then, "I will not execute the fierceness of My anger. . . . For I am God, and not man, the Holy One in your midst; and I will not come with terror" (Hosea 11:9 NKJV). God has great love and compassion on His children, and because He has promised to save you from a fate in hell, He will keep you safe in the day of judgment.

This doesn't mean you can live however you please, though, or utterly disregard His commands. You'd be very ashamed to be in His presence if you did. "And now, little children, abide in Him, that when He appears, we may have confidence and not be ashamed before Him at His coming" (1 John 2:28 NKJV).

UNDOING DEATH

Where, O death, are your plagues?
Where, O grave, is your destruction?
HOSEA 13:14 NIV

God declared, "I will deliver this people from the power of the grave; I will redeem them from death" (verse 14). The Israelites were well aware that dead bodies decomposed in tombs until they were completely destroyed. "They die and return to the dust" (Psalm 104:29 NIV). People eventually become dust, blown in the wind. But since God has promised to bring them back to life as resurrected bodies, He asked, "Where, O grave, is your destruction?" In that day all the destruction of the grave will be reversed.

You commonly hear that death is final. It *would* be final if not for the miracle-working power of God. He will undo the grave's work and redeem ("buy back") His people from death. The Bible promises, "Your dead will live, LORD; their bodies will rise—let those who dwell in the dust wake up and shout for joy.... The earth will give birth to her dead" (Isaiah 26:19 NIV). Long-dead bodies will re-form in supernatural form and rise to live forever.

God asks, "Where, O death, are your plagues?" Old age, sickness, and death *are* very real plagues to the billions of people in the world today. They take a heavy toll on humanity and cause a great deal of grief and tears. But one day "he will swallow up death forever. The Sovereign LORD will wipe away the tears from all faces" (Isaiah 25:8 NIV).

NOT PICKED CLEAN

If grape-gatherers had come to you,
would they not have left some gleanings?
OBADIAH 1:5 NKJV

========

There was a law in Israel that when you sent grape gatherers into your vineyard during harvesttime, they were *not* to meticulously gather every grape; they were to leave some pickings for the poor and the stranger, the fatherless, and the widow. You were not to scour or "glean" your vineyard after the pickers had finished their work (Leviticus 19:10; Deuteronomy 24:21). This merciful law showed God's consideration for the poor. But God told His bitter enemies, the Moabites, that when He judged *them*, He was going to utterly finish them off. . .and not even leave a small remnant. God has great mercy and compassion upon His own people, even when they're deserving of judgment. "He has not dealt with us according to our sins, nor punished us according to our iniquities" (Psalm 103:10 NKJV). As Ezra the scribe pointed out, "You our God have punished us less than our iniquities deserve" (Ezra 9:13 NKJV). This is because His plan for His people is restoration. He wants to redeem you from your sins, time and time again, so you can continue to serve Him.

God is merciful and compassionate, and He has no desire to beat you into the ground, even when you've sorely disobeyed. When you're going through a time of chastening, pray to Him, "In wrath remember mercy" (Habakkuk 3:2 NKJV). God will have mercy, and He will restore you.

GOD'S BURDEN IS LIGHT

Dear people, how have I done you wrong?
Have I burdened you, worn you out?
MICAH 6:3 MSG

God had a complaint against His people: They were persistently disobeying Him, after all He had done for them. And His requests hadn't been unreasonable or burdensome. The Bible declares, "He has shown you, O man, what is good; and what does the LORD require of you but to do justly, to love mercy, and to walk humbly with your God?" (Micah 6:8 NKJV). Yet to these few demands, the Jews said, "Oh, what a weariness!" (Malachi 1:13 NKJV).

Many people feel that it's a burden to serve God. The apostle John wrote, "For this is the love of God, that we keep his commandments: and his commandments are not grievous" (1 John 5:3 KJV). In fact, when you boil them down to their most basic form, God's commands are easy to understand and live out. Paul quoted several of the Ten Commandments then said, "And if there is any other commandment, are all summed up in this saying, namely, 'You shall love your neighbor as yourself'" (Romans 13:9 NKJV).

God has no intention of laying heavy burdens on you and wearing you out. And even of your work for Him, Jesus says, "Take My yoke upon you and learn from Me. . .and you will find rest for your souls. For My yoke is easy and My burden is light" (Matthew 11:29–30 NKJV).

LIVING AND EXUDING LIFE

If a person defiled by contact with a dead body touches one of these things, does it become defiled?
HAGGAI 2:13 NIV

Moses wrote, "Whoever touches a human corpse will be unclean for seven days" (Numbers 19:11 NIV). God added, "Command the Israelites to send away from the camp anyone. . .who is ceremonially unclean because of a dead body" (Numbers 5:2 NIV). Touching a dead body automatically defiled a person. So Haggai asked some priests the question, if a defiled person touched any food, did the food become defiled? They answered that it did. Then Haggai said, " 'So it is with this people and this nation in my sight,' declares the LORD. 'Whatever they do and whatever they offer there is defiled'" (Haggai 2:13–14 NIV).

Before you were saved, you were spiritually dead and defiled in God's sight. Isaiah declared, "We are all as an unclean thing, and all our righteousnesses are as filthy rags" (Isaiah 64:6 KJV). Like Lazarus, who had been in the grave for four days, you had a spiritual stink (John 11:39), and even your best good deeds had the stench of death on them. Like the ancient Jews, whatever you offered to God was defiled.

But God brought you back to life, thoroughly cleansed you from the inside out by washing you with His Holy Spirit, and clothed you in pure white robes of His righteousness. Now, as you continue to walk in His Spirit, loving God and others, your entire life exudes His life-giving Holy Spirit.

CONTRIBUTORS

Quentin Guy writes from the high desert of New Mexico, to encourage and equip people to know and serve God. He currently works in publishing for Calvary Albuquerque and has cowritten such books as *Weird and Gross Bible Stuff* and *The 2:52 Boys Bible*, both of which are stuck in future classic status. A former middle-school teacher, he serves with his wife as marriage prep mentors and trusts God that his children will survive their teenage years. Quentin's devotions appear on days 75–111.

Glenn A. Hascall is an accomplished writer with credits in more than one hundred books. He is a broadcast veteran and voice actor and is actively involved in writing and producing audio drama. Glenn's devotions appear on days 112–148 and 259–294.

Ardythe Kolb is a wife, mother, and freelance writer, with three books and devotions or stories in over a dozen compilations. She serves on the board of Heart of America Christian Writer's Network as the editor of its monthly newsletter. Besides writing, she volunteers as a CASA for abused children. Ardythe's devotions appear on days 149–184, and 186.

Iemima Ploscariu is a history researcher who spends most of her time in Sacramento, California. She is passionate about all things historical. Along with her freelance writing, she also works at her local public library. Iemima's devotions appear on days 223–258.

Ed Strauss is a freelance writer living in British Columbia, Canada. He has authored or coauthored more than fifty books for children, tweens, and adults. Ed has a passion for biblical apologetics, and besides writing for Barbour, he has been published by Zondervan, Tyndale, Moody, and Focus on the Family. Ed's devotions appear on days 38–74, 185, 187–222, and 331–365.

Tracy M. Sumner is a freelance writer and editor living in Beaverton, Oregon. An avid outdoorsman, he enjoys fly-fishing on world-class Oregon waters. Tracy's devotions appear on days 1–37.

Lee Warren is published in such varied venues as *Discipleship Journal*, *Sports Spectrum*, Yahoo! Sports, Crosswalk .com, and ChristianityToday.com. He is also the author of the book *Finishing Well: Living with the End in Mind* (*A Devotional*), and he writes regular features for *The Pathway* newspaper and *Living Light News*. Lee makes his home in Omaha, Nebraska. Lee's devotions appear on days 295–330.

SCRIPTURE INDEX

OLD TESTAMENT

NEW TESTAMENT